MY FATHER'S WAR

Finding Meaning in My Father's World War II Military Service

MY FATHER'S WAR

Finding Meaning in My Father's World

War II Military Service

Helaine Hartman Cohen

Acknowledgments

I would like to thank my family for supporting and encouraging me. A special thanks to my son, Brandon, who helped me with the basic research and some of the early writing.

The National Archives in Maryland and the Library of Congress house many of the original military records and both are special places. The staffs there were helpful and knowledgeable. The World War II Museum in New Orleans has a wonderful collection of oral histories, as does the Veterans History Project at the Library of Congress.

I am grateful to Gay Walley, my editor, who carefully helped me reshape and strengthen my book. Thanks for your encouragement and praise. Betty Ann Sharp and Rachel Moser both read my manuscripts and were supportive. Thank you.

Finally, Roland Gaul in Luxembourg spent several days taking us to the battlefield sites, the remnants of war still there, and the memorials to American troops. We found pillboxes, a super-bunker, trenches, monuments, and many reminders that war once scarred the beautiful countryside. He also shared many stories about the people who lived on both sides of the Sauer River during the war.

About the Author

Helaine Hartman Cohen is a retired CPA who developed an interest in World War II after learning about her father's experience in Europe during that war. After several years of research on his battle experience and his life as a POW in Germany, she began to write about it. She received a master's degree in World War II Studies and has been writing about various facets of the war. She is currently working on another book that will explore the impact of women on the war effort during World War II.

Table of Contents

Introduction

During the early morning hours of February 7th, 1945, the XII US Corps under General Manton Eddy, which was part of General George Patton's Third US Army, launched an offensive from the area of Echternach, Luxembourg, over the swollen Sauer and Our Rivers into a heavily fortified area of the Siegfried Line in Germany. Their objective was the capture of Bitburg, Germany.

The crossing of the Sauer (Sure) and Our Rivers was brutal by all accounts, so brutal that it has been a source of pain and conflict for many who made the crossing and for those who called for it and commanded it. In my father's regiment, only 15 to 20 men of approximately 400 men, who attempted the crossing, survived. The crossing was mishandled, yet it was also, in concert with a strategic surround of the Germans, part of a very effective campaign. The war was won shortly thereafter.

At the time, Europe was experiencing a difficult winter which was uncommonly cold and snowy, and the thaw that occurred during the preceding week resulted in melting snow that led to more challenging road and river conditions. River levels were abnormally high and contained strong currents, and nearby roads were broken and muddy. On the German side of the river, the terrain included steep cliffs and heavy fortifications, including barbed wire, mines, trenches, and fortified, well-armed pillboxes. In addition, there were limited supplies for troops. It took several days of intense fighting, but ultimately the Americans managed to build several bridgeheads over the Sauer and Our Rivers across from Luxembourg, thus enabling the XII US Corps to enter and gain a foothold in Germany. This was the beginning of what was known as the Eifel Campaign.

According to my father, a member of the first battalion of the 417th Regiment in Patton's Third US Army, the initial crossing of the Sauer River in the Echternach area led to a large loss of life amid difficult fighting conditions. Recorded accounts of this action are often incomplete and sometimes contradictory, but most agree that dozens of boats attempted to cross the river on the first night, and few of them made it across. Many men were killed by artillery fire, swept away by the currents, or sunk due to the heavy packs they had on their backs. By the end of the first day, only a few dozen men in the XII US Corps were safely across the rivers despite over 1,000 troops making the attempt.

My father began to talk about his wartime experiences decades after World War II. Prior to that, I knew of his POW status only because my paternal grandmother presented me with a gift when I was a teenager. It contained two blue boxes, designed in a similar manner as jewelry boxes. One was labeled Purple Heart and the other was labeled Silver Star. Inside the box with the Silver Star was a clipping from a newspaper (probably from a New York City newspaper) that said:

> "T/5 Frank J. Tonto of 2081 Second avenue, overseas nine months with the 301st Engineers of the Seventy-sixth Infantry Division, revealed that he was one of the company of engineers which last February 7 built the first bridge across the Saar River. The 417th and the 385th Infantry Regiments of the Seventy-sixth cracked the Siegfried Line and crossed the Saar, Tonto said, despite Gen. George S Patton's statement that only a green outfit would try to cross the Saar. "They were damned green, too," Tonto said, "but they were the first to get across." Two treadway bridges which they built near Echternach that day were knocked out by the Germans, Tonto related, but the third held and the infantry crossed."

My grandmother told me that my father gave the medals to her when he arrived home and said he did not wish to see them again. The clipping was the only indication of what he went through. She counseled me against asking him about anything related to the war. I did not even tell him that I had his medals for over a decade beyond their receipt. And I still do not know who Frank Tonto is.

When I was growing up, we did not mention Germany or General George W. Patton, Jr. I understood that these subjects were not for discussion. My father, without specifying why, let it be known that he had nothing good to say about Patton.

My father first started talking about his war experiences several years into his second marriage when I was an adult and had children of my own. The descriptions were brief. He was part of Patton's Third Army as a "regular soldier". He said he was in the 417th Regiment, which was part of the 76th Infantry Division. On February 7, 1945, which happened to be his nineteenth birthday, he was sent over the Sauer River from Echternach, Luxembourg, into Germany. It was his first military action.

According to him, 1,200 soldiers were sent over the raging river in boats that night. Most boats capsized, and all but a few troops died. At first, he told me only about 15 men survived the crossing. At another time, he said it might have been 22 who successfully survived the crossing, indicating that his memories were only partially reliable. In large part, he said the deaths occurred because the troops were carrying 70 pounds on their backs, and they sunk under the weight of the packs after the boats capsized. My father barely mentioned that he was taken prisoner during the operation. It was obvious that my father was still too traumatized to discuss this subject in detail. I would have to fill in the blanks on my own.

From the limited descriptions of what happened to my father, I developed a list of questions as I struggled to understand the mysteries of what my father experienced during World War II and why there was such a large loss of life. Some memories seemed to haunt him decades later. Then there were questions about my father's medals, the Purple Heart and the Silver Star. The Purple Heart is easy to explain as it is usually given when a soldier is wounded or killed during an action. The Silver Star is awarded "for gallantry in action"[1]. It is the third-highest military decoration for valor in combat and is considered above the Bronze Star awarded for meritorious or heroic acts. What did my father do to receive these honors?

I kept thinking about the issue of the unusually high number of casualties. Only later did I start to think about why this all happened, who was responsible, and was the action avoidable. I did not even begin to ponder the POW experience until years later when it became clear that this part of the war experience in POW camps like Stalag IX-B was often missing from the literature and did not approximate the TV show Hogan's Heroes or the movie The Great Escape. And how would I corroborate information with his story?

In his later years, my father discussed his battle experience at Echternach three times, only once on tape. And he said little about his prisoner of war experiences. I learned that the river he crossed was the Sauer River, not the Saar River. He insisted over 1,100 American soldiers attempted to cross the river that night, a number given to him during the repatriation process after he was released from his POW camp, and that he was one of only two dozen men known to have successfully crossed on that first day of the operation.

To me, it was intriguing that so large a loss of troops was not recognized in official army records. I always wondered whether my father had the number of casualties wrong. Furthermore, I wondered why this action was not more known. As one person I spoke with said, "Why this is so, we can only speculate today: The cause most probably rested on the fact that this regiment had heavy losses at the Luxembourg-German border, the crossing of the Sauer River, and the conquest of the Siegfried Line at the beginning of the combat in January and February 1945. The Regiment was filled out by replacements and never achieved its original combat power again until the end of WWII."[2]

The location and timing of this action have also been a question for me. Official records of the 417th Regiment have verified the Sauer River as the location and the date of the action. Many books discuss Montgomery's troops being the first to breach the Siegfried Line into Germany in February, but he began the attacks farther north a day after the Sauer River crossings and days after the First US Army and other elements of the Third US Army advanced into Germany. I could not find references to the offensive by the 417th Regiment in the memoirs of General Dwight Eisenhower, and only a few short sentences were written by General Omar Bradley. Another inconsistency is that military maps reference action in that area as between February 8th and March 21st, not February 7th. Finally, I always wondered why my father blamed Patton for what he called "a suicide mission."[3] I thought that this offensive would be a result of planning and authorization by military leaders higher up the chain of command.

The crossing of the Sauer River - in tandem with the crossing of the Our River not far away - by Patton's troops is not a well-known story. The harsh conditions of some prisoner-of-war camps, especially my father's camp, are also not well known, probably because so many POWs refused to talk openly about their experiences in captivity. My father cursed Patton until the day he died and never looked at the medals he received.

After my father, Roland Hartman, died, I began to seriously investigate his story. I wanted to understand what he experienced, what he witnessed, and where it fit into the war. Finding meaning for what he endured was also important. I read World War II history books and searched the internet for information on the crossing of the Sauer River. I began with limited information on his affiliations and found only a few brief written accounts on his action. It was hit or miss for a while. As a CPA trained in accounting and tax returns, I was not knowledgeable about the military, and my understanding of World War II was limited.

Roland told me he was a member of the 417th Regiment in C Company. I learned the 417th Regiment was a component of the 76th Infantry Division, along with the 385th and 304th Regiments. I discovered the Orders of Battle for the 417th Regiment and 76th Infantry Division and learned the division was part of the XII US Corps during the action in February, which was part of the Third US Army under General George Patton. The Third and First US Armies were assigned to the 12th Army Group under General Omar Bradley at that time.

I then contacted the US Army Heritage and Education Center at the US Army Barracks in Carlisle, PA, and they supplied me with a brief 14-page history of the 417th Regiment. In 2008, even before my father died, I found myself visiting the National Archives in College Park, MD, to read the actual battle reports, after-action accounts, and other documents for the crossing of the Sauer River. The operations into Germany from Luxembourg became more real from these original documents.

As I located additional documents and viewed oral histories of the soldiers involved in this action in February 1945, it was clear to me that the story of the 417th Regiment's crossing was only part of a larger operation. To understand what happened during this action and what it meant, especially the fiasco of the first day, I realized that it was important to examine the whole operation, both in terms of the other units involved and for the length of the operation. The context within the war setting was also missing. Roland's story may have diverged from the battle scene after the first day, but there were other stories related to the crossing that enhanced the meaning of the Sauer River crossing. The XII US Corps persevered, figured out ways to successfully make the crossings, established multiple bridgeheads, and advanced into Germany.

Additionally, I learned that it was not just the infantry that was involved in these crossings; they were supported by artillery and chemical units, armored units, engineers, intelligence and reconnaissance groups, medical personnel, signal companies, and people in the supply chain who transported supplies, ammunition and food to the front. Fighting a war is a communal effort.

As my research continued, I enlarged the research to include the other divisions involved in this action and the entire battle, and then I pivoted to understanding Roland's journey through the prisoner-of-war system in Germany, which was also worth telling. That experience must have been equally brutal for him. I learned that he ultimately was held at Stalag IX-B in Bad Ord, Germany, often mentioned as the worst stalag in the German system. Slow starvation and unsanitary conditions were a way of life there.

However, reconstructing what happened does not explain why these events happened or the significance and impact of those operations. I eventually expanded my search to obtain a better understanding of the context in which these events occurred. This was the only way to appreciate how various motivations, objectives, perspectives, planning, leadership, logistics, location, and uncontrollable factors contributed to the action. Like the war itself, it was a complex and ever-changing situation. Also, I had no understanding of how this river crossing contributed to the war effort at that time and its impact on future events and people. Each soldier has a unique story, and no matter what happened, it had some effect on the outcome.

The result of this research is an examination of one military operation by the XII US Corps at the beginning of February 1945, why it happened, how it impacted future operations, and how it affected the people involved. Ultimately, the men of the XII US Corps learned from the challenges of that first day and adapted to successfully complete their mission. To me, this gave meaning to the initial losses suffered by the 417th Regiment and other troops in the XII US Corps along the Sauer and Our Rivers. After the crossings, the survivors then advanced through the remainder of the war. It was a complex, well-coordinated, and dynamic set of events that contributed to the ultimate outcome of the war. And for each individual involved and each unit of participants, there were different perspectives and experiences with individual memories and meanings.

Although today I cannot know my father's exact experience during the war, I have come to understand the circumstances of these crossings, the reasons and motivations for the operations, what actually happened, the impact, and perhaps what it meant to my father and others who served there. This book then traces the paths of different units and men and how they met the challenges of crossing the Sauer and Our Rivers, followed different paths to the end of the war, and saw the victorious end of the war in the European theater. My own journey through this project involved completing a master's program in World War II and researching this project thoroughly with the help of my son. At times, it was like a mystery story with side tales, contradictory accounts, evolving sets of questions, extreme suffering, and heroics. As I continued, I came to understand more about all that was involved strategically, as well as finally understanding the reality of what my father must have gone through.

Roland's Story, Part I

This is my father's story, as he told it to me. Some of it can be verified in World War II records and the stories of other people who took the same path. Roland Hartman was born and raised in New York City. As a teenager, his friends called him Clint. His father was an antique dealer and his mother was a housewife. He had a brother who was four years younger than him named Alan. After he turned 18 years old in 1944, Roland tried to enlist in the navy or air corps, but he was rejected due to his color blindness. Disappointed, he joined the military after the army drafted him a few months later. He was sent to basic training in the spring of 1944 in Cash Landing, Florida. According to Roland, the period of his basic training was difficult, not because of the training but because of difficulties interacting with many of the other men with him. He claimed they "disliked anyone and anything to do with the Jewish religion." He claimed he was once physically jumped by a group of them. He also talked about his life within his military unit:

> "They were coal miners or steel workers and I wound up in the center of the company area almost every week with a fight sponsored by the captain of the company as the final answer to any argument that came. I never lost one of

those boxing matches. I never really got hit. These guys only knew how to hit by winding up and swinging as hard as they could possibly swing. I was always smart enough to step away from them and being able to jab and that was all I could do. But I did lose one fight. I lost a fight to a man of my like size and weight by the name of Hennessey."[4]

This story is not unique; other Jewish soldiers in World War II also reported the need to fight other fellow soldiers.[5] Roland later noted that these fights might have helped forge bonds with the other men in his unit.

After basic training, he was sent to Camp McCoy in Wisconsin for ranger training. During that time, he became a black belt and made one parachute jump. Despite his training, he was sent to Europe in November 1944 as an infantryman in the 417th Regiment's 1st Battalion (Company C), one of three regiments in the 76th Infantry Division. This was probably due to the shortage of infantrymen and the need for replacements. The 1st Battalion of the 417th Regiment departed Camp McCoy on November 13th, 1944, for Camp Myles Standish in Taunton, Massachusetts. They arrived there three days later. At that time, the troops did not know where they were going. The soldiers were outfitted with clothing and equipment and were given additional training. Many were given passes to visit nearby Boston before shipping out.[6]

The regiment departed Boston on November 24th on the USS Marine Raven for Europe. Roland remembered the crossing of the Atlantic Ocean took "17, 18 or 19 days" and was part of a convoy. "The first five days were horrible weather where everybody on the ship was ill, seasick, including me.… Occasionally, the soldiers could see the smokestack of a German submarine in the water."[7]

Army records indicate that a convoy of approximately 30 ships transported other elements of the 76th Division on the USS Sea Owl, USS Brazil, and the USS Black Warrior. They docked in Plymouth, England, on December 4th and then moved by train to Bournemouth, where they received more training and inspections and were issued additional equipment. They experienced for the first time the British fog and blackouts.[8]

According to Roland, he remained in Great Britain for approximately three weeks before being shipped to France. They crossed the English Channel on January 11th and landed in Le Havre, France. Their first stop was in St. Hellier, France, 60 miles away. Roland recalled that elements of the 76th Infantry Division then traveled to Belgium (on January 22nd) to help relieve the 101st Airborne after Bastogne had been freed. He said their regiment played a minimal role there. Roland remembered that the weather was "cold as hell at that time," and there was "loads of snow, loads of it." After Belgium, Roland remembered moving to Luxembourg.[9] They arrived there on January 25th.

Roland's first military action began on his 19th birthday, February 7, 1945. He said that "General Patton sent us on a suicide mission. That's all it was, [it] was a suicide mission." When asked why he called it a suicide mission, he replied, "You cannot send a group of men with any kind of sincerity across a river at flood stage flowing at least 25 or 30 miles an hour in a torrent downstream in small boats… [with] everybody wearing full winter uniforms [and] with every possibility of anything you can carry with it."[10]

The assault boats, Roland remembered, were row boats with about eight oars each. They had been stacked in a park near the river in Echternach in anticipation of the crossing. Snow was on the mountains at that time, and he knew that the melting snow was rushing into the river, causing flooding and fast currents. As he recalled it, the small, beautiful stream became a torrent of water. He also noted that the Germans had planted barriers to prevent the crossing, including firings from tanks and "a monster bunker with 10-inch concrete walls for the protection of their own men."[11]

Preceding the actual crossing, he remembered there was an artillery display. Then, during the crossing, the Germans traded fire with the Americans. "And the Germans lit up the sky like daylight with whatever it was, uh, shells whatever they had." He later described them as flares.[12] He called the German 88 the "finest, most efficient weapon in this war."[13]

The 417th Regiment moved into the park, where the boats were stacked and prepared for the river crossing. As they moved onto the river, their boat was deluged by raging water. "At this time the beautiful evening became alive with firing of 88… I watch[ed] boat after boat being hit by shells and torrents of machine gun fire… I saw as 3 boats in back of us [were] hit by fire, the boats turning over by the torrents of water…."[14] Despite the firings and the raging river, Roland's boat neared the German side of the river.

During the one interview with Roland on tape, he refused to talk about how he made it to the German shore. "That is not something I really want to speak about. I'd rather not speak about that." He later briefly discussed what happened. Roland's boat almost made it across. As the assault boat carrying his unit over the river approached the shore, his commander told him to get out of the boat and pull the boat to shore. After he climbed out of the boat, German fire hit the boat, perhaps making Roland the lone survivor from that boat. He managed to walk through the remaining few feet, which had mines and barbed wire, to shore.[15]

"Me and one of my buddies are ordered to
jump from the boat and pull it to shore side,
An 88 shell lands in the center of the boat and
I see my friends, buddies being torn apart. The
screaming. They are very quickly being taken
downstream by the torrents of water…but
orders probably saved our lives because we
could not swim in the swirling torrent [where]
we were. Five feet from German side, we hit a
cleavage so we could straighten ourselves….
Somehow I survive and I find myself alive. The
river has become almost alone, I see no boats
just wild water. I am now on shore in a small
pool of melted ice and I see 2 other men who
are alive."[16]

Roland estimated that the gear he carried into the boat
weighed between 80 and 90 pounds. It included a bazooka and
a burp (machine) gun, as well as ammunition and a backpack
with other personal supplies. He understood his mission to be
"one of the first soldiers to enter Germany on the last push
into Germany."[17] The problem was the weight that pulled the
men down into the water. Roland noted that "Probably the
only reason I am alive today [is].... I had the presence of mind
to realize that with all the things strapped on me as they were
and we were close enough to shore that I figured I might sit on
the bottom on my legs and walk to the shore. Because
everybody tried to swim. And that is why they all died. So many
of them."[18]

Roland was also lucky because the German side of the river contained a minefield lined with barbed wire. He avoided these obstacles and made his way through the last few feet of water to reach the shore. There he found himself with two other men he did not know in a similar situation; however, much of their equipment was gone. According to him, "Very few of us got to the other side." He felt like he "was one of the three men to invade Germany."[19] The quiet he described on reaching the shore following the chaotic and loud crossing still haunts even me. One of my first questions on hearing this was: what happened to all the soldiers that night?

The Setting for the Battle: Luxembourg

I decided to visit Luxembourg and the Echternach area to understand the setting for my father's story of war. It's hard to imagine all the horrors that took place there. Today it is a peaceful farming area with walking tours of an ancient city and hiking areas nearby to enjoy the countryside. The Sauer and Our Rivers are narrow rivers, not rushing torrents that meander through the green landscape. There are tall hills, narrow roads with switchbacks, farms and pastures, and small villages. If you look further and across the rivers into Germany, you find the remnants of war: there are foxholes and trenches hidden in the wooded areas and half-hidden pillboxes in odd places. Some are still intact. There are also majestic views from the hilltops overlooking the area; these highpoints were also used to survey the area and assemble artillery sites during the war. It was a most elucidating trip since my guide, coincidently named Roland, was a local expert in the history of World War II in that area.

Luxembourg is a small sovereign state with a rich history dating back to 963 AD. It is landlocked, currently situated northeast of France, south of Belgium, and west of Germany.

The state was not always independent, however, since it spent time as part of the French, Dutch, and German empires throughout the Middle Ages and Renaissance Era. Indeed, while the state as we know it now approximates Rhode Island in geographical size and has an estimated population of only 628,000 people,[20] Luxembourg's true populace stretched out beyond its borders, intermixing with the populations of its neighbors. The borders were often in flux as states in Europe warred with each other and land exchanged hands. Nevertheless, the people of Luxembourg maintained their own heritage throughout the years while appropriating some customs from the surrounding areas.

Echternach, the oldest city in Luxembourg, is located along the Sauer River in northeast Luxembourg. The city dates back to 698 AD when the Abbey of Echternach was first founded and a town developed along its outskirts. It is older than Luxembourg itself. Today it is a small town with a population of approximately 5,000 people. Today's Echternach still has a vibrant town square with beautiful architecture that was renovated after the destruction of World War II; the Abbey itself remains in excellent condition. The area around the city is serene, with long walkways and biking trails along the river and through the mountains nearby. Dancing processions are held all across the town once a year, and the event (held on Whit Tuesday) attracts tens of thousands of tourists. Looking at it in this context, it is hard to imagine it as the location of a deadly conflagration for the men involved in breaching the Siegfried Line in February 1945.

The town of Echternach, as we know it today, is vastly different than it was years ago. Today, it is a peaceful town. The tranquil terrain around the city and its surrounding towns is both beautiful and menacing due to the facets of its geography. Located on the southern end of the Ardennes Forest, the houses and structures that make up the towns of Echternach and Echternacherbrück are located along flat ground and are surrounded by hills, mountains, valleys, and plateaus covered by densely populated forests. These hills are not rolling, shallow gradients but mean, steep rock faces. The near-sheer cliffs that rise up not far from the banks of the Sauer River make traversing the area extremely difficult. Getting from one place to another often requires taking multiple twists and turns aimed at either traveling through valleys between the small mountains or creating a shallower slope for scaling the cliffs. During the war, the hills provided many different vantage points for both sides, allowing both the Americans and Germans to not only view the other side extremely well but also to place artillery and pillboxes in locations featuring clear firing lines and strong defensive measures. Any aggressive action required the capture of these high points to assure the army's view of the area and to deny vision to the enemy.

The forests themselves also make the area extremely strong for anyone on the defensive. While the high points could provide a vision of the area in general, the forests provided cover for individual soldiers and fortifications within. The Germans were able to use the woods to disguise the locations of various pillboxes along the cliffs, and the roads that wound through the forests provided them with a multitude of options for ambushing American soldiers attempting to traverse them. Machine gun nests, mine fields, and carefully concealed foxholes (many of which were still visible 75 years after they were dug) provided an extra layer of defense beyond the initial barrier of pillboxes overlooking the river, as demanded by the protocols of the Siegfried Line itself.

It is also crucial to understand the role of the Sauer River. The river stretches entirely across Luxembourg and then forms part of the border with Belgium on one side of Luxembourg. Approximately 107 miles long, the river is extremely thin, rarely exceeding 100 feet in width. One exception is in the western part of Luxembourg, where a dam was built in the 1950s, creating an artificial lake. The river flows slowly, generally moving east to west, with very little traffic along the way. The banks consist of large brush that can be as much as 100 feet wide on each side. Some of the hills begin to rise near this edge, meaning that there can sometimes be as little as 200 feet between the river shore and a steep incline.

On a beautiful, sunny day, one can now bask in the serene beauty of the area and assume that the Sauer River is just a placid, narrow river that is not much of an obstacle to anyone in the area. The river on which Echternach lies meanders to the northwest of the town, creating the natural border between Luxembourg and Germany. If one drives along its bank, they realize that at different points, the river heads not only north but sometimes east, west, or south instead. At one point, the river moves south, then east-west, and then north, creating a German salient surrounded on three sides by Luxembourg. Nearby, the town of Bollendorf-Pont is surrounded by Germany on three sides.

Traveling approximately 10 miles (by road) to the northwest of Echternach on the Luxembourg side, one would pass through the small towns (or villages) of Weilerbach, Bollendorf-Pont, Grundhof, Dillingen, and then Wallendorf-Pont. It is in that area that the Sauer River meets the Our River. The Sauer River heads to the west at that point and the Our River goes in a more northern direction. The river today is generally about 30 yards wide and slow moving. On either side, you can see raised banks and vegetation (brush). There are small roads near the edges on both sides. After the roads, there are often high cliffs and hills that sometimes rise to over 150 feet tall, often heavily wooded, although you can sometimes see some rocks. There are small roads heading up the hills, often switchbacks with sharp turns hiding under the vegetation. It is not hard to imagine that, from above the cliffs, the Germans had an excellent view of the American troops as they crossed. Evidence exists even today of the heavily fortified Siegfried line, for there are still partially destroyed pillboxes along the country roads and trenches and foxholes in the heavily wooded areas. Several farms still exist in the area, such as the Ammeldingen Farm just over the river in Germany, where the terrain flattens. And there are plateaus atop hills, such as in Biesdorf, Germany, which provide magnificent views of the area tens of miles away.

Prior to February 1945, the border between Luxembourg and Germany had already seen several crossings. In September 1945, when the First US Army was stationed in this area, troops crossed over into Germany in a number of locations and established a bridgehead. Due to supply shortages and a shift in priorities, the American troops eventually withdrew to the Luxembourg side of the border. In December, the southern attack for the German's Ardennes Offensive (also called the Battle of the Bulge) occurred in Luxembourg, but there were only small gains, and much of that gain was erased quickly. In January, there were additional attempts to cross the river into Germany with limited success. At the same time, the 5th Division crossed the Sauer River in the Diekirch area, not far from where it meets with the Our River within the borders of Luxembourg.

As February began, Patton's Third US Army was preparing for another crossing of the Sauer and Our Rivers, this time into Germany. The Luxembourg that the American soldiers encountered in early 1945 was different than the country preceding the war and today. Bombings and fighting in the streets had already destroyed many of the buildings, and much of the population was evacuated or fled the area for safety purposes.[21] There were minefields, pillboxes, military camps, and other obstacles of war visible throughout the area.

Prelude to Battle: January 1945

January was a month of transition for Allied forces. It would take most of the month for the Allied forces to reduce and eliminate the bulge created by the Germans in December during the Battle of the Bulge. January was also the month for intensified planning at all levels by the Allies for their future operations. On some days during the month of January, the cold and snowy winter weather that plagued the Allies since the fall appeared to be improving, but the effects of the bad winter continued to affect operations. Patton noted in one letter, "The whole country is covered with snow and ice."[22]

Decades later, many men continued to talk about that cold, wet winter that made the war that much harder for the combatants in 1945. Harold J. "Lindy" Lindberg, who was in the 304th Regiment, remembered the cold freezing water in his canteen and was unable to drink until it thawed in the mornings.[23] After finding himself in the river on one occasion, he realized that such exposure, even for a short period of time, would lead to freezing to death.[24]

During January, the 76th Infantry Division arrived in the European theater to join the action. The 76th Infantry Division was activated in 1942 but remained in the United States until its move to Europe in 1944. Major General William Schmidt took control shortly after activation and remained in command until the end of the war in Europe. The division, which included the 304th, 385[th,] and 417th Regiments, was initially assigned to the Fifteenth US Army of the Twelfth US Army Group when they arrived in Europe, probably to complete their training and prepare for combat. They were reassigned to the VIII Corps in the Third US Army several days later in a reserve capacity and relocated to Belgium. At the end of the month, the 76th Infantry Division relocated to Luxembourg on the front lines. The Third US Army issued a new Operational Directive dated January 26, 1945, that adjusted the boundaries between the Third US Army corps and specified that the XII US Corps would assume control of the 76th Infantry Division.[25]

The XII US Corps also consisted of the 5th Infantry Division, commanded by Major General S. Leroy Irwin, and the 80th Infantry Division, commanded by Major General Horace L. McBride. Both divisions arrived in France during the summer of 1944 and fought their way through France. The 80th Infantry Division was involved in the battle to relieve the 101st Airborne Division in Bastogne during the Battle of the Bulge and moved into Luxembourg in January 1945. The 5th Infantry Division, which briefly crossed into Germany in December 1944, fought in Luxembourg to reduce the southern attack in the Battle of the Bulge and was positioned south of the 80th Division. Both divisions were veterans of river crossings. On January 22nd, the 76th Infantry Division advanced into Belgium and three days later reached a location on the southern flank of the corps on the Sauer River in Luxembourg, where they relieved the 345th Infantry Regiment of the 87th Infantry Division. The crossing of the Sauer River would be the first combat experience for the 417th Regiment and the 76th Infantry Division. Colonel George E. Brunner was commanding the 417th Regiment.

Context: The Political and Military Situation in Early 1945

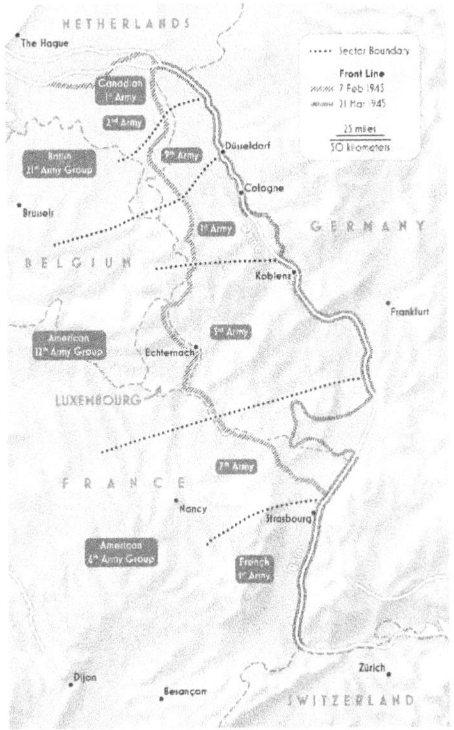

Allied front -February to March 1945

I learned early on in this project that context is important. The XII US Corps was not operating in a vacuum; there were military actions up and down the Allied front. One action or the conditions surrounding that action can affect many other units along the front and even reshape the thinking of the planners and leaders.

On the strategic planning level, Allied leaders were looking toward the end of the war at the beginning of 1945. Roosevelt, Churchill, and Stalin, their staffs and military chiefs, were in Yalta on the Crimean coast, discussing the end of the war in Europe and how the Allies would manage Europe afterward. They were concerned with surrender terms and post-war issues. To them, the question was not if they won the war but when. When asked to estimate when the war in Europe would end, there were estimates that ranged anywhere from the summer of 1945 to the beginning of 1946. Conditions for surrender and post-war issues were important issues, but there were many other topics to address relating to the treatment of Germany, what post-war Europe would geographically look like, territorial shifts and national identities in Europe, how the region would be governed, the treatment of displaced persons and released POWs, war reparations, and the new world organization (the future United Nations).

By the end of 1944, the United States Army had over eight million personnel deployed around the world, with approximately 2.7 million personnel in the European Theater. The 21st British Army Group, comprised of British, Canadians, Polish, and a small number of other nationalities, had several hundred thousand additional troops. There were approximately 85 divisions at the disposal of the Allied forces, with 71 Allied divisions available to fight at that time in

Europe, including 61 American, 16 British, and 8 French divisions. Some divisions were understrength due to casualties and a shortage of replacements.[26]

At the beginning of February, the 21st British Army Group was located in the Netherlands (Holland) on the northern flank of the Allied lines. Field Marshal Bernard Montgomery was the commander of this army group, which included the Canadian First Army, the British Second Army, and the Ninth US Army. At that time, Montgomery was planning Operation Veritable, a drive from Nijmegen southeastward between the Rhine and Maas Rivers to clear the western side of the Rhine River. A second operation, Operation Grenade, was to launch approximately two days later when the Ninth US Army would cross the Roer River near Julich (west of Cologne) and then advance northeast to the area of the Rhine River near Dusseldorf. If successful, the two actions would also capture the Ruhr industrial area in Germany. This would reduce Germany's ability to produce the equipment and supplies required by the troops in battle and would also eliminate many German troops from battle. General Eisenhower instructed Montgomery that Operation Veritable was to start no later than February 8th.[27]

To the south of the British was the Twelfth US Army Group under General Omar Bradley. The army group contained the First US Army under the command of General Courtney Hodges and the Third US Army under General George Patton. The First US Army, located north of St Vith and west and south of the Roer River Dams in Belgium, was tasked with protecting the right flank of the Ninth US Army during Operation Grenade. They were to advance from the area of the Roer River to high ground between the Erft and Rhine Rivers as the Ninth US Army's attack progressed; then the First US Army could seize the strategically important dams in that area.

The Third US Army was located to the south of the First US Army in Luxembourg. Both armies were already in action. Patton was directed to be on an aggressive defense meant to create enough action to pin down German forces in their area and not allow them to relocate to the north, where the main action was.

To the south of the Third Army was General Jacob Devers' Sixth US Army Group. Situated in France east of Metz, it was composed of the Seventh US Army on the northern flank next to the Third US Army and the French First Army. They were in the process of eliminating the Colmar Pocket and settling in on the western banks of the Rhine River, which separated France and Germany in that area.

On the Eastern Front of Germany, the Soviets were moving closer. In the middle of January, they had entered Warsaw, Poland, and were advancing to the Oder River in eastern Germany, approximately 100 miles from Berlin. The Allies understood that the strong Soviet offensive on the eastern German frontier had affected the German war effort by creating casualties and decreasing German manpower strength. The Germans felt compelled to transfer some of their troops from their western front to the eastern front to defend against the aggressive Soviet offensive.

The Third US Army recorded the strength of the German army they would be facing at the beginning of February, just before their Eifel campaign:

> "An estimate of enemy strength in Third U. S, Army zone at this time showed 27,000 combat effectives (the equivalent of three and one-half divisions) and sixty tanks or assault guns, opposing III, VIII and XII Corps, while 18,000 troops (the equivalent of two divisions) and forty tanks or assault guns, were opposing XX Corps [to the south]. To this total of 45,000 St Vith troops (the equivalent of five and one-half divisions) and 100 tanks or assault guns, could be added to the estimated tactical reserve held by the enemy in the Army's zone of advance, consisting of Panzer troops, fifty tanks and 5,000 infantry, the equivalent of one and one-half divisions."[28]

Bradley later wrote about the situation at the end of January, indicating that the German troops were "decimated units, poorly trained, and understrength, but those deficiencies were heavily offset by his Siegfried Line defenses. Except in that 40-mile gap where we had penetrated the Siegfried Line to the Roer, this cordon remained intact from Arnhem to the Swiss border." [29]

Following SHAEF's (Supreme Headquarters Allied Expeditionary Force's) orders for the European Theater, orders filtered down from the Twelfth US Army Group to the First and Third Armies and then to various corps and divisions commanders. Upon receipt of the instructions issued by the Third US Army, commanders from the XII US Corps, the 80th, 5th, and 76th Infantry Divisions, and their regiments were expected to plan operations in a coordinated manner to cross the Sauer and Our Rivers from Luxembourg with the objective of advancing to and then seizing the town of Bitburg in Germany. The 80th Infantry Division was on the northern (left) flank of the corps, the 5th Division was in the center, and the 76th Infantry Division was to the south on the right flank. The 417th Regiment was temporarily assigned to the 5th Infantry Division for additional support. The remaining regiments of the 76th Infantry Division were held in reserve.

The XII US Corps was ordered to begin an assault against the Siegfried Line in the middle of the night on February 7th. The lay of the land directly across the river made this a logistical nightmare for the entire corps. Directly across from Dillingen was a large, uninhabited hill covered in dense forestry. This meant that the Corps' assault would be broken up into two separate sectors, a plan that would be both beneficial to the assault but also potentially more dangerous.

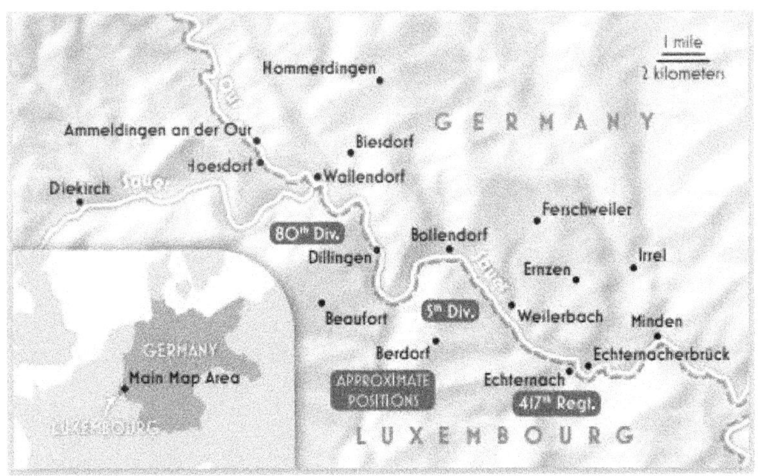

XII Corps Sector Early February 1945

The rough, uninhabited terrain, which had no strategic value, would provide a sense of safety for the units directly next to them because it protected them from a potential flank from German troops; but because passage through the terrain was so difficult, the two sectors on either side of this forested area were very much on their own and could not assist one another as they advanced. The sector to the north, which was focused on the German town of Wallendorf, was to be handled entirely by the 80th Infantry Division and its supporting troops, with little or no immediate assistance available from the 5th and 76th Infantry Divisions in the southern sector.

The attack plan against the Siegfried Line consisted of multiple phases. The first stage was the initial crossing utilizing only some regiments in each division with the goal of establishing a bridgehead. Since the Germans had destroyed most of the bridges over rivers as they withdrew from France, the infantrymen would have to cross the rivers in boats, secure the opposite shoreline, and dig-in. If possible, they were to engage the enemy and reduce pillboxes with sight over the river. Engineers attached to each regiment would be used to help ferry the troops across the rivers and then return the boats to the Luxembourg side to be used again. Additionally, engineers were needed to construct temporary footbridges and treadway bridges to cross the remaining troops, equipment (including tanks and vehicles), and supplies.

Once the troops were across, the men were to begin assaulting key strategic locations in the area. Depending on the unit's location, the targeted location could be a town or simply a hill allowing an excellent view of the surrounding area. After securing temporary bridges for the initial assault over the rivers, the engineers would then work to construct stronger treadway bridges for vehicles and tanks to cross in support of the infantry and long-lasting Bailey bridges for use beyond the assault.

Each regiment had multiple objectives during this operation. The initial objectives were usually close to the river and were designed to reduce the German troops' ability to defend the West Wall. Once certain objectives were achieved, the units would move toward their next goal, usually farther inland, until reaching their final objective. Upon completing that mission, one of the regiments held in reserve would relieve the men of their position and continue the assault.

Directions for the operations around the Sauer River and Our River crossings were sometimes confusing because the rivers meander in multiple directions as they move through Belgium and Luxembourg. The Sauer River generally flows eastward until it reaches Wallendorf, where it meets the Our River, which flows in a generally southeastern direction until it joins the Sauer River. Once both rivers merge in Wallendorf, the Sauer River generally flows north to south in Luxembourg, but it does flow from east to west in a few locations as well. In the area between Dillingen and Bollendorf, the Sauer River generally meanders south and east from Wallendorf to

Dillingen, then moves south to Grundorf, then north, and then east to Bollendorf. Dillingen and Bollendorf are actually east and west of each other. Therefore, troops trying to advance east into Germany might find themselves crossing a river from south to north (not east to west) or find themselves north or south of other troops along the river (not east or west). To conceptualize this better and understand where places were in relation to other places, I also learned to study the maps of the area and even make a few maps of my own.

Preparations, Operations, and the Allied Front: February 1-6

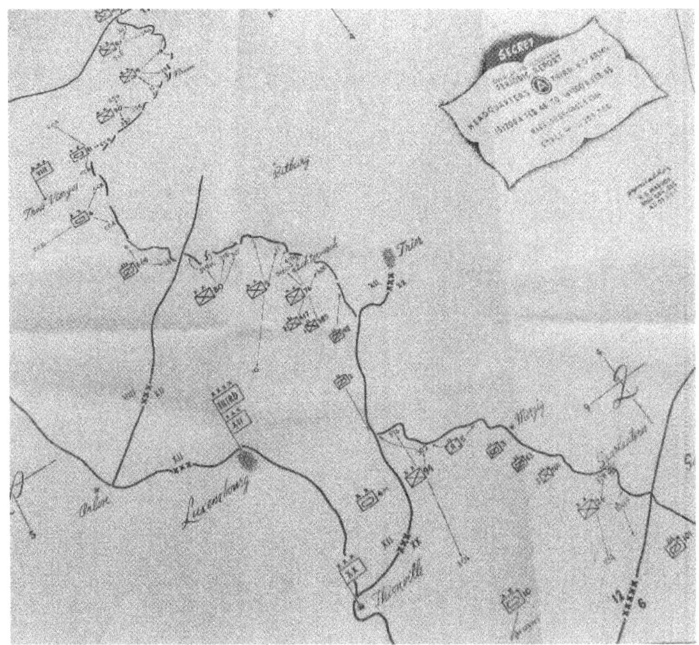

Third Army Planning Map: February 1945

During the first week of February, there were activities to the north and south of the XII US Corps all along the Allied front, but Eisenhower and his commanders were busy planning future actions and overseeing several operations in progress along the Allied front, including the First US Army's V US Corps operation south of the Roer River and its dams, the Third US Army's VIII US Corps attack on the Siegfried Line from the Belgium area, and the Sixth US Army Group's continued efforts to eliminate the Colmar Pocket to the south. At the same time, the 21st British Army Group was planning Operations Grenade and Veritable in the north, and the XII US Corps was preparing for the crossing of the Sauer and Our Rivers into Germany by planning, training, and reconnaissance activities.

On the military commander level, the generals were busy at the beginning of February visiting troops and planning their next operations. Eisenhower was busy issuing letters of instruction for the Allied armies and conferencing with Generals Montgomery, Bradley, and Devers. Bradley then met with army commanders Hodges, Patton, and Simpson at Spa to discuss Eisenhower's orders and coordinate planning activities. Bradley relayed the news from above that the main thrust into Germany would be in the north by the 21st British Army Group with the Ninth US Army under British control. Current operations by Hodges' First US Army and Patton's Third US Army would be allowed to continue until February 10th and perhaps beyond that date, depending on casualties and their consumption of ammunition.[30] Both Hodges and Patton often met with their commanders to share plans and coordinate operations. At the same time, Bradley and Patton often found time to visit various units on the front. Patton wrote he wanted to encourage his troops and to understand exactly what was occurring on the battlefield.

Patton, who loved to study military history and often wrote in his diaries about what he learned, visited the remains of Bastogne and Houffalize on his way to the Spa meeting and noted that Houffalize was completely destroyed during the Battle of the Bulge, even more than St. Vith. He wrote a poem about Houffalize to memorialize the destruction:

> *O little town of Houffalize,*
> *How still we see thee lie;*
> *Above thy steep and battered streets*
> *The aeroplanes sail by.*
>
> *Yet in thy dark streets shineth*
> *Not any Goddamned light;*
> *The hopes and fears of all thy years*
> *Were blown to hell last night.*[31]

Sometimes, the generals and their personal friends would meet briefly for other reasons. On February 5th, Patton was called to Bastogne, where he met with Eisenhower, one of his oldest friends, and Bradley. He discovered that it was for purely social reasons. They had their picture taken together amid the ruins of the city.

North of the Third US Army, the 21st British Army Group under Field Marshal Montgomery was planning for Operations Grenade and Veritable at the beginning of February. Field operations were limited in this sector at that time. South of the 21st British Army Group, the First US Army of the Twelfth US Army Group continued the advance begun on January 28th toward the Roer and Urft Rivers and the seven dams in that area. In the first four days, the army took several towns to the south and west of the dams and reached the Our River and the German border. By the end of January, the First US Army crossed the Our River in two locations and crossed the German border in at least four locations.[32] By February 4th, the First US Army took control of the area west of the Paulushof Dam on the Urft River and moved northeast to reach Urft Lake and the site of the Urfttalsperre Dam. The army now controlled the entrances to two dams and was close to a third dam.[33]

On the northern flank of the Third US Army, the VIII US Corps was situated to the east and southeast of St. Vith, near the Our River. They began a new drive to the east toward Prum on January 29th, with the joint objectives of protecting the right flank of the First US Army and also penetrating the border between Luxembourg and Germany. The corps captured several towns east of the Our River near the border between Belgium and Germany. By the end of February 1st, they advanced four miles into Germany and were moving eastward toward the town of Bleialf, one of their objectives. This action was considered the main operation for the Third US Army at that time.

The next day, the VIII US Corps received word their objectives were changed and were redirected toward Prum and the Prum River. Some of their southern sectors were reassigned to the III US Corps.[34] Acting on intelligence that there were a number of unoccupied pillboxes in their sector, the VIII Corps began an assault from the northern part of the corps sector in the Schnee Eifel area and captured ten pillboxes on their way to capturing the town of Brandscheid.[35] The advance continued as the corps captured the town of Habscheid to the southwest of Brandsheid, Grosskampenberg to the west, and strategically important high ground northeast of Brandscheid. The corps was now less than ten miles to the west of Prum. The III US Corps was located to the south of the VIII US Corps and north of the XII US corps in early February. The corps took a defensive position between the Cleve and Our Rivers. Their orders were to maintain an aggressive defense against enemy troops in their sector area with the goal of prohibiting the enemy from moving elsewhere along the front. The corps reported no other operations but were told to be ready to attack northeast or east towards the Kyll River if necessary.

The 80th Infantry Division entered the war in Europe at the beginning of August 1944 when they landed at Utah Beach and were assigned to the Third US Army's XII US Corps. The division was responsible for the capture of Argentan on the east of the Falaise Pocket in August and participated in the Third US Army's drive across France. They were also active in the attack against the German bulge created by the Ardennes Offensive, fighting in Luxembourg and at Bastogne. By the beginning of 1945, the experienced division had participated in several operations and crossed multiple rivers. The 2nd Battalion of the 318th Regiment received a Battle Honors Unit Citation for its action around Bastogne at the end of December 1944.

The 80th Infantry Division's sector in February included the area to the north of the unoccupied forest in Germany and extended south opposite the forest itself. They were located in the Luxembourgish town of Reisdorf, south of the junction of the Sauer and Our Rivers, where the Sauer River provides a natural border between Luxembourg and Germany. The 319th Regiment was to the left (north) of the 318th Regiment, which was situated in Dillingen directly south of the unoccupied forest. This made their station relatively secure yet poorly situated for an effective assault. The regiment's crossing site was actually northwest of Dillingen in an area where the men could then move due north toward more desirable locations in Germany.

The 319th Regiment's assault plan called for a river crossing at 3 AM on February 7th in conjunction with a crossing at the same time by the 318th Regiment farther south. These crossings were timed to be approximately two hours after the troops in the XII US Corps' southern sector began their own attacks against the Siegfried Line. The 2nd Battalion of the 319th Regiment planned to cross the Our River near the Luxembourgish town of Hoesdorf, northwest of Reisdorf (also known as Kleinsreisdorf). The 1st Battalion was to move northeast from Reisdorf to the junction between the Sauer and Our Rivers and then cross the Sauer River close to Wallendorf. After crossing, the 2nd Battalion was to proceed up the overlooking ridge to capture this dominating terrain. Similarly, the 1st Battalion was to secure the high ground before daylight and, then, when darkness lifted, work back towards the river, clearing pillboxes along the way.[36] After the initial crossing, the engineers would construct a footbridge on which the 3rd Battalion would cross.[37]

The 318th and 319th Regiments' assaults were to be preceded by an artillery barrage beginning approximately 30 minutes before the crossings. It was primarily a diversionary tactic; at times, the artillery would aim at the crossing site, but often the guns would focus farther inland toward enemy gun locations. In doing so, the artillery hoped to draw fire away from the crossing site and onto themselves, allowing the infantry to cross without enemy fire focused on the river.

Meanwhile, the 318th Regiment was to assault the Siegfried Line farther southeast by crossing the Sauer River just outside of Dillingen, Luxembourg. From there, the unique terrain would force the troops to divide themselves between moving east and west along the southern side of the hill on the German side of the river. The 1st Battalion would remain in reserve. The 3rd Battalion was to head east toward Bollendorf in the 5th Infantry Division sector. They were to assist them in the capture of that town and then move back west into position near Biesdorf, which was the 2nd Battalion's main objective.[38]

Like many other plans, the 318th Regiment's plans were designed to be conducted as swiftly as possible. The regiment wanted to strike quickly at what it considered to be the most important high ground within the sector. Unfortunately, the operation failed to account for extreme delays in crossing the Sauer River. If the attack was delayed in any way, the difficulty in completing the mission would rise considerably.

Both the 318th and 319th Regiments sent specially trained reconnaissance teams over the river to gather intelligence to aid in their planning. The usual goal of these reconnaissance missions was to gather "all possible information of the strength and disposition of enemy troops on the eastern side of the Sauer River, location of pillboxes and guns and any other military fortifications."[39] These attempts did not yield the desired information.[40] Fortunately, while the location of the enemy would remain foggy, the 80th Infantry Division knew ahead of the attack just how limited the Germans' resources were. The Siegfried Line may have contained a vast number of pillboxes and structures to be used in defense of Germany, but those resources could only be used successfully with adequate manpower, which had been severely diminished in the aftermath of the Ardennes Offensive.[41] Intelligence estimated that the American troops outnumbered their foes by over three times as many men. While the Germans held an advantage in position along their defensive line and a surprise factor of hidden locations, they lacked the manpower to fight on even terms with the US army. This also meant that one of the strengths of the Siegfried Line, the redundant defense system, would be underutilized.

The 80th Infantry Division was a veteran of river crossings and had developed a set of procedures to improve their efficiency and efficacy in mounting assaults across rivers. However, once the actual crossing was attempted, each regiment had its own unique procedures.

The 319th Regiment decided that each boat would consist of a 13-man team. A full squad of nine men would be passengers on the boat while a three-man engineering crew operated the boat. A fourth engineer was part of the assault team, and his responsibility was to hold the boat in place while the others loaded into the boat, then help release the boat once it was ready. The boat was to move across the river, drop off the nine-man squad, and then return with just the three engineers.[42] Additionally, there were detailed plans for the storage of the boats for the crossing, the procedures to retrieve the boats from the dispatch point, how they would be dispatched to the point of embarkation, and how the boats would be launched at the control point.[43] This plan contrasted slightly with the crossing pattern for the 318th Regiment, which used a smaller crew manning the boats.[44] Their plan called for only two men to be in charge of the boats rather than four, a mistake that would ultimately come back to hurt the American troops during the assault.

The 80th Infantry Division held their 317th Regiment in reserve. They were to be used later in the operation.

The 5th Infantry Division arrived in Europe even earlier than the 80th Regiment by landing on Utah Beach in early July 1944. Originally part of the V US Corps of the First US Army, they were reassigned to the XX US Corps of the Third US Army in August. During the breakout operations from Normandy, they captured Angers. While driving across France, they crossed the Seine River at Fontainebleau and the Marne River to seize Reims. The division reported heavy casualties (perhaps 1,400 troops) during operations to establish a bridgehead over the Moselle River in September. Later, they captured Fort Driant, the last fort to fall around Metz in December. That same month, the division crossed into Germany and reached the Saar River before the Battle of the Bulge. The 5th Infantry Division was part of the Third US Army's drive against the German bulge during December and was reassigned to the XII US Corps on December 21st. On January 18th, 1945, the 5th Infantry Division crossed the Sauer River near Diekirch, Luxembourg, and then drove toward the Our River farther north. All these locations were in Luxembourg. They were now planning a second crossing of the Sauer River farther south, this time into Germany.

The 5th Infantry Regiment was responsible for the assault in the southern sector of the XII US Corps, located south of the unoccupied forest and reaching down to the ancient town of Echternach. They recorded their plans differently than other units in the XII US Corps and emphasized different elements and details of the attack. The 5th Infantry Division chose to utilize the 10th and 11th Regiments for this action, allowing the 2nd Regiment to remain in reserve. These two regiments were located on the Sauer River northeast of Echternach. The 76th Infantry Division's 417th Regiment was placed temporarily under the command of the 5th Infantry Division to cover the far-right flank of that corps near Echternach. The 76th Infantry

Division's 304th and 385th Regiments were held in reserve at the beginning of the operation, as was the 4th Armored Division, which was also part of the XII US Corps at that time. The 417th Regiment was stationed in Echternach itself.

The plan for the 10th Regiment called for the initial crossing to be made by the 2nd Battalion in the dead of night near Weilerbach (north of Echternach and south of the German town of Bollendorf). The other battalions would then cross. Once they crossed, the 2nd Battalion was to head due north to Diesburgerhof, a town northeast of Bollendorf, while the 3rd Battalion was to occupy ground northwest of the town, thereby protecting the flank and cutting off Bollendorf from the rest of Germany. Once those two objectives were secured, the 1st Battalion would swing back southwest to take Bollendorf, a key objective of the operation.[45] Attached to the 10th Regiment was the 133rd Engineer Battalion, which was tasked with operating the boats and building a bridge across the river to expedite troop movement after the initial crossings were made. They also had the support of the 5th Division Artillery, as well as a battalion of men operating smoke generators for obscuring enemy vision. After the initial breach, the 10th Regiment planned to have air support drop in supplies for the troops.

The 11th Regiment was located along the Sauer River to the right of the 10th Regiment near the town of Berdorf. Their right flank was protected by the 417th Regiment. Their plan was to cross the Sauer River just after midnight on February 7th. The 2nd and 3rd Battalions would cross the river simultaneously, with the 2nd Battalion on the left and the 3rd Battalion on the right. The 1st Battalion would be held back in reserve. After crossing, the troops were to make their way north toward the high ground on the German bank.[46] The 3rd Battalion would swing east and capture the German town of Ernzen. The 2nd Battalion would move north toward Ferschweiler to protect the flank of the 10th Regiment as they captured that town and then drive north toward the Prum River to establish a secure area in preparation for the next river crossing.[47] The troops were directly supported by the 7th Engineer Combat Battalion, which was in charge of operating the boats needed for the assault and building bridges across the river. The 19th, 30th, and 31st Field Artillery Battalions and a unit of chemical engineers were also attached to provide support and smoke for the assault.[48] Unlike the 80th Infantry Division plan, they did not detail how the initial crossings would utilize the engineers.

The 417th Regiment of the 76th Infantry Division did not enter the war in Europe until they arrived at Le Havre, France, in January 1945 and were assigned to the XII US Corps. They were sent into defensive positions along the Sauer and Moselle Rivers in the vicinity of Echternach. The regiment was unique in the XII US Corps in that it was composed mostly of green soldiers who had never seen combat before.

The 417th Regiment in Echternach was temporarily attached to the 5th Infantry Division militarily but was still attached to the 76th Infantry Division administratively. Their job was to cover the right flank for the XII US Corps operation. The recorded plan of attack for the 417th Regiment was less detailed than the other regiments in the Corps. They recorded that they would cross the Sauer River north of Echternach on the night of February 6-7th by stealth and establish a bridgehead. This would allow the engineers to construct footbridges and, later, a Bailey bridge across the river to further enhance the Allied troops' ability to cross the river. Once the entire regiment was across, the troops were then to push east and northeast toward the Prum River. The small German town of Echternachenbruck, across the Sauer River northeast of Echternach, was to be captured along the way, but ultimately the goal of the 417th Regiment was to establish control of the area south of the Prum River near the towns of Irrel, Menningen, and Minden.[49] The plan noted that each battalion had multiple objectives that functioned as checkpoints before their final objective, a point north of Minden and south of Irrel (086382), which was considered the most important goal. Once the regiment captured this objective, they would be relieved by the 385th Regiment. According to the commanding officer of the 417th Regiment:

> "The 1st Bn, crossing initially, was to organize across the river, reduce the pillboxes [sic] as it advanced, and seize the high ground (067377) about 2000 yards north of the crossing site. The 2nd, following in the wake of the first, was to sweep directly east along the steep escarpment, clear the pillboxes in its path, and advance to its objective, the high ground midway between ECHTERNACH and MINDEN (075366). The 3rd Bn, upon crossing was to assemble and organize in the ravine on the left flank of the regiment, then move on order between the 1st and 2nd Bn to the regiment's final objective (086382)."[50]

Attached to the 417th Regiment were various supporting units, including the 160th Engineer Combat Battalion, the 91st Chemical Battalion, the 901st Field Artillery, and the division's own artillery. Additionally, air support was expected to resupply the troops that made it across the river.

The area of the crossing site was extremely perilous for a variety of reasons. The terrain itself provided various obstacles. The approach to the river on the side of Luxembourg is extremely hilly, and the scarcity of roadnets to the crossing sites was extremely difficult to manage. There was only one approach leading to the crossing site where the 417th Regiment embarked, so maintaining cover was key to disrupting enemy fire along the predictable pathway to the river.[51] Furthermore, the hilly area on the opposite bank meant that after crossing, the men would have limited vision of the enemy, and the enemy could use their strong vantage points against the Allied soldiers, both while in Luxembourg and once they crossed onto German soil.

On the other side of the river was a flood plain that extended about 200 yards to the foot of an escarpment which rose almost vertically to a height of about 150 feet above the river. On the left flank of the regimental zone, a draw ran northeast, leading gradually upwards to the top of the escarpment.[52] This meant that the soldiers had to move slowly and methodically to safely approach areas suspected to be German strongholds.

The crossing pattern the 417th Regiment chose differed from that of the 10th and 11th Regiments. The latter two chose to cross small portions of their initial battalions by boats as a means of stealthily acquiring control of the opposite shore. The small group of men (never more than a company) was to control the area while the engineers were to construct a bridgehead that would allow the rest of the battalion across. The 417th Regiment, however, chose instead to cross an entire battalion by boat, hoping to fully gain control quickly. The risk of crossing a large number of men immediately was much higher than the risk taken by the 10th and 11th Regiments in crossing reconnaissance platoons and single companies. It ultimately proved to be a decision that led to a large number of casualties, but at the same time, it may have saved the operation.

Activity by the XII US Corps in Early February

At the beginning of February, the 80th Infantry Division of the XII US Corps was located between Bettel and Bollendorf in Luxembourg. They were actively patrolling their sectors, probing the German defenses in the area, and preparing for their upcoming operations. Periodically, they would receive enemy artillery and mortar fire.[53] The 319th Regiment sent patrols to the area near the Our River to check approaches for the crossings and several days later practiced river crossings.[54] The engineers organized themselves for the crossings and for the construction of bridges across the river.[55] There were also some limited-objective attacks in the 80th Infantry Division sector to clear the town of Hoesdorf, Luxembourg, on the west bank of the Our River.[56] This was to ensure that the Germans were pushed back to the east bank of that river.[57] Prior to the assault, the 319th and 318th Regiments sent reconnaissance teams along the river to scout out the enemy defense system, gain information on the terrain, and determine enemy positions. The 318th Regiment made two attempts, but neither attempt yielded the desired information.[58]

The reconnaissance team for the 319th Regiment attempted to scout the area on the German side of the river, but the heavy fog and dense forest on the opposite side made observing from Luxembourg nearly impossible. Other troops crossed the Sauer River near Moestroff to test conditions rather than to scout the area, but operations were conducted in very different conditions from what they would eventually face as the men had no time limit, crossed without the cover of darkness, faced no enemy fire, experienced no drift from heavy river currents[59] and was done in an entirely different crossing location than where the men would cross on February 7th. There was little information gained by these attempts. The 318th Regiment also tried to gather information by establishing listening posts, but the battalions failed to pick up any useful communication from the German side, and the thick woods in the vicinity of the town of Biesdorf made observation of opposing troops difficult. Additionally, the Americans unsuccessfully attempted to obtain a new German prisoner to gain information, either through the capture of an enemy reconnaissance team member or by sneaking across the river to capture a German patrol.[60]

The 5th Infantry Division, located to the south of the 80th Infantry Division, did not chronicle much of their preparation during the first few days of February except to note they prepared for the assault and patrolled their sectors. This was also true for the 417th Regiment. On February 3rd, the artillery units for the XII US Corps remained active by firing harassing charges at enemy buildings and towns. The 417th Regiment recorded that they were officially attached to the 5th Infantry Division for operational purposes during the first week of February and moved into position next to the 5th Infantry Division near Echternach.

Obstacles Affecting War: Weather, Geography, and the Siegfried Line

To truly understand the difficulties faced by the men of the XII US Corps in breaching the Siegfried Line, it is imperative that we know more than just the battlefield itself. I developed a healthy respect for how outside influences and the weather, terrain, and Germany's fortifications can play a part in shaping how the battle is fought and the outcome of the operation. Leadership cannot avoid considering these obstacles and other uncontrollable influences, as the planners sometimes have to adapt their strategy to overcome them.

Remains of pillboxes in Germany near the Sauer

The weather influenced operations during much of the European campaign. Rain, wind, snow, ice, and other forms of bad weather decreased visibility for land and air operations and led to flooding and muddy roads. In some cases, bad weather canceled ground operations, and at other times it limited supporting air operations - which were beneficial or harmful to offensive or defensive positions, depending on how much each side was affected by the inability to use air support due to difficult conditions brought on by the bad weather. The Allies required good weather conditions to carry troops across the water to land on the beaches of Normandy. Bad weather on June 5th delayed the invasion of Normandy by one day and almost delayed it for a full month. During the actual landings, some boats were blown off course and landed in the wrong locations. On the other hand, bad weather could ground air support for the enemy.

During many of the Allied operations in 1944 and 1945, the weather was uncooperative and dictated how the war was conducted. There was intense cold as well as heavy freezing rain and snow through much of the winter beginning in November 1944. Eventually, the troops encountered muddy roads and flooded conditions. Air support and bombing missions were curtailed at times, and tanks sometimes bogged down in the mud. The adverse weather continued for months. Eisenhower noted the problems in his memoirs, but he decided at that time that operations should continue:

> "By November 1 many of the rivers were out of their banks and weather conditions along the whole front slowed up our attacks. In spite of these conditions we proceeded with the general plan of building up great bases and communications to the borders of Germany, closing the Rhine with initial emphasis on the left, preparing for the destruction of the German forces west of the river, throughout its length, and getting ready to launch the final assaults toward the heart of Germany."[61]

"Damn the weather, it is starting to rain." Patton wrote in his diary on December 3rd.[62] Six days later, he noted, "It is still raining. The Saar usually 50 feet wide is now 300, but that won't stop us."[63] At one point, Patton tried another approach: "The weather was so bad that I directed all Army chaplains to pray for dry weather."[64]

Bad weather, the Allies learned, could also be used as a tactical weapon. The Germans timed their Ardennes Offensive to coincide with bad weather so that the Allies could not rely on air operations for support. During the encirclement of Bastogne, bad weather prevented air drops of supplies for the surrounded American troops. This problem presented itself again for the XII US Corps in February.

The cold, wet weather lingered into the next year. Patton noted the problem in January when he wrote: "The whole country is covered with snow and ice."[65] Towards the end of the month, however, there was a period of warmer weather. This caused different problems, as the melting snow began to flow into the rivers, widening them until they reached flood stage in some places. It also increased the speed and intensity of the river flow. Roads became muddy and sometimes collapsed from all the water:

> "With the advent of bad weather, road
> maintenance presented additional problems to
> the Services of Supply because of the shallow

foundations of many of the European roads, particularly in Belgium. In numerous instances our heavily laden trucks broke completely through the surfaces of main highways and it seemed almost impossible to fill the resulting quagmires with sufficient stone and gravel to restore them to a semblance of usefulness."[66]

Patton continued to record the bad weather in his diary. On January 18th, he wrote: "Things are a little slow just now mostly due to utterly vile weather. Yesterday Eddy jumped off in a London fog which turned to rain and sleet. We are going forward but are mostly delayed by the ice.[67] Two days later, he recorded that "The weather could not be worse. It is snowing like hell again now."[68] Eight days later, Patton wrote: "We are starting a new attack to day and it is snowing like Hell. However, I think that the Germans are in a bad way and that we will be able to get through. Unfortunately we have to storm the Siegfried line as a starter."[69] The issue of the ongoing bad weather continued to affect the planning process, for there was concern about flooded areas, damaged roads, and the need to reduce air operations.

At the end of January, the forecast for most days still included bad weather, creating the possibility that operations such as the Sauer and Our River crossings could be nightmares. Several accounts state that the Sauer flooded above the brush on the sides of the river, which then reached almost 100 yards in width and rose to be six to twelve feet deep, far greater in width than the normal 30 feet during a peaceful day. As the Americans began preparations for the assault, a steady bout of rainy weather set in. With the increase in water from the thaw and the rain, the Sauer River began to develop a strong current between 8 to 12 miles per hour.[70] While one could easily swim across the river in a matter of seconds on a peaceful day, any attempt to do so in February of 1945 would be foolhardy due to the terrible weather, bad river conditions, and the possibility of frostbite from exposure.

The weather was especially difficult for the infantry's three major support groups: the engineers, the artillery, and the air force. First, the current was the bane of the engineers, who became frustrated by the Sauer River's tendency to force the boats they were operating off course and to wash out sections of the bridges they were tasked with constructing. Both jobs became harder and took longer than anticipated. Additionally, it was their job to repair broken roads, often destroyed by the muddy quagmires, adding to the workload. Second, the artillery required clear lines of sight to find locations on which they could fire. Mist, fog, and smoke blowing in the wind often obscured the enemy on both sides. In some inopportune moments, the smoke actually moved in odd directions due to the wind, allowing enemy vision that would normally have been obscured. Finally, the pilots involved in air support faced difficulty staying on course, which led to off-target landings, bombings, dropped supplies, and smoking. In some cases, plane missions were canceled due to concern about their chance of success in the harsh weather.

Geography was also an important factor in planning. I learned that the terrain in the area of Echternach dictated the type of operations to be conducted and the equipment which could be used. The hills and ridges around Echternach and the Sauer and Our Rivers played a role in planning operations.

Mountains, tall cliffs, and high ridges often required skills to climb and provided vantage points to survey the area below. Forests provided hidden locations for observation and concealed artillery from aerial view. The First US Army spent months trying to clear the Huertgen Forest because troops could not be sure what was below the trees or even around the corner, and ravines and gorges were difficult to move through.

Control over the limited roadways and the intersections of major roadways was always of importance. In some locations, such as in forested areas and mountain ranges, the only way to advance was via the roadway system, and in some areas, such as on the German side of the Sauer and Our Rivers, roads were limited. If you controlled the roads or the intersections of roads, such as in Bastogne and St. Vith, you controlled the traffic flow: blocked intersections blocked the advance of the enemy.

There were many rivers in this area, and the Germans often destroyed the bridges when withdrawing to obstruct the Allied advance. This was the case in Luxembourg. In the Sauer and Our River crossings, it was necessary for the engineers to construct new bridges to move troops over the rivers faster and to allow tanks and other equipment to move into Germany. Tank warfare, an important component of Patton's overall battle strategy, played only a small part in this operation. As they waited for bridges to transport them to Germany, they could only offer fire support across the river. Once over the rivers, there were no flat plains that were optimal for tank warfare. The terrain would not be as amenable to the mobile warfare Patton's troops excelled in, and disabling the heavy Siegfried Line fortifications could not always be done by artillery alone. As I discovered in the many accounts of the crossings into Germany, American troops developed various methods for destroying the pillboxes and many obstacles that composed the Siegfried Line. Their ingenuity and perseverance were admirable. It was a community effort that sometimes invited artillery from other places to come in and help.

Germany's fortification system along the Siegfried Line was the most dangerous part of the operation due to its defensive measures. The Siegfried Line itself was a series of strong protective measures along the German border designed to repel any and all Allied troops attempting to make their way into Germany. It was a complex system consisting of countless pillboxes, trenches, minefields, barbed wire fences, and other obstacles.[71] The area where the XII US Corps troops, and most notably where the men of the 5th Infantry Division were located, was considered the most heavily fortified area within the entire Siegfried Line. In particular, the defenses opposite Echternach were extremely strong and considered by many as impregnable. Vantage points afforded the Germans excellent locations for pillboxes that could blast the river should anyone attempt to cross, and intelligence reports suggested that the far bank of the river was also laced with a large anti-personnel minefield. The Germans, in fact, were so confident in their defense of the area near Echternach that they were shocked when they discovered that the 417th Regiment had even decided to cross.[72]

The English term "Siegfried Line" is confusing because it really refers to two separate German defense systems. The first Siegfried Line was constructed in the middle of the First World War within France by the Germans after they had already managed to push themselves forward. It was a subsection of the more famous Hindenburg Line established by the Germans in 1916. The second Siegfried Line, and the one usually referenced here, was a series of fortifications constructed by Adolf Hitler in the 1930s along the border of Germany and its neighbors to the west; for this reason, it is often referred to as the "West Wall."

The bunkers and strongholds positioned within the multiple levels of the Siegfried Line defense system provided a multitude of important measures. First, they housed and protected the troops positioned along the Line. Built using a combination of concrete and steel, their pillboxes usually housed anywhere from 6 to 12 soldiers, including one officer. Smaller pillboxes often contained only two rooms: an inner room for quarters containing bunks, supplies, and other items needed for the troops living there and an outer room facing the opposition that had a vision for firing on the enemy. They were often camouflaged as houses or garages or built into hills for additional protection and were surrounded by minefields, booby traps, and other defensive measures.[73] There were different designs based on the specific landscape, but each one generally had a series of embrasures aimed outward for enemy observation as well as some aimed backward in case the enemy managed to move behind the bunker. The embrasures were gun ports intended to prevent the assaulting team from making it to the pillbox doors, and many had bullet traps aimed at stopping the opposition from firing into the bunker. The bunkers also featured complex ventilation measures, especially in pillboxes that contained heavy weaponry that emitted large volumes of smoke when fired.

The size of the embrasures for each bunker varied, usually based on use. Wider embrasures allowed for a greater angle of fire. In some cases, the embrasure was so large it allowed troops an almost 180-degree angle of fire, giving them the ability to fire at anyone coming their way. The drawback to such large embrasures was that they exposed pillbox inhabitants to enemy fire and grenades if the enemy closed the gap. In other pillboxes, the embrasures were simply small holes rather than long strips of open window. This afforded the defenders more protection, but it hurt their offensive power by reducing the angle of fire. Additionally, these holes would only work with certain small weaponry; larger holes or strips were necessary for heavy machine guns or artillery. Embrasures of this nature were also outfitted on the outside with a stepped slope, which allowed for an increase in the angle of fire while limiting the bullet trap effect that draws in and increases the accuracy of enemy fire.

Many pillboxes featured elaborate tunnel and trench systems that provided safe, fast movement between bunkers. Bunkers in specific locations, often on high ground with excellent vision, functioned as command posts charged with issuing directives to other pillboxes nearby. Although orders could be transmitted by radio, many of these command posts were connected in some way to those other pillboxes. One such command structure, the Katzenkopf, was located on a hill overlooking Irrel, north of the Prum and Sauer Rivers. Beneath the confines of this pillbox, which could house as many as 84 men, was a series of unfinished tunnels designed as a method for express resupply from inner Germany.

In theory, the Siegfried Line pillboxes were intended to provide a strong defensive position for any troops stationed within them; however, many of these pillboxes were of poor quality. German General Siegfried Westphal later remarked in his memoirs that the defensive structures were woefully inadequate:

> "The majority of emplacements had concrete roofs of only eighty centimetres thickness which afforded no protection against heavy shells. Many of the positions only had loopholes at the front and were thus at a tactical disadvantage... Because of the short time available it had been impossible to fit the emplacements into the terrain as well as the tacticians desired. Many of them lay not on the more favourable rear slopes but on the front slopes of the hills... One particularly worrying feature was that some of the emplacements possessed no loopholes at all and could therefore only be used as shelters."[74]

Bunkers were not the only strongholds within the Siegfried Line defense system. In addition to pillboxes, the Siegfried Line featured machine gun nests located throughout the forests outlining the roads in Germany. German troops also dug many foxholes around them and obscured them for the express purpose of punishing unwary soldiers passing by. Many nests were located in defensive positions atop hills, in which the gunner and his spotter could lay continuous fire on troops moving into his line of vision. Some were close to the roadways and were instead used for short bursts of fire, after which a trench system would allow the ambushing Germans to escape quickly.

Pillbox location within the Siegfried Line was also a key element in the defensive structure. Several pillboxes in high locations were so remote that they were not particularly useful for firing purposes, but their view of the enemy location was so spectacular that they were used primarily as spotting posts. This use differed from pillboxes located closer to the action, where soldiers had to be more accurate in firing their weapons. These pillboxes, besides being connected, were often close enough that they could see each other. In many cases, the Germans built embrasures facing out in the direction of those other pillboxes, allowing them to fire on the pillboxes should Allied forces manage to capture them. In some locations, there could be as many as six or eight pillboxes per acre.[75] This created a redundant defense system that could slow down any assault, even if the attacker was able to make positive gains in attacking the West Wall.

Besides these fortifications were a series of traps and obstacles aimed not at supporting the German soldiers but at simply doing as much damage to any opposing assault force as possible. Most dangerous were the minefields all across the Siegfried Line. Many of these fields were filled with both anti-personnel mines to take out infantry and anti-tank mines used to disarm any assaulting vehicles. Some minefields were located directly on roadways and in forests, and others were placed in strategic locations around the pillboxes to thwart any flanking members unaware of the mines.

Another common obstacle was barbed wire fencing on the line. This obstacle had one of two effects. It forced a soldier to spend time carefully cutting the wire, where he could be injured coming into contact with the fence or exposing himself to enemy fire, or it funneled the soldiers toward desirable locations where the Germans could fire on the advancing troops. A fence that directed enemy soldiers into an undetected minefield was an especially effective deterrent. If that combination failed to harm the enemy, it often slowed him down, allowing any Germans nearby to retreat before they were overrun.

The use of dragon's teeth was a unique deterrent along the Siegfried Line that symbolized the Siegfried Line itself. These large concrete structures were placed in the ground in locations that were under observation by German heavy weaponry. They were pyramidal in structure and placed in rows (perhaps as many as five rows), giving them their nickname based on aerial views of the structures. The teeth essentially created an obstacle course for any tanks or vehicles attempting to travel through the area. Enemy armored vehicles were forced to move through the area slowly, if at all, allowing Germans on high ground to fire accurately on the opposing vehicles with anti-tank weapons. Andrew Adkins, who was in the 317th Regiment, remembered the dragon's teeth as staggered and spaced in such a manner that a tank could not drive through. Interspersed among the teeth were minefields, barbed wire, and pillboxes that were virtually impregnable to artillery and set in such a way as to give the Germans interlocking fire across the entire front."[76]

Due to the large number of hills and mountains on the border between Luxembourg and Germany, few dragon's teeth fields were located in the vicinity of the XII US Corps. Some of these fields were farther inland, where flatter ground dictated a necessity for man-made vehicular obstacles. Like the Siegfried Line as a whole, the goal was not to stop the enemy right at the border but to draw them into a disadvantageous situation whereupon the Germans could use reserves to punish the enemy for its poor positioning.

Other Troops in Support of the Infantry: Artillery, Engineers, and Medics

The assault across the Sauer and Our Rivers was not done by the infantry alone. Too often, we forget about the support groups in an army, and many of them died on the front. Artillery and chemical units in each division provided cover for the crossings, killed enemy soldiers in their path, and helped in the destruction of pillboxes. Engineers were multi-talented and ferried men across the river, cleared mines, and built bridges so that tanks, equipment, and men could easily move across the river. Medical personnel tended to the injured and even ran toward the front and the danger rather than staying away. Other groups, such as supply units, also operated in support of the river crossings. Each group was important in ensuring the success of the operation. Years later, many veterans remembered and shared their experiences of what life was like on the frontline in Europe.

The use of artillery was key to the success of operations in Europe. Artillery includes large-caliber guns and weapons that could be fired from behind enemy lines to reach a distant target. Unlike small arms, which include guns and rifles, artillery employs heavy machines that fire shells, cannons, rockets, and mortars. The use of artillery began centuries ago when the use of gunpowder and cannon balls was developed. Today, we talk about large-mounted firearms, such as howitzers, that can launch long-range fire at targets they cannot see miles away and are capable of bringing down buildings. Artillery power, therefore, supports the infantry by adding power and range of firings that the infantry's small firearms cannot match.

During World War II, artillery was effective in both destroying active enemy artillery and counter-attacking German troops in their trenches and on the battlefield. It had both defensive and offensive applications. Often located six or more miles from the front, artillery could neutralize enemy actions or cause large casualties and massive destruction via heavy bombardments. When directed accurately, some artillery fire could take out an enemy artillery gun, an outpost, or an attacking infantry group located over ten miles away.

Artillery supported infantry operations in many ways. Preparatory firings on the enemy before a planned attack weakened enemy positions and blocked the enemy from using specific sites. They also protected and covered friendly troops in action and destroyed enemy installations. Firings harassed the enemy when used sporadically, and when aimed at unrelated targets, it created stress on the enemy and prevented sleep.

Military engineers also worked closely with the infantry and spent much of their time on the front lines. In general terms, it was their job to make sure that any obstacles that could impede the progress of the advancing Allied army be removed, anything that could enhance the Allied advance be done, and any obstacle that could hurt the enemy be used. This would include creating their own obstructions against the enemy. The army engineer handbook in 1943 defined what it meant to be an engineer:

> "You are an engineer. You are going to build bridges and blow them up. You are going to stop tanks and destroy them. You are going to build roads, airfields, and buildings. You are going to construct fortifications. You are going to fight with many kinds of weapons. You are going to make sure that our own troops move ahead against all opposition, and you are going to see to it that enemy obstacles do not interfere with our advance. You are an engineer."[77]

To enhance the mobility of the Americans, engineers were responsible for constructing and maintaining buildings, roads, airfields, hospitals, ports, and other structures needed by the armed forces on a routine basis. Bridge building was especially important as the Germans often destroyed bridges over rivers as they retreated to slow down the Allied advance. Roads often required maintenance due to bad weather conditions or overuse. They also were rebuilt to accommodate large tanks and other military equipment. Engineers were also tasked with clearing areas that contained mines, roadblocks, trenches, snow, dragon's teeth, debris, and other impediments to the military advance. Conversely, they might find themselves creating similar minefields and obstacles to create problems for the Germans. New roads, outposts, trenches, fortifications, and fencing were also built by the engineers. When necessary, they would even destroy a bridge, road, or building to protect the Allied troops or impact an operation.

The danger surrounding the work that the engineers did was no more apparent than during their work in Echternach and the crossing of the Sauer and Our Rivers in February 1945. They built bridges, ferried infantry across the river, eliminated mines, did explosive work, and repaired roads. During these activities, they were subject to enemy fire and other dangers. Engineer Willard Chapman remembered working on a bridge over the Sauer River, which was near completion when a loose boat floated down the river and severed a cable that held the bridge in place. They lost the entire bridge after hours of work.[78] In the attempted crossings in the 417th Regiment sector, so many engineers were lost in the 160th Engineer Battalion by the end of the second day that they were replaced by the 282nd Engineer Battalion. Thomas G. Manos, an engineer in the 5th Division, received a Silver Star for his work in crossing the Sauer River between February 5th and 9th. His unit made reconnaissance crossings to gain information prior to the action. During the operation, the swift current and intense enemy fire made it impossible to construct a footbridge across the Sauer River, but he braved the enemy fire completely exposed while coordinating and directing crossings by means of assault boats. This helped establish the bridgehead despite the swift current. Once across, they then used mine detectors to eliminate mines and boobytraps.[79]

Engineer combat groups were versatile, but it was dangerous work. They used bulldozers to clear streets, but they also did demolition work when necessary. They could not build a bridge before all the mines in the area were removed, and sometimes they were doing this while they were being shelled with mortars. Sometimes they did not get all the mines and people died.[80]

Combat medics also operated on the front lines. They took care of the men in the field and then sent them back behind the frontlines to the aid stations, battalion field hospitals, or other hospitals to receive treatment.[81] They were respected and appreciated by everyone who recognized their willingness to enter an active battlefield to aid the wounded.[82]

As one soldier wrote: The courage and superhuman strength exhibited by the men who brought in the wounded could never be paralleled."[83]

They carried no guns, only first-aid kits, and wore Red Cross bands in the hope that they were safe from fire. Their job was to identify the wounded on the battlefield, evaluate their medical condition, provide immediate first aid (such as bandaging a wound and providing pain medication) to stabilize them, and then evacuate the men from the place where they were wounded. As a combat medic, Marvin Kruse viewed his job as to "prevent shock, stop bleeding, and evacuate them out of the line of fire and then get them back to the aid station where they could be treated further."[84] They carried two bags on both sides with supplies. Ben Antonio noted that there were so many men he took care of that he could not remember them all. He learned "you take care of the worst guy first, but we cried a lot."[85] He also learned that he had to make choices: if he knew the man would not make it, he would give the man a shot of morphine and move on to the next wounded soldier. The least wounded soldiers were taken care of last.[86]

Medics were constantly in action during battles, and they often worked at night to try to get the wounded out because daytime fighting made it difficult to reach the wounded. If the battle stopped at night, they were often involved in finding, treating, and evacuating casualties they could not reach during the day. Even then, it was dangerous. Sometimes they were searched by the Germans.[87] During the crossings of the Sauer River, they were involved in a motor assault boat operation for the evacuation of the wounded. They flew a large Red Cross flag to avoid enemy fire. "No one bothers to linger long enough to tie up the boats- probably because the landing points are directly under Siegfried Line pillbox guns."[88] Jessee Dye talked about how he would have to go out to get the injured with firing from both sides in what he called a no man's land.[89] They were constantly in demand and rarely had time off. Carl Hatfield noted that he went for a solid month without changing his clothes, and it was cold at the time.[90] Ben Antonio claimed he never got a change of clothes until near the end of the war.[91]

Outfitting the Troops: Weapons and Equipment

Infantry units carried with them into battle a variety of equipment. Standard military gear included an assortment of possessions for various purposes. But most crucially, each soldier was outfitted with a primary weapon as well as a secondary weapon, such as knives and pistols. Each soldier's primary weapon dictated his role in battle. They also carried a shovel to dig foxholes. The majority of infantrymen carried weapons that fell into three categories: machine pistols, semiautomatic rifles, and automatic rifles.

Each class of weapon had its own advantages and disadvantages. Machine pistols were mid-weight, fast-firing weapons with large ammunition clips capable of firing out hundreds of rounds a minute, but they lacked the range or armor-piercing capabilities of rifles. The Colt automatic pistol, developed and used during World War I, was often the standard issue in World War II. However, it was more suited to personal defense, given the development of more sophisticated weaponry.

Semiautomatic rifles were light yet strong weapons that could be fired extremely accurately but at a far slower rate. The Garand Semi-automatic Rifle M1, one of the most widely used American semiautomatic rifles, could be used operationally at 656 yards, or three times the distance of the Tommy Gun. The gun's effectiveness was counterbalanced by a lower firing rate.[92]

Finally, automatic rifles combined the distance of the semi-automatic rifles with the firing speed of a machine pistol. Unfortunately, these weapons were extremely heavy and bulky and required a set up involving bipods or tripods in order to provide stability for firing accurately. Light rifles, such as the Browning Automatic Rifle (BAR), could be carried and operated by one person but featured lower clip sizes than their heavier counterparts. The BAR itself featured a 20-round clip and, in practice, could fire 60-80 rounds each minute.[93] Heavy machine guns, which required one person to operate the gun and another to change out ammunition clips or belts, were extremely heavy and required a period of setup time.

Select infantry also carried a variety of other weapons into battle besides standard firearms. Flamethrowers were uncommon but used effectively on both sides: defensively as a deterrent for entering pillboxes as well as offensively in large fields for smoking out ambushing enemies hiding in heavy brush. Most crucially, infantry also carried explosives designed either to combat enemy vehicles (armored or unarmored) or to blow holes in enemy defense systems. Satchel charges, for example, were used in extremely close quarters; when troops assaulted an enemy stronghold, they were placed near doorways in order to create an entranceway for the troops to attack the soldiers inside the bunker or pillbox. Many also carried grenades.

There were two forms of ranged explosives. The first was propelled rockets that were fired directly at enemy vehicles. As the war continued, the United States developed a reusable version of the German panzerfaust, a single-use weapon consisting of a long tube that fired a missile with a large, bulbous head. It was called the bazooka. On the Siegfried Line, these bazooka rocket launchers became useful in the assault on pillboxes, where they were fired into small openings to stun the inhabitants.

The other ranged explosives commonly used by the infantry were mortars. Unlike bazookas, they were capable of firing at large distances. Although artillery could easily outclass them in this area, mortars were more mobile and thus more flexible in their use. They were easily transportable and were usable with little setup. Additionally, mortars not only could be used to detonate explosives among enemy troops but could be fit with specific payloads aimed at emitting large amounts of smoke. When placed in strategic locations, this allowed the infantry to obscure their movement. Finally, mortars fired in a high arc rather than a straight line toward the opposing troops, allowing the men operating them to occasionally hide their location by firing from cover.

Artillery and heavy vehicles also played important roles in warfare at the time. Each division maintained its own heavy artillery units. These weapons were the strongest howitzers available on the ground, capable of firing up to 10 miles away. They were not particularly mobile, however, and as a result, they were set up in strategic positions of strength prior to the start of a battle. Field artillery, on the other hand, consisted of lighter weapons that could still outrange any weapons in the hands of an infantryman and be used effectively against armored units, but they did not have the strength or range of their heavier counterparts. Instead, these guns were more mobile and could be moved around a field of battle to get into a better position. Tank destroyers, or "TDs," made up the bulk of field artillery units during World War II.

There would be no tank destroyers without the tanks themselves. They were armored vehicles that were a combination of powerful weaponry protected by heavy armor with mobile capabilities that allowed them to be used on the front lines of combat. The M4 Sherman medium tanks, with their use of combined firepower, was one of the most massed-produced tanks of the war. They played only a small part in the crossing of the Sauer River.

Finally, it is important to note that the breaching of the Siegfried Line was not a battle fought in two dimensions. The sky was itself a part of the battlefield, but aircrafts played only a small part in the breaching of the Siegfried Line for several reasons. First, the German defense was actually quite strong. Unlike the Maginot Line, the Siegfried Line's inherent design allowed the Germans to defend their airspace quite effectively. But more crucially, the weather was problematic for flying during the operation. Early aviation was risky in poor conditions, and because of the heavy rain and wind, the chance of success for any mission was lower than normal. As a result, there is little in the way of aviation technology that is relevant to this operation, with the exception of the difficulty of resupplying the troops.

The importance of bridges in war should be considered. The Germans blew up bridges over rivers as a way of delaying the Allied troops from advancing and to hinder the advance of vehicles and tanks. The stories of the Sauer and Our River crossings demonstrate that the use of boats was not always possible if the rivers were swollen and ran fast. There were several types of bridges built during World War II. The ponton bridge was a temporary floating bridge built to generally carry lighter traffic, such as soldiers on foot. They often had wooden decks on floating devices such as boats strung together. The treadway bridge was a floating bridge with two tracks for a roadway. It was capable of transporting smaller tanks. Permanent fixed bridges required posts or buttresses on the sides of the river, which supported the span over the river. Bailey bridges, for example, were prefabricated steel structures. They could carry larger and heavier loads.

Crossing the Sauer and Our Rivers; February 7-11

I spent a long time trying to understand exactly what happened at the beginning of February 1945 along the Sauer and Our Rivers. There were many perspectives to consider. Planners and generals look at the big picture and how all actions coordinate with each other. On a micro level, the men are trained to do what is asked without thinking about the broader issues. In the end, the event is recorded based on what they see and what they experience. Success is measured by the advance forward. The after-action reports do a remarkable job of recording what happened, but the oral histories and first- hand accounts talk about the fears and bravery of the men on the front-line. I read about and heard men talk of their camaraderie and support within their units and how they learned to keep their heads down and their fear in check. I decided to document not only what happened during the action but the chaos and the experience of the men who were there. The analysis of understanding what happened would have to come after.

With preparations now complete, the XII US Corps, composed of approximately 75,000 soldiers, began their assault across the Sauer and Our Rivers and into Germany as planned, although they knew that the weather in Luxembourg would not cooperate during the second week of February. During this period, the weather conditions were often cloudy with intermittent rain and sometimes impaired visibility. The milder temperatures continued to add water to the flooded Sauer and Our Rivers and washed away roads in the area. At times, air support was non-operational, which affected air missions and the ability to supply American troops in the field. The weather also impacted artillery and smoke firings, some of which were misdirected.[94]

The action began with artillery lighting up the night sky prior to actual crossings. This was not unusual, as there had been artillery firings from both sides of the river for days. The Germans, however, did not believe that an attempt to cross at the most fortified point of the Siegfried line was likely.

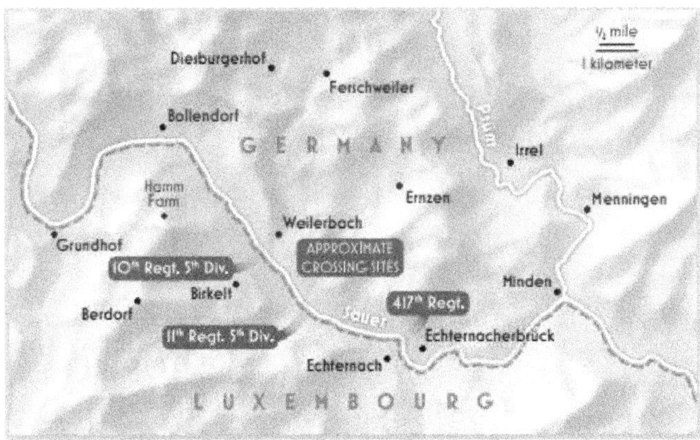

5th Division and 417ᵗʰ Regiment Crossing Sites

February 7

In the 417th Regiment sector, the regiment chose to cross the entire battalion containing approximately 900 troops by boat to fully gain control in Germany. The risk of crossing a large number of men at once was much higher than the risk taken by the 5th Infantry Division in crossing reconnaissance platoons and single companies. It ultimately led to a very high number of casualties, but at the same time, it led to a different outcome than the 5th Infantry Regiment.

Pushing off at 1 AM on February 7th, 40 boats consisting of A and B Companies plus part of C Company made their way across the river. The boats crossed in waves; 16 boats with men from B Company pushed off initially, followed by 16 boats filled with men from A Company, and then the last 8 boats consisting of elements of C Company. The goal was to get many of the men across quickly and quietly, then return the boats to the Echternach side so they could be reused by the rest of the regiment.[95]

As in the other XII US Corps locations, the assault did not go as planned for the 417th Regiment. The operation hinged on the ability of the 1st Battalion to maintain stealth throughout the operation. The men initially succeeded in that respect, as the engineers successfully hid the boats within Echternach the night before the attack, and the men of the 417th Regiment successfully reclaimed them and made their way to the river. The enemy fired mortar and artillery, as it had done on previous nights, while the men of B Company were at the river, the success in maintaining the secrecy of the operation only meant that the fire was directed at the town of Echternach itself rather than the troops on the river.[96]

Unfortunately, the secret could not last forever. Sources differed on when the Germans became aware of the approach, but their awareness ultimately made the crossing more perilous for the men than the operation intended it to be. According to one account, while B Company was in the middle of the river and A Company was getting into its boats, the enemy began to light up flares that illuminated the crossing site. This caused the Germans to see and then shoot at the men on the river. Because the zone was suddenly hot, confusion erupted and, as a result, "Some of the boats were damaged, others were swept down the river, while still others capsized. Men that made the crossing were scattered, and after regrouping, action reports indicate the effective fighting force of the 1st Battalion consisted of 56 men and 3 officers from A Company, 52 men and 2 officers from B Company, and a handful of men from C Company."[97] Given that each company began with an approximate strength of between 180 and 200 men, large numbers of troops were casualties or missing men.

In the heat of battle, primary sources provide contradictory accounts of the facts on the first night. Military records contradict each other on the assertion that multiple boats were lost. The 417th Regiment's journal reported at 1:37 AM on February 7th that 39 of the 40 boats were across the river, and the history of the 417th Regiment for the year 1945 also claims that same number, possibly because the latter cited the information from the journal. If all but one boat made it across, the assertion that "some of the boats" were damaged while "others" capsized is inconsistent. However, there are multiple accounts indicating that multiple boats capsized and were destroyed by enemy fire. On the other hand, if 39 of 40 boats made the trip across, the two companies would presumably have more than a third of their respective troops across the river, which did not happen if the companies had between 150 and 200 men. Additionally, if 40 boats set out to cross the river, hundreds of men (over two companies) must have made an attempt in those 40 boats, which usually carried at least ten to twelve men per boat. Additionally, the commanding officer of the 1st Battalion recalled that C Company's effective fighting strength on the far shore had "dwindled to 78 men and two others."[98] I find it odd that half a company, crossing in eight boats after the cover is supposedly blown, managed to have a stronger force than either of the two companies that crossed under the cover of darkness in 16 boats each.

The 160th Engineer Combat Battalion provides its own account of the crossing:

> "Approximately 400 men started the first wave of which approximately 350 were successful in reaching the far shore. By 0110 the first wave was reported across. As the men jumped out of the boats on the far shore they tripped flares and set off AP mines. By 0115 the enemy were firing flares all along the river, illuminating the river."[99]

If this telling is correct, more men made it across initially than believed; this suggests that casualties also occurred after the crossing. Of course, the engineers also said that the enemy was not aware of the troops until after the men had crossed. This differs from other accounts, which suggest that the Germans contested the crossing itself.

The men in the 417th Regiment told their own story of the crossing. In addition to the official records, there exist individual accounts and a published regiment account of boats being capsized from the strong current and boats being hit by enemy fire and sinking. It is a story of chaos and casualties. The artillery fire lit up the sky and some boats on the river took direct fire and sunk. Out-of-control boats were carried down the river by the swift current as artillery fired on those boats. Overturned boats dumped men in the freezing river, leaving the men trying to swim but often sinking under the 70 or more pounds of weight on their backs.[100]

> "The assault boats were filled each with twelve to sixteen men. Midstream, the boats drew fire from the nazi pillboxes on the hill of the German shore. The boat behind one in which rode Pvt Harry Goedde sank under a direct hit, and its occupants swept downstream. His own boat started to drift toward the very spot where a nazi machine gun was spitting fire from the bank. The men tried frantically to restrain their course by grabbing for rushes along the water's edge but swamped the gunwales. Along with his companions, Goedde shed his equipment and plunged into the icy water. Several were immediately carried away by the current. A medic called for help, and Goedde, a confident swimmer, took him in tow until they both made shore. Meanwhile, on the Luxembourg side, a building had been set afire by a German shell. Wet and shivering, from under the protection of weeds, Goedde watched the warm fire. In its glare, he could see the assault boats coming across and the Germans opening up on them. A shell threw up a sheet of water, a boat lurched crazily, and the men spilled into the freezing, racing river. He could see their heads bobbing and arms flailing. Then they were carried out of the radius of light and he could see them no more ..."[101]

This account is in line with Roland's account of his crossing and the destruction of his boat. He talked about the artillery fire and the screaming of men in the river.

Additionally, other men from the 417th Regiment also mentioned that troops sunk in the river because of the weight they were carrying. Richard Scott of the 5th Division later said, "if you have heavy boots or galoshes, 2-3 layers of clothes, you have a helmet, and you have ammunition and all the stuff you own practically on your belt and your back, you know what is going to happen, there is no way you can stay up. And so they drowned."[102]

The disagreement on details suggested to me that what happened to the men that night is only part of the mystery; I now began wondering how many men were lost during this first day of the operation, when they were lost, and how they were lost. How could it be that a total of 108 enlisted men made it across from two and one-half companies that likely had at least 170 men each to start? Clearly, not everyone that failed to make it across that night was a casualty. Some of the men who were in boats that capsized were able to swim back to the safety of the southern shore. Those men were not considered casualties. They became part of the next assault crossing. Still, the Germans had begun to take aim at the crossing site with machine gun fire and artillery blasts, peppering the boats and the unfortunate men within them. It is not hard to imagine that many of those men became casualties. There are also accounts of men in the water unable to return to shore. Kingsley Roberts Jr believed that the casualty rate for that one battle was 75%.[103]

Michael J Debacker, a medic in the 301st Medical Bn in the 76th Division, said: "We lost over 500 men in Luxembourg."[104] According to an article written by Al Pollack, a member of the 417th Regiment, "The attacks continued for many days. Hundreds died from drowning and direct murderous fire and mines."[105]

Roy Martin, a member of C Company in the 417th Regiment, was one of the few who crossed the Sauer River successfully on the first day. He saw some action before being wounded and spent several days in the cold waiting to be evacuated to an aid station. He was told that only 16 men made it across alive that day.[106]

What all the sources agree on, however, is that those were the only men of the 417th Regiment to successfully cross that night. No matter how many boats made it across, none except the evacuated injured returned to the Luxembourg shore afterward. Due to the swift current, the engineers operating the boats had a difficult time navigating the boats on the way over to Germany. Those loads were with a full crew of soldiers weighing down the boats. Once the infantrymen disembarked, the boats became lighter and became more vulnerable to the push of the river's strong current. The engineers soon discovered that it was impossible for the skeleton crew to make the return trip. They made several attempts to paddle the boats across to Luxembourg, and every attempt failed.[107] Furthermore, the crossing site became increasingly hotter as German artillery pounded the river and both banks. The increasing danger forced the troops to bunker down, wait for things to cool off, and find replacement boats for the next crossing attempt.

Although the crossing stalled, the assault was still the most successful crossing among the three divisions in the southeast sector of the XII US Corps assault. With two full companies and half of a third sent across, the force was easily the strongest to make it across that day, even if the companies suffered large numbers of casualties in doing so. This afforded the 1st Battalion the ability to attempt something that no one in the 5th Infantry Division was able to do on February 7th: they moved forward toward their goals.

Once the troops in Germany regrouped, a mixture of A and B Companies of the 417th Regiment immediately set forth toward their objective north of Echternach. The column moved up the nearby hill toward the top of the draw, where the men planned to establish control. They deftly avoided the landmines in the vicinity, braved German mortar and artillery fire, and soon reached what they took to be the objective.[108] Unfortunately, the morning hours of February 7th brought a dense mist which, combined with the low amount of light, caused the men to lose track of where they were. It was not until around 10 AM, once the fog lifted that the men realized they were still 200 yards south of their objective. They quickly advanced north up the hill, captured some German weapons in the area, and dug-in on the high ground. At this point, Company A was reporting casualties of 20%.[109]

Meanwhile, the rest of the 417th Regiment was trying to figure out how to get across the river. The engineers held 30 boats in reserve prior to the attack, and with the 40 boats sent over no longer operational, the regiment was forced to use those reserves. However, only a few additional attempts were made to cross the river on February 7th. The regiment requested smoke generators in the vicinity to help cover the men along the river. Unfortunately, the generators that arrived only had enough smoke to cover 4 hours.[110] Because of this short time frame, the smoke was used mostly to help the engineers construct the bridge across the river instead of transporting men over by boat.

The river, already a menace to the engineers for ruining the boat crossings, also plagued the engineers throughout their bridge-building efforts. The current continuously washed out areas of the footbridge that the engineers were constructing during the night of February 6-7th.

> "It was some time before they were able to get
> a cable across. Even then the current washed

<blockquote>
the first one away. A second cable was established but once again the pressure pulled out the "dead man" mooring it. Finally, a bridge was constructed and then attempts were made to float it in place. About that time assault boats from the crossing hit the bridge and broke it apart. The failure to get a footbridge in made it necessary to cross all the troops by boat."[111]
</blockquote>

The construction of the footbridge itself involved tying together several boats and then placing boards atop them. With the boat supply dwindling and reserves already being pressed into action, the engineers were forced to cannibalize the footbridge and take it apart so that the boats could be used to cross men during the next crossing.[112]

The attempts to traverse the river that day were mostly met with failure. As morning rolled around and darkness faded, the wind began to blow the smoke in a less-than-ideal direction. With the ability to provide cover in daylight lost, all crossing operations ceased until nightfall, when the cover of darkness could once again obscure the 417th Regiment's approach to the Sauer River.[113]

As darkness appeared, the American troops in Germany started to face trouble. Already understrength due to the rough crossing operation, the troops that dug-in at their initial objective point soon encountered heavy resistance. At 3:55

that afternoon, the Germans pushed forward with a counter-attack aimed at recapturing the high ground the American troops seized. A group of German infantrymen, supported by three tanks, moved toward the American troops, who responded with small arms and bazooka fire. A combination of strong resistance and luck helped the men of A and B Companies repulse the German counter-attack. One bazooka shot hit the German tank head-on, completely knocking it out. A second tank became inoperable after it was caught in mud and could not move. The Germans promptly abandoned it. With only one tank left, the Germans retreated.[114]

As dusk approached on the Luxembourg side of the river, the engineers began taking measures for the next crossing. They managed to procure a total of 14 boats (eight storm boats with up to 55 horsepower and six assault boats with up to 22 horsepower) and planned to use them in combination with guide ropes operated by engineers on both sides of the river; this would allow the engineers to cross the river and provide a method for the boats to make a return trip to Luxembourg. Unfortunately, German artillery fire stymied those plans. The continuous fire eventually fell on the boats themselves. By 6 PM, four of the six assault boats were hit, and multiple storm boats were damaged.[115]

That evening, the 417th Regiment reassessed its battle plan. The initial goal was to cross each regiment in full before starting the next one. With A and B Companies already in position at their initial objective but suffering from severe losses, regimental command ordered instead that the 2nd Battalion begin crossing before the remainder of the 1st Battalion, leaving behind elements of C and D Companies, as well as the battalion's commanding officers. Instead of moving toward their own objectives, the 2nd battalion was to move to the 1st Battalion's position and provide them direct support.[116]

As night fell, the 2nd Battalion moved in to attempt a new crossing. In the hours preceding the assault, enemy artillery continued to rain down on Echternach. That fire continued as the men went across in the nine boats still available.[117] G Company, with a heavy machine gun platoon attached, commenced crossing at 2030 in the remaining boats, some of which contained solid ice. Four hours later, three platoons and the heavy machine gun platoon successfully reached the other side, but only one of the storm boats remained in serviceable condition.[118] The crossing operation was once again suspended. As a result, the boats were put to a different use: helping establish the footbridge. This, too, proved to be frustrating.

> "The remaining power boat was employed in
> an attempt to put in a cable for the footbridge.

<blockquote>Four times during the night a cable was secured on the far shore, but twice it was ripped out by boats which drifted from the crossing site of the adjacent unit upstream and twice by capsized boat loads who grabbed the ropes attached to the cable."[119]</blockquote>

In the 5th Infantry Division zone, crossing over the Sauer River in February was far more difficult than their January crossing of the same river near Diekirch. The regiments chose a different crossing pattern than the 417th Regiment assault. The 10th and 11th Regiments attempted to cross only a few boats at a time, while the 417th Regiment chose to cross much of the regiment early in their operations. The attack by the 10th Regiment commenced at 1:30 AM on February 7th. The 2nd Battalion was initially slated to begin a half hour earlier, but there was a slight delay with the boats. The first group from company E reached the river at 1:50 and pushed off 15 minutes later. This was late in comparison to other infantry regiments, who each reported that at least one company had managed to start crossing by 1:45.[120]

The 10th Infantry's Executive Officer, Lt. Col. William Breckinridge, had two more explanations for the delay in the initial crossing. The first focused on natural terrain, which included step cliffs, ravines, and a lack of roadnets which impaired troop movement. This was coupled with enemy fire, "which emanated from pillboxes on the far side of the river. Despite the unfavorable natural features, the 10th went ahead with plans for the attack."[121] Breckinridge's second explanation was that the troops were actually blocked from moving along the road because of Allied troop movement. Elements of the 11th Regiment got lost and, in moving along the single road that the 10th Regiment had at its disposal, blocked troops attempting to move toward the river. This delayed them by approximately one hour.[122]

The 2nd Battalion of the 10th Regiment faced stiff resistance in its initial crossing. The plan called for a stealth attack on the river under the cover of darkness. After the troops started across the river, artillery was supposed to provide covering fire. Unfortunately, the delay in troop movement was costly; the artillery fired at the appropriate time, but the troops were not in the proper position.[123] The Germans were able to properly utilize the extensive Siegfried Line defenses along the Sauer River that featured several pillboxes located along the bank with excellent sight of the river. The Germans set up a machine gun in one such pillbox across from the crossing site and consistently harried the troops making their way across. The troops reported that German artillery fired at them once every 2-3 minutes.[124]

As in other regiments in the XII US Corps operations, the crossing was further complicated by the terrible condition of the Sauer River itself. They quickly discovered that the thawed snow and ice along the Sauer River dramatically increased the width of the river. The strong current that soon developed made life hell for the engineers steering the boats. Gene Currivan of the New York Times wrote that "The current was so swift that the assault boats had a difficult time staying upright. Rubber boats bobbed around like corks, while wooden craft, though much easier to handle in the rough water, were twisting and turning as if battling rapids."[125] It was reported that boats capsized simply because of the current, and the soldiers were forced to swim back to the Luxembourg shore. Others were blown so far off course that the engineers decided to turn back for fear of landing in an extremely perilous location on the German side of the river.

At 3:55 on the morning of February 7th, the 2nd Battalion of the 10th Regiment was still unable to make any headway. The initial crossing by E Company failed completely, and Company G, the second of the companies to begin the assault, was halted by machine gun fire several times. At one point, they noted that there were three separate machine guns from the opposite bank firing on them and five boats were already lost. They requested covering fire at 4:40, and General Irwin commanded that artillery be used to help the soldiers at the crossing site. At

5:00 AM, when the troops finally started to receive support, the 2nd Battalion noted that they had already lost 13 boats and were in the process of receiving 12 more.[126]

Over the next few hours, the 2nd Battalion attempted another crossing. By 8:05 that morning, they determined that the crossing was once again largely unsuccessful. Two boats from Company E successfully across, but the rest sank. Unfortunately, the nine men on the German side of the river were cut off with no means of communication with fellow soldiers remaining on the western bank of the Sauer River. Stranded, the men lay on the bank for hours while waiting for allied soldiers to also cross the river and provide support. By 11:00 PM that night, they still had no contact with the other side, and the 10th Regiment began organizing a patrol to reach their position to determine what the nine men may have learned.[127]

The 3rd Battalion was preparing for its own assault. They were informed just after noon on February 7th that they should be ready to cross the Sauer later that night. They started up the road toward the river around 10 PM, with L Company beginning the assault an hour later.[128] The 3rd Battalion's assault, which began approximately 21 hours after the attempt by the 2nd Battalion, was even less successful. Initially, the river was the biggest obstacle, with the current posing the biggest threat to the boats. The crossing was further slowed because the battalion was extremely disorganized; only half of L Company was actually attempting to cross as the calendar moved forward to February 8th. The other half was still in transit to the river as of 3:15. By 4:30, when the rest of L finally arrived, 2 more boats were rendered unusable while the company attempted to cross.[129] As a result, the 3rd Battalion stalled, and after a full day of battle, the 10th Infantry failed to cross the Sauer River.

The defeat of the 10th Regiment in crossing the Sauer on February 7th was, in many ways, unsurprising. This was not the first time that Allied troops had made it to the Sauer, nor was it the first time they had engaged the Siegfried Line. The poor weather conditions and the logistical failures in coordinating the assault led to disaster in crossing the river.

The 11th Regiment operation called for a reconnaissance platoon of the 2nd Battalion to cross the Sauer River by boat ahead of the rest of the men without any fire. This would allow the attached engineers to more easily construct footbridges that could be used by the rest of the battalion. Eight men made it across this way, but unfortunately, no other men were able to cross. The engineers then attempted to push an assembled bridge across the river, but the river itself did not cooperate. The river was much wider than normal, having been flooded by a combination of the steady rain and the thaw that melted the snow and ice on the ground during previous weeks. A strong current developed due to the river's expansion, resulting in the bridge washing out and forcing the men to regroup.[130]

Once some of the men were across, artillery planned to lay down covering fire so that the troops could make it into defensible positions against enemy pillboxes. Unfortunately, the collapse of the footbridge delayed the crossing of the men, and the artillery ended up firing at the appointed time, thus eliminating the element of surprise for the 2nd Battalion. The enemy fired back, making the crossing site even more hazardous. F Company tried to cross early on February 7th by boat, but the enemy harassment was so strong that they could not even assemble the necessary number of boats to begin the assault.[131]

The 3rd Battalion of the 11th Regiment fared far worse in their own initial crossing attempt. They were located approximately 500 yards south of the 2nd Battalion, and their reconnaissance platoon did not enjoy the benefit of stealth during their crossing attempt. They began receiving enemy fire at 1:40 AM as they made their way across the river by boat, and the intense fire from machine guns, artillery, and mortar scattered the American soldiers on the southern shore of the river.[132] The men making their way over to the river found that no bridge had been built, and no men from the reconnaissance platoon made it across the river either. As a result, L Company organized an assault at 6:45 AM on February 7th, but the attack was pushed back due to enemy fire.[133]

Meanwhile, the 1st Battalion waited in reserve for the first two battalions to cross and establish a bridgehead. Normally, the men would be idle during this time, but after the initial crossing failed, the 1st Battalion was put on alert that their orders could change. This began a three-day odyssey of perpetual vigilance and almost no action for the 1st Battalion. During this period, the men were notified multiple times of scheduled assaults across the river, yet each time the attack was canceled by their superiors. The first of these orders was an alert at 11 AM on February 7th that the 1st Battalion was to move to the bridgehead established by the 417th Regiment and cross there. Those orders were canceled that night in favor of allowing the 2nd and 3rd Battalions more time to conduct their own assaults, with the 1st Battalion once again following their lead.[134]

To the south, after regrouping, the men of the 11th Regiment decided to undertake an attack later that evening on February 7th. All attempts by the 7th Engineers to construct footbridges for both battalions during the day failed, in part due to the raging river and partially due to the enemy's constant artillery barrage on the crossing zone. Friendly artillery answered in response, with the 19th Field Artillery, in particular, raining down fire on the enemy in record fashion. With no restriction on ammunition, Battery B fired an incredible 1,519 rounds in a 24-hour period. The enemy's fire eventually died down that afternoon, and the American troops used this brief lull in the action to take advantage of another crossing attempt.

At 6:30 PM on February 7th, both the 2nd and 3rd Battalions of the 11th Regiment began separate assaults. The 3rd Battalion sent K Company over with elements from M Company, but more than half the boats washed out, and the men in those boats were forced to return to the Luxembourg shore. 3 boatloads managed to make it across by stealth, and 28 men from K and M Companies began to establish a bridgehead in the 3rd Battalion's sector. They dug in and waited for reinforcements from I Company, but unfortunately, the swift currents along the Sauer River once again foiled the efforts of the men trying to cross the river. Worse, the men of I Company were not nearly as quiet as their comrades in K Company, and screams from men as the river capsized their boats alerted Germans to the attack area. At that point, the two sides once again engaged in an artillery duel, and no more men from the 3rd Battalion managed to make it across despite several attempts through early morning on February 8th.[135]

The 2nd Battalion fared little better in its assault. F Company pushed off at roughly the same time that K Company did, but once again, the Sauer River wreaked havoc on the boats. Even though F Company sent ten boatloads of men across, only four managed to complete the crossing. The Germans soon discovered the men along the shore and opened fire and, in doing so, actually provided relief for the eight men of the reconnaissance patrol who crossed over the night before. Amidst a heavy gunfight between the elements of F Company on the far shore and the Germans, the eight men returned to the Luxembourg side of the Sauer River while the men of F Company resumed the role of establishing a bridgehead.[136]

The 10th and 11th Regiments were forced to wait several days to advance toward their objectives because they were unable to get a fighting force across the river. This was different than the 417th Regiment, however, which was strong enough to strike forward immediately on the first day of action.

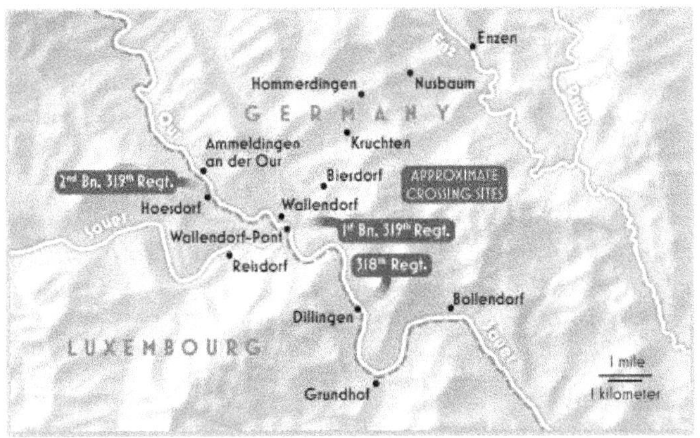

80ᵗʰ Division Crossing Sites

In the 80ᵗʰ Infantry Division sector, to north of the 5ᵗʰ Infantry Division and south of the III US Corps, the 319ᵗʰ and 318ᵗʰ Regiments commenced their assaults on the Siegfried Line on time. Artillery in support of both regiments rained down fire on the German side of the Sauer and Our Rivers during the hour before the attack set for 3 AM on the morning of February 7ᵗʰ. In the 318ᵗʰ Regiment's sector, the shelling began as early as 2:10; in the 319ᵗʰ Infantry Regiment's area, the artillery began 20 minutes later. At first, this did not seem to be unusual, as both sides had traded fire with each other throughout their brief standoff initiated when the Allies had pushed toward the German border in late January. This time, however, the artillery barrage was stronger, aimed at buttoning up the German defenses or drawing their fire toward themselves and away from the infantrymen, who began to march from their quarters to the assembly areas for the upcoming assault approximately 15 minutes before H-Hour.

The 318th Regiment's offensive was spearheaded by the 2nd Battalion, which was scheduled to cross as soon as the artillery preparation ended. The 1st Battalion would follow as soon as the 2nd Battalion was across, and the two would then fan out toward their objectives. The men carefully made their way into position by the boats, which had been set up the day before for immediate use once the men arrived.

At 0300, F Company jumped off from the southern shore of the Sauer River toward the north. Paddling the boat was a challenge for the engineers in charge, as the NCO commanding the boat had to shout orders to them on the fly as the boat was caught in the heavy river current, and the engineer on the right side was often required to make two paddles for every one on the left side to combat the drift from the current. The men were not subtle in crossing and made no attempt to lower their voices because the Germans were preoccupied with the artillery barrage preceding the crossing.[137]

After 20 minutes of fierce struggles along the river, F Company reached the far shore, although they were nearly 500 yards downstream from where they had started. The only obstacle during the crossing was the river itself, as the Germans did not fire on the men at all. F Company successfully landed on the far shore but immediately suffered its first blow as the men on the far right side of the company attempted to disembark. Because of the extreme drift, the men landed in the middle of a minefield, and as the men left the boat, they triggered explosions around them. The entire 12-man crew became casualties as 9 men were killed and 3 men were wounded in the blasts.[138]

The remaining men of F Company immediately began to march back upstream, away from the minefield and toward a designated assembly area that had been the original landing zone before the river drew them off course. It was at this time that the 318th Regiment's practice of using one fewer engineer in each boat came back to haunt them. The boats' crews were responsible for securing and beaching the boats on the German shore for use should the men have to retreat back across the river, but unfortunately, the Sauer River had other ideas. The boats were swept down river, and the men were stranded.[139]

The loss of the boats was especially damaging to the operation, as F Company soon discovered that they would actually be left on the far bank on their own for some time. Though F Company had been fortunate enough to avoid enemy fire during their crossing, the same could not be said for

E and G Companies, which were set to start their own crossing immediately after F Company made it across successfully. The Germans unleashed a torrent of fire on the woods near the shore, driving back the men from those companies in the staging and assembly area.[140] Furthermore, the companies faced difficulties simply carrying the boats to the shore, as the banks were slippery and the bank's steepness prevented the men from reaching the river.[141] By the time E and G Companies were ready to cross, it was close to noon, daylight had broken through for quite some time, and F Company had been in Germany alone for several tense hours. It became apparent to them that if they were to reach Biesdorf, they would have to do it without the support of the rest of the battalion.[142]

Meanwhile, upstream along the Our River, the 319th Regiment of the 80th Infantry Division was launching its own offensive against the West Wall. Unlike the 318th Regiment, which planned on crossing one battalion at a time across a single site, the 319th Regiment set up two locations to be used simultaneously by the 1st and 2nd Battalions. The artillery preparation started off at the same time, but its attention was split between the two sites. Still, the support was directed at disrupting the enemy as much as possible:

> "The corps artillery concentrated on communications, counterbattery missions and

CP's while the division artillery hit the immediate objectives to neutralize the enemy fire and dislodge or destroy his troops. Fifteen minutes before H-hour our artillery was placed immediately opposite the crossing site and, after the crossing operation started, about 0320, our artillery continued to fire for an hour and a half. This fire had been planned to be shifted ahead of the advance in 200 yard increments about every 20 minutes."[143]

The 2nd Battalion's crossing began just after H-hour arrived, and from the beginning, it was a disaster. The artillery preparation in support of the infantry was not enough to dissuade the Germans from countering with their own fire, and the resulting exchange threw the men on the river into a state of confusion. Commanders had to be extra forceful in getting the men in line for the crossing. The darkness and the tough slope only added to the confusion as men began slipping down the slope while carrying the boats toward the river.[144] By the time the men were actually at the river's edge, the assault was already behind schedule and disorganized.

Once at the river, the crossing faced extreme resistance that the 318th Regiment was fortunate enough to avoid. The river's current was even stronger in this section of the river, and while it was merely a nuisance for the 318th Regiment in blowing them off course, it was hazardous for the men of the 319th Regiment. The current capsized several boats, while others were lost as German counter-fire tore through them. Approximately half the boats launched in the first phase of the attack were lost, although the crew was able to swim back to safety, and the ones that managed to make it across were blown off course and then beached. The engineers realized that without crew weighing down the boats, there was no realistic possibility of returning the boats to the southern shore.[145]

Engineers supporting the 319th Regiment described the hazards of crossing that first day as follows:

> "Each boat crossing was a nightmare, as the boat left shore the current would catch it and send it rushing crazily downstream, sometimes it would catch a snag and capsize throwing the men into the swirling waters. Sometimes the boat would be hit by shrapnel from a near miss or be riddled with machine gun fire, but somehow most of them reached the far shore. The infantry would leap out of the boats and almost immediately begin to push ahead through the barbed wire and the minefields while the engineers started back once more into the racing water and shellfire and again the current would carry the boat further downstream. Once again on our side, we would have to work the boat back upstream to the original starting point. That was a terrible experience, working along the bank, slipping and stumbling in the dark, dragging the boat along against the current, then suddenly that desperate hunted feeling when a flare would light up everything."[146]

As a result, the aggressive assault plan of the 80th Infantry Division was severely delayed. The initial plan called for assaults on the towns opposite the Our and Sauer Rivers on the day of the assault, but not enough men made it across in the first attack to make those plans feasible. Approximately 60 men from each of F and E Companies, the first two companies assaulting the Siegfried Line in the 2nd Battalion, were in Germany on February 7th, and, in doing so, the men lost a considerable amount of equipment. The most the men could do was to move away from the shore and into Germany by a few hundred yards, capture an enemy pillbox in the vicinity, and then dig in and wait for reinforcements.[147]

The 1st Battalion of the 319th Regiment, crossing closer to Wallendorf, had an easier time crossing the river but still faced several complications. The Germans put up stiffer resistance against the 2nd Battalion near Hoesdorf, allowing the 1st Battalion to cross without the same heavy fire battering them. Despite only mild resistance, the 1st Battalion, led by C Company, was unable to get across the river smoothly. It took four hours for C and B Companies to successfully cross the river. By 7 AM, the command group was also with them, but A Company lagged behind, losing 40 men without even reaching the river. Only three or four boats remained after the vast majority of the ones used by the first two companies were lost. As a result, the 1st Battalion was at limited strength while on the far shore.[148]

Worse still for the 1st Battalion, the crossing site placed the men quite literally between a rock and a hard place. On the German shore, a flat flood plain separated the river from a road connecting the towns of Wallendorf and Ammeldingen. On the opposite side of the road, less than 40 feet away, a 200-foot cliff rose steeply up from the flat bank. This essentially walled in the men, who were stuck between this cliff and an angry, raging river. When day broke, the Germans could see where the men of the 1st Battalion were, and the Siegfried Line defense systems kicked into full gear. It became clear that staying in this position was not an option. The men would need to charge the hill and eliminate the pillboxes before enemy fire could cripple them.[149]

The decision to charge against the enemy from the bank was quite successful and was a major reason why the 319th Regiment was able to gain control over its sector. The men rushed the hill and captured several pillboxes lining the cliff despite the enemy fire. This allowed the men to dig in near the crest of the hill, where they next faced a German counter-attack. They successfully repulsed the German team and maintained control over the hill overlooking the crossing site. This was especially important because it managed to reduce fire directed onto the river. That evening, A Company was quickly able to move across the river without the threat of German fire and capture Wallendorf itself, and the engineers attached were able to work on a bridge more successfully.[150] Still, this left the 80th Infantry Division behind schedule. Even though they successfully crossed some men that first day and established a bridgehead, the lightning quick moves that were planned for interior locations such as Biesdorf were not feasible.

The delay in the attack was significant in not only helping the Germans maintain their defenses in the short term but also in helping them analyze the American assault operations. As noted earlier, the Americans planned to take objectives as soon as they were across the river, and they were to do it by taking particular routes through the rugged terrain. As the men stalled while taking their predefined paths, the Germans were given time to determine the way in which the Americans were attacking the Siegfried Line's defenses. This allowed them to shift soldiers to certain locations that they believed the Americans were planning to attack. As a result, the already slow progress caused by the poor crossing pattern was made even slower as the assault avenues were now more heavily defended than previously expected. To counter this problem, orders changed. The 2nd Battalion in the 319th Regiment was ordered to capture specific high ground closer to E and F Company's locations rather than to continue toward their initial objective farther inland.[151] With movement slowed and resistance heavier than expected, a more cautious approach was deemed the more prudent course of action.

In the meantime, the 318th Regiment, to the south of the 319th Regiment, was embroiled in an intense firefight in its sector starting as the mist rose on the morning of February 7th. While the 319th Regiment made headway that day in capturing pillboxes across the river, elements of F Company of the 318th Regiment's 2nd Battalion remained alone along the German side of the Sauer River for a significant period of time while E and G Companies were raked with fire and unable to cross the river in support. Worse, these men were in complete disarray:

> "The Bn CO then directed E & G companies to infiltrate to F company's crossing site. (978413). After arriving at the site the men were sent across, a boat or possibly two at a time. An enemy MG position about 50 yards downstream made the crossing double difficult. Any boats that drifted down were immediately raked with fire. The engineers on hand at the original crossing claimed to have no knowledge of assault boats and as a result the infantry had to maneuver [sic] the boats themselves. Late on the afternoon of the 7th more engineers arrived and took over the ferrying operations.[152]

At this point, the battle grew even harsher. "Small arms, automatic weapons, self-propelled guns, artillery, and nebelwerfer batteries" rained down from Germany on the men trying to cross the river. The fire, combined with the swift current and the Americans' disorganized crossing pattern, wreaked havoc on the men trying to cross. No one was able to cross during the day, but by 11:00 on the evening of February 7th, the rest of the 2nd Battalion was across. The plan had been for the entire regiment to cross and capture Biesdorf by this point. Instead, the regiment only managed to cross a single battalion, which made its mission to simply clear out the surrounding area and create a safer point of passage for the remaining battalions to cross more difficult.[153]

After the first day of action, the entire 80th Infantry Division remained behind schedule and scattered. Only parts of each crossing team successfully crossed on the initial push, which resulted in a shortage of men for the push against the Siegfried Line's outer fortifications.

The 318th Regiment also discovered that advanced intelligence on the terrain in their sector was inaccurate and led the men into a trap:

> "The 1/25,000 WALLENDORF sheet used by F Co is not accurate for the terrain where the crossing was made. Along the stretch of highway where the company regrouped there was an abrupt cut to the road leaving a sheer

bank about 20 feet high on the east which masked the company from observation and fire from the wooded slopes rising east of the road and the river. The WALLENDORF map shows a secondary road or path running down to the river at approximately 980413, then looping back to the north and winding through the woods to the east of BIESDORF. In actual feet this forest road came down to the river bank and the hard surfaced highway at a point further south than shown on the map. So F Co… entered the wood road where it intersected with the hard surfaced highway and began to move up and around the slope. The 3rd Plat already was off the hard surfaced road and down the forest road when, just at the west curve of the loop, two enemy machine guns in pits on either side of the road opened up on the point squad. The two bazookas of the 3rd Plat were brought up and fired all their ammunition but were unable to knock out the enemy."[154]

Late on the first day, the 1st battalion of the 318th Regiment moved to the high ground on the Luxembourg side of the river. They remained there during the night, ready to cross the next day.

At the end of the first day of operations, the XII US Corps could only report partial success. Some troops had crossed the river, but many failed in their attempts, and others did not ever get the opportunity to try. In the case of the 417th Regiment, some infantry who crossed had also begun to advance toward their objectives. Both the German defense and the raging rivers combined to prevent the construction of bridges. Patton wrote that neither he nor Eddy was pleased with the progress but recognized the negative impact of weather on the operation.[155]

General Patton visited units in his Third US Army almost every day. On February 7th, he drove to the VIII US Corps sector and noted how some roads were impassable. Patton wrote in his diary that night: "All troops not actually fighting are working on the roads."[156] Given the bad weather and the bad road conditions, Patton gave permission to General Eddy, commander of the XII US Corps, to stop operations if necessary. Patton recorded in his diary "…he continued to attack. They are making fine progress."[157]

Roland's Story II

After a turbulent crossing of the Sauer River, Roland Hartman found himself on the German shore with two other Americans he did not know. He was surprised by the silence and lack of activity on the German shore. He knew the objective was to knock out a pillbox approximately 1,000 feet up on the side of a big hill, which he referred to as a "mountain."[158] Assessing the situation and the tall snowy hill next to them, the three men decided to "team up and get toward the top of the mountain. We no longer have any guns or equipment."[159] He noted that they were also wet and tired.

The three men "started climbing through the melting snow and once in a while saw an exploding shell or machine gun fire." But there were complications, for Roland discovered that the bazooka he was carrying was inoperable and "some of the fire dodging us came from the rear (our own men)."[160] In addition, they found that the top of the mountain had a sheer cliff on top, making it impossible to move toward the other side. During the climb, one of the three men was killed either by fire or by a landmine he stepped on. The two remaining men continued on their mission. Approximately half-way up the mountain, not far from the concrete bunker they were seeking, Roland was hit by a shred of phosphorus fire in his wrist. He unsuccessfully tried to reduce the burning using the melting snow. Eventually, his new buddy (as he called him) used a small rock to pick off the phosphorus shred, giving Roland immediate relief.

> "I, Roland Hartman pvt…[am] climbing, sliding on the melting snow…while bombarding continues. When will all this end? Now another prob[lem] takes place, I know nothing and I do not know the consequence… a flare of potassium hits my wrist and I am burning alive, I can't shake it off. Finally my new buddy picks up a pebble and grinds the

area, literally grinding the spot and stopping the pain."[161]

Roland's story is a little less clear at this point. In one version, he participated in the reduction of a pillbox. In another version, it is only mentioned that a pillbox was "destroyed by an explosive charge." Could this part of my father's experience be related to his Silver Star? The injury to his wrist from the flare would justify the Purple Heart. Trying to take down a pillbox almost alone might qualify for a Silver Star, depending on what happened and his part in this event.

The two men completed the climb to the top of the mountain, only to find that the top of the mountain contained a gully which made further progress impossible. Now on the run and trapped, a German patrol discovered the two Americans and took them captive.[162] The two prisoners were taken to a bunker and then put on stretchers. Eventually, a German doctor was brought in to tend to their injuries. Besides the phosphorus burn, Roland was hit by shrapnel in the head and stomach. He had a head injury and some hearing loss.[163] "I was not in great shape. I was very bloody. But not life-threatening wounds, I was lucky." Decades later, Roland still remembered the bunker. He called it huge; the walls were ten inches thick. The two prisoners remained there for several days before being transferred to other locations.[164] During this time, the Americans were separated, and Roland never saw his buddy again.[165] He also noted that his fingers permanently lost some sensation, possibly from the exposure to cold weather. At some point, one of the Germans took possession of his watch.[166]

February 8

As Roland began to adapt to his new status as a prisoner of war, the Americans below and across the river continued their attack on Germany. It is not clear if he understood at that time that the battle to cross the Sauer and Our Rivers by the XII US Corps continued or that the Americans were slowly increasing the number of troops on the German side of the rivers and were enlarging bridgeheads. He must have heard, if not seen, the battle going on below him and on the river. It is also not clear how long he remained with the Germans at the front before he was sent into the German POW system, although he mentioned he was there for several days.

In the 76th Infantry Division, the 2nd Battalion of the 417th Regiment located an additional 18 boats for the next crossing after losing 39 boats the previous day. The new attack was set to start in the early morning hours of February 8th. Each of the 18 boats was to carry 15 men, 3 of whom were to return to Luxembourg to pick up another dozen men. The attack was planned to be under the cover of darkness once again, but German firings set a house on the Echternach side of the river on fire while the 2nd Battalion was preparing to launch. The inferno "silhouetted all activity along the river," making it difficult for the men to maintain cover as they made their way up the only road to the crossing site.[167]

Approaching the river was no easy task for the men in the 2nd Battalion. The damp weather created miserable travel conditions, and the weight of the equipment exhausted the men as they made their way to the crossing site. Once there, they still had to deal with the German artillery, which continued to mercilessly maintain steady fire on Echternach. The last two boats carried to the river received direct hits, reducing the number of usable boats to only sixteen.[168]

E and F Companies began the first crossing of February 8th at 4:30 AM, and once again, the assault did not go as planned. Two boats were riddled with artillery fragments almost immediately after push-off and barely made it 6 feet out. At least 6 boats never made it across, and only one boat returned to Luxembourg to be reused by the two remaining companies seeking to cross that day. H and I Companies were forced to return to Echternach and await new orders for crossing at another time.[169]

Shortly after this crossing attempt failed, the 1st Battalion received word that the Engineers scrounged up additional assault boats for a new crossing. At 6:30 AM, the remaining men of that battalion, consisting of part of C Company, all of D Company, and the battalion command group, packed tightly into the small number of boats made available to them. The battalion still intended to cross everyone at the same time rather than sending the men across in waves, and some boats contained as many as 18 men.[170]

The crossing was once again hotly contested. The battalion requested that the 4.2 mortars within the 91st Chemical Battalion launch smoke onto the far shore to help obscure the enemy's vision of the crossing site. Unfortunately, this request was not fulfilled, and enemy artillery, mortars, and small arms fire littered the crossing site. The boat containing D Company's mortars received a direct hit from enemy artillery. Most of the crew were lost, and the 6 mortars in the boat fell into the river and were subsequently washed away by the strong current. This loss was catastrophic for the battalion, which would now have to complete its mission without any mortar support.[171]

The 417th Regiment did meet with some success on this day. The command group, as well as C and D Companies of the 417th Regiment, managed to cross the river, losing only two boats in the process. As of 8:25 that morning, A and B Companies were still on the objective they had reached the day before. Upon arriving on the German side, the troops that had just landed quickly made their way up the ravine on the way to rendezvous with the troops near the objective.[172] On the way, the battalion command became aware of just how dire the situation was: nearly every pillbox in the vicinity was manned, and two officers of C Company informed the command that they were under fire from German small arms and machine guns.[173] Furthermore, the troops of A and B Company, who had arrived the previous day, had repulsed a second counter-attack supported by tanks. By 10:15 on February 8th, the troops from the second crossing began moving toward the regiment's third objective.[174] The infantry troops were moving beyond the river and into ground action to establish a bridgehead.

Roland had a friend, also in C Company, who did not cross over the Sauer River until the second day, February 8th. He also experienced the same chaos Roland described, the swollen waters, German firings that destroyed boats, men trying to stay alive in the swirling waters, and disarray on the German side of the border. But he also talked about men arriving on the other side of the river, coming together, and an upward assault on a hill across from Echternach to eliminate the pillboxes. Despite some setbacks, the group made progress.

At the river, the 160th Engineers furiously tried again to establish a footbridge for the remaining troops of the 2nd and 3rd Battalions despite an extraordinarily high number of casualties. It was reported that "By 0530 [on the 7th of February], only one officer and 38 enlisted men were still accounted for at the crossing site out of the original 135 men and 4 officers."[175] The loss of engineers manning the boats and the attacks the engineers endured trying to build the bridge diminished the engineers' capacity to function.

The engineers were so undermanned that units within the 160th Engineer reserve were put into combat to support the engineers who were unable to complete the mission on the first day. One last ditch effort to establish a cable across the river at 4 AM failed when a direct hit from enemy mortars destroyed the cable. The engineers were forced to shift their priorities: when it became apparent that the remaining troops would have to be ferried over the river, the 160th Engineers directed all boats to be beached upon crossing over to Germany, as attempting to cross them back over to Luxembourg for more men would only result in the boats capsizing due to inadequate weight.

Additionally, an assessment of the 160th Engineers group determined that the unit was in trouble. The commanding officer made the call at 5 AM on the 8th that he no longer had sufficient men at his disposal to continue with the assault. An hour later, the 282nd Engineers were called in to relieve the 160th Engineers, who reported 3 dead on the operation, 50 missing, 39 wounded, and at least 90% of the men soaked in water.[176] While this last point may seem like a minor grievance, it was a large threat due to the conditions of the operation. The cold weather had already forced many men out of the battle due to frostbite, trench foot, and other foot injuries. The troops soaked in water were easily at risk of hypothermia as they were dunked in the river repeatedly and were given no respite due to the constant rainy and cold conditions.

No additional efforts to bridge the river were made on February 8th, and the 2nd Battalion still had 289 men, almost one-third of their troops, waiting to cross the river at 12:30 PM. On the German side of the river, the troops that made it across were still very much divided. Remnants of A and B Companies had not yet reached the objective point that troops from the two companies had held for the past 24 hours, and the two groups had no contact with each other. The companies continued to report casualties, including the Executive Officer of B Company, who was wounded in the head and was returned to the 1st Battalion's command post.[177]

Despite these problems, the 417th Regiment conducted some operations during the day. Allied airplanes made several flybys over the German border region. Some planes had instructions for dropping supplies, including medical supplies, at specific coordinates that could be safely retrieved by the men of the 1st Battalion. Others were reportedly involved in "dive-bombing" the town of Ernzen, which was one of the major objectives for the 11th Regiment on the immediate left flank of the 417th Regiment.[178]

The men across the river, led by the 1st Battalion's commanding officer, Lieutenant Colonel Clarence A. Mette, Jr., remained bogged down as they tried to hold the objective point established by the first troops to cross the river. At one point, the men became involved in a tense negotiation with German soldiers over medical evacuation. The negotiation, unfortunately, ended with some wounded Americans being captured by the Germans:

> "….an American medic who was a prisoner of the Germans came to the battalion commander [Mette] from a pillbox at ERNZERHOF (058370) which contained 15 wounded American prisoners. The German officer requested medical supplies for his wounded captives. The CO told the medic to return to the German officer with the demand to produce the American prisoners in two hours at the end of which time the box would be plastered with artillery. 15 minutes thereafter the medic returned with a request by the Germans to allow a German ambulance to pass through the lines and remove both German

and American wounded to German hospitals. The CO replied that he wanted the American wounded. After the receipt of these, he would grant safe conduct to a German ambulance to pick up the enemy wounded. Shortly thereafter the American wounded were passed through the lines and a German ambulance removed 3 enemy wounded. As the ambulance moved out, wounded from Cos A and B were placed in the German vehicle."[179]

As night fell on February 8th, crossing operations restarted. The remaining men on the Luxembourg shore, consisting of part of the 2nd Battalion as well as the entire 3rd Battalion, prepared for another crossing. The 2nd Battalion organized 25 assault boat teams and prepared for crossing at 9 PM.[180] Smoke generators were set up 45 minutes prior to the assault to allow for cover during the crossing operation. This time, every boat made it across the river. The crossing site was not as heavily contested by the Germans, who appeared to instead be focused on the men who held the high ground in German territory. The river was still a problem, but the engineers operating the boats were able to navigate the boats well enough that they only drifted 30 yards downstream.[181] The battalion noted that they experienced fewer casualties than usual that night, but unfortunately, the battalion commander became a casualty himself.[182]

Patton wrote about the crossing of the Sauer River in his book, "War as I Knew It." He wrote:

> "The 5th Division jumped off on the morning of the seventh at 0100 and crossed the Sauer River. Due to the rapid current and flood conditions, there were a great many boat casualties and probably more than sixty men drowned.
>
> One combat team of the 76th Division (417th, commanded by Colonel George E. Bruner), attacking on the right of the 5th Infantry Division, did a better job getting across than the 5th in getting across the river because they did not realize how dangerous it was. After they got across, they did very little for about three days-probably recovering from the shock of their own heroism."[183]

In the 5th Infantry Division sector, the assault by the 10th Regiment's 3rd Battalion began approximately 21 hours after the attempt by the 2nd Battalion. Initially, the river was the biggest obstacle, with the current posing the biggest threat to the boats. However, a burp gun started firing on them at around 2:30 AM, puncturing another boat; and the disorganization of the battalion led to only half of one company attempting to cross early while the other half failed to arrive on time. By 4:30, when the rest of L Company finally arrived, 2 more boats were rendered unusable.[184] As a result, the 3rd Battalion crossing stalled.

The 2nd Battalion of the 10th Regiment launched another attack late in the morning of February 8th. At 10 AM, E Company set off for the east bank and successfully managed to get across in the next hour. By 11 AM, the entire company was on the opposing bank, relieving the 9 men who had made it across the day before. Upon crossing, E Company encountered enemy troops bunkered down in pillboxes. After engaging the enemy, the Company established a foothold, and by 12:45 PM some of the German soldiers began withdrawing from their pillboxes. G Company soon followed E Company across. Half of the Company was over by 1:30.[185]

The Germans pushed back, however. The crossing of the Sauer River itself was a two-part process; the troops that crossed first in the boats were tasked not only with clearing enemy objectives but with helping establish a bridgehead for the attached 133rd Engineer Battalion while the engineers constructed footbridges to help the troops cross more easily. While E Company of the 10th Regiment was able to neutralize one pillbox immediately in their vicinity, the opposition was still able to fire at the 133rd Engineers. By 5 PM, the Germans were able to fire consistently on American troops at the 2nd Battalion crossing site, leading to the realization that the Americans would have to change landing locations. The engineer report for that day noted that "Two of the boats succeeded in crossing, but casualties for both Infantry and

Engineers were so high that the crossing was postponed and that site abandoned… Company C [of the 133rd Engineers] relieved Company B at 1700 hours 8 February on the assault crossing work."[186]

The remainder of February 8th was filled with failure on multiple fronts for the 10th Regiment. The 2nd Battalion lost its last boat at 6:40 PM. The 3rd Battalion fared even worse, with only 3 boats sent across on an alternate route.[187] At the end of the day, the 2nd Battalion had a precarious foothold on the opposing bank, while the 3rd Battalion had almost nothing to show for the day's work. The defeat of the 10th Regiment in their early attempts to cross the Sauer was, in many ways, surprising. This was not the first time Allied troops made it to the Sauer, nor was it the first time they engaged the Siegfried Line. However, poor weather conditions and logistical failures in coordinating the assault led to disaster in crossing the river. Despite these setbacks, the men that made it across were well dug in, and they even managed to capture some prisoners of war.[188]

Farther south, the 2nd Battalion of the 11th Regiment fared little better than the previous day in its assault. F Company pushed off, but once again, the Sauer River wreaked havoc on the boats. Although they launched ten boatloads of men across the river, only four managed to cross. The Germans soon discovered the men along the shore and opened fire. Amidst a heavy gunfight between the elements of F Company on the far shore and the Germans, 8 men of the reconnaissance patrol who had crossed over the night before returned to the Luxembourg side of the Sauer River while the men of F Company resumed the role of establishing a bridgehead.[189]

The next assault attempt by the 11th Regiment occurred at 5:30 PM on February 8th. The remainder of F Company, along with G Company, successfully crossed the river in the 2nd Battalion sector, but not without cost:

> "At 1730 on the 8th, G Co started to cross (under a smoke screen) but received MG fire from pillbox No 3. The company commander, Capt Dursk, was hit and 25 of his men wounded on the crossing. The only man not hurt in the boat with Capt Dursk was the radio operator. Capt Dursk ordered the boat to continue across the river so that his company would have communication. G Co finished crossing by 1830."[190]

The crossing for both F and G Companies of the 11th Regiment occurred under severe fire for over 2 hours. No other men were able to make it across, and the troops that made it across were low on supplies. The soldiers dug in and attempted to stay under cover while machine guns and mortar fire blanketed the area, but it became necessary for soldiers to brave the open area to gain the supplies needed for fighting back against heavy German fire.

> "…as pillboxes increased their rate of fire, Pvt. Armand LeTourneau exemplified the true courage of those infantrymen whose mission it was to move into the very teeth of the enemy fire. He regained control of the craft and frantically paddled near shore, then leaped into the river and shore-beached the assault boat while machine bullets cracked by… [Letourneau] displayed distinct heroism when he emerged from cover in the midst of fire, worked his way back to the boat and returned with two armloads of ammunition with which he opened furious fire, and, in conjunction with others, succeeded in silencing a pillbox machine gun."[191]

The extreme danger presented by the German fire halted the American advance, and the remainder of the 2nd Battalion was forced to retreat once again.

While these operations were conducted, the 1st Battalion of the 11th Regiment remained in reserve, providing some covering fire for the men trying to cross the river. The men were alerted that they would attempt a crossing later that day at 6:00 PM after the 2nd Battalion successfully crossed the Sauer River, but the attempt was canceled when it became apparent that they were not going to be able to cross. The weary men of the 1st Battalion had been on alert for three straight days and said they had not slept during that time. Upon hearing the news, they immediately went to bed.[192]

Over the course of the day on February 8th, the engineers working with the 11th Regiment tried valiantly to install the footbridges necessary for crossing the troops over in mass, but once again, enemy fire and the Sauer River current made life difficult for them. They tried to run cables across the river to help the assault boats deal with the current, but those attempts were also unsuccessful.[193] The most crucial set-back, however, was the 133rd Engineers failure to construct the bridge across the Sauer River. The constant harassment from enemy troops made life difficult for the soldiers. While the 10th Regiment successfully eliminated one pillbox that day, engineers were still bombarded with fire from the other pillboxes that were not yet reduced. Even more damaging to engineers' efforts was the Sauer River itself. The strong current frequently caused parts of the bridge under construction to become detached. Ropes used to anchor the pieces to the riverbank were often cut, sometimes resulting in whole sections coming apart and drifting down river. The engineers even tried to utilize a partially destroyed bridge as an "expedient footbridge" by placing boards and timber over the gap of the remaining bridge, but that also failed, given the size of the gap and German fire on the bridge area.[194] As nighttime came, engineers ceased their efforts for the day. The bridge was still far from being completed. Nevertheless, despite the strong defense of the West Wall by the Germans and deterrents from Mother Nature, there was still a successful crossing of two companies within the 10th Regiment.

In the 80th Infantry Division zone, the rains ceased early in the morning of the second day of the attack on the Siegfried Line. The Third US Army's after-action report only noted that the 80th Infantry Division enlarged their bridgeheads.[195] The 80th Infantry Division reported that crossings in both the 318th and 319th Regiments continued, and both bridgeheads were enlarged. They also noted an increase in the number of fortifications that had been reduced, which had decreased the heavy enemy fire opposing the American assault. The difficulties in building bridges were also highlighted, including the strong currents and heavy enemy fire.[196] The 80th Infantry Division G-2 report briefly noted that there was still heavy artillery fire directed at the bridging sites, and there were also small arms and gun fire aimed at the attacking forces who crossed the rivers.[197]

Under cover of darkness, engineers in the 80th Infantry Division helped ferry supplies across the river and bring back wounded soldiers.[198] Even with these difficulties, the 80th Infantry Division's after-action report indicates pillboxes were "encountered and reduced" and the two battalions across the river expanded the bridgehead.[199] It was a busy day for the engineers. The 150th Engineers, with the support of the 1135th Engineer Group, made several unsuccessful attempts to build a bridge across the Our River in the vicinity of Wallendorf in the 319th Regiment sector. The strong currents and enemy fire still worked against them when trying to build a treadway bridge. A footbridge was built during the early morning hours, enabling a few troops and supplies to move across the river before the bridge was destroyed by the swift current. Just before daybreak, they were able to get a cable across the river but were forced to stop the building effort during the daylight hours.[200]

The original plan for the engineers called for them to build several bridges in this area, including two footbridges, an infantry support bridge, and a treadway bridge. Their mission was delayed for days.[201] Without the bridges, the troops of the 80th Division were forced to continue attacking across the Sauer and Our Rivers utilizing boats. By the time the 1st Battalion of the 318th Regiment was ready to cross, only a few assault boats remained for crossing the river.

On the second day of the assault, the 318th Regiment continued to cross the Sauer River at Dillingen, south of Wallendorf, using the remaining assault boats. Unlike the 5th Infantry Division's difficulties, most of the 3rd Battalion of the

80th Infantry Division succeeded in crossing during the day and joined the 2nd Battalion, who crossed the river during the night. The two battalions were actively engaged that day in battlefield warfare. They worked together to clear woods and the high ground overlooking the river of enemy troops. The 3rd Battalion moved to the south toward Bollendorf to clear the forested peninsula surrounded by the Sauer River between Dillingen and Bollendorf and thereby enlarge their bridgehead over the river.[202]

On the German side of the river, troops from the 2nd Battalion of the 318th Regiment turned toward the north. Under mortar and artillery fire, the troops moved up to a crest overlooking the river. As the battalion began to attack downward away from the bridgehead, they encountered an elaborate fortification system of defenses developed by the Germans. There were pillboxes camouflaged as houses, barns and haystacks, foxholes and trenches hidden in dense foliage, and minefields and booby-traps. In the first hour, the attack was chaotic. There was extensive enemy artillery and nebelwerfer (smoke propeller) fire. An after-action report for the 318th Regiment referred to the action as "into the gaping jaws of Hell."[203] Between the hours of 1300 and 2300 (1:00 in the afternoon to 11:00 at night), they were only able to advance 1,200 yards.[204]

While some troops in the 2nd Battalion of the 318th Regiment were able to advance, others could not and were separated from their comrades. Sensing an enemy counterattack was approaching, the 2nd Battalion stopped and waited for the Germans to advance to approximately ten yards of their position. The Americans then fired into the approaching enemy troops, killing 25 Germans and forcing the remainder of the Germans to run in retreat. The battalion then dug in for the night.[205]

In Luxembourg, the 1st Battalion of the 318th Regiment, which had been in reserve in Diekirch, moved to the high ground near the crossing site in anticipation of their going over. Unfortunately, enemy fire and other problems left them with only four assault boats at their disposal for the crossing. Then, German heavy artillery fire set off one pole charger. The troops, realizing the crossing would be a difficult one, elected to abandon some of their equipment (including the pole charges) to increase their chances of making a successful crossing. After the crossing began, the Germans situated north of the crossing site continued to fire on the boats with artillery and mortar fire and even used a captured American AT gun.[206]

In the Wallendorf area, the 319th Regiment also enlarged its bridgehead on the high ground in Germany. The mission for the 1st Battalion was to clear the ridgeline, which would eliminate the enemy's ability to directly see the site for the building of a bridge planned for this area. The fighting was chaotic. Company A crossed the raging Our River before daybreak and captured Wallendorf. From there, they advanced uphill, where they were pinned down by intense fire from pillboxes in the area. B Company bypassed the area of the pillboxes to reach the high ground but found themselves separated from the rest of the battalion. Several pillboxes were disabled that day, but the troops learned that indirect fire on the pillboxes did not do much damage to them. The battalion listed 25 casualties for that day.[207]

The 2nd Battalion of the 319th Regiment encountered strong enemy fire; however, they managed to defend their bridgehead.[208] It was evident that the enemy held a vantage point from which to see the entire Allied front in this area and used it to successfully fire heavy artillery concentrations. As a result, there were few additional crossings that day; only 27 men managed to cross in this sector. They had expected that a bridge would be built by now to allow the remaining troops to cross via bridges as opposed to the boats now being used, but like many of the units in the XII US Corps, they were behind schedule. Communication was also an issue for the battalion. While the radio worked at night, there was no wire for other communication with the troops on the other side of the river. Additionally, there was poor reception on the German side of the river due to the reception-blocking terrain. The remainder of F Company was finally ferried over the river around midnight.[209]

The 3rd Battalion of the 319th Regiment was ordered to cross the river at Wallendorf during the morning of the second day. Enemy artillery destroyed some of the boats to be used for the crossing, but engineers continued to locate additional boats. Despite the use of a smoke generator, the heavy enemy fire still made the crossing difficult. The 3rd Battalion attempted to cross again later in the day on February 8th, but the first boat took a direct hit from enemy fire, and all were killed, which resulted in all further crossings being canceled until after dark.[210] Another attempt was made just before midnight.

There was an unfortunate episode as well that day. As the 319th Regiment troops were heading west on their way down from Kleinsreisdorf (also called Reisdorf) to Wallendorf, the 318th Regiment opened fire on the Germans, lighting up the night and revealing to the Germans the position of the advancing troops. As a result, the Germans fired their own artillery and nebelwerfer at the 319th Regiment, killing several American troops.

The Americans used the cover of darkness that night to send supplies over by boat to the troops of the 319th Regiment now in Germany and evacuate soldiers injured by the attacks.

Engineers once again attempted to build bridges across the wide, raging rivers in the 80th Division sector. The current was still strong, and the Germans continued to fire on the engineers and their constructions. Like the 5th and 417th Infantry Divisions in Luxembourg, the engineers were still unable to complete any type of bridge over the rivers by the end of February 8th.

The 80th Infantry Division attached the 51st Armored Infantry Battalion to the 319th Regiment to provide additional support for the attack to the east of Bettel and to protect the regiment's left flank. Additionally, the 53rd Armored Infantry Battalion was attached to the 318th Regiment to support its right flank.[211]

The Alternative Experience

Roland missed being part of the successful conclusion of the XII US Corps attack on the Siegfried Line from Luxembourg. Had Roland not been taken prisoner, he would have experienced the assault on the Siegfried Line defenses, which had been regarded as impregnable, and the enlarging of the bridgehead to the Prum River. The path not taken included German pillboxes and minefields, artillery fire, battles in heavily forested areas, and strong German defenses by troops not yet ready to retreat or surrender. In the next three days, most of the remaining frontline infantry troops in the XII US Corps were able to cross the Sauer and Our Rivers into Germany, and operations shifted to overcoming the Siegfried Line defenses and advancing toward their planned objectives.

Roland never understood the broader picture of what the river crossing was about in the context of an elongated Allied front advancing into Germany and then ending the war in a coordinated manner. His crossing was just the beginning of an operation that eventually brought the Third US Army to the Rhine River. Overcoming the Siegfried Line was a meaningful accomplishment in tandem with advancing Allied troops extending from British and American forces to the north of the XII US Corps to the American and French troops to the south in France. He, however, was stuck in a German prisoner-of-war camp which we will get into shortly. For now, we shall follow the American troops as they braved and vanquished the Siegfried Line. For me, this part of the story gave meaning to the initial struggles on the first day of the crossing.

February 9-11

In the 417th Regiment's zone, the regiment continued to move the 3rd Battalion into Germany after the completion of the 2nd Battalion crossing. Two companies crossed in the morning of February 9th. The crossings were not without complications as boats still overturned and drifted downstream, and men became disorganized in the dark. One squad ran into a minefield."[212]

The attempted crossings of the Sauer River had already generated large casualties. The two companies, which usually had a strength of 180 to 200 men each, could only account for 98 men in one company and 60 men in the other, and a third company had two entire platoons, comprising approximately 50 troops each, missing. Several companies were still waiting in Luxembourg to cross. The lone exception for crossing during the day of February 9th was a single boatload containing the 2nd Battalion's executive officer and his attached party, which crossed at 2 PM to provide some direction to the battalion after losing its commanding officer.[213]

There were losses of several other commanding officers in each of the three battalions, including the commanding officer of the 3rd Battalion, who was reported across the river on the night of February 8-9th but soon became a casualty. While elements of the 1st and 2nd Battalions held the initial objective point north of the Sauer River, the men were missing the leadership to direct them to where to go next. The 417th Regiment's executive officer, Lieutenant Colonel R. D. Boerem, had not yet crossed the river, and the troops on German soil remained scattered and disorganized. This left the 2nd and 3rd Battalions moving in the wake of the 1st Battalion[214] instead of advancing toward their own objectives until leadership arrived to reorganize and direct the whole regiment.

While little progress was made toward the objective points, the men across the river were engaged in heavy combat with the Germans operating the Siegfried Line defense system. They reduced several pillboxes in the vicinity of the crossing site itself. One pillbox was particularly troublesome and was essential for establishing control in the area. Unfortunately, it had killed seven men who attempted to bypass it.[215] After several failed attempts to reduce the pillbox, the American troops adjusted their methods of attack and finally succeeded:

"In the assault of the pillbox, the first efforts were directed at closing the ports with small arms fire. With the enemy buttoned up, fragmentation grenades were dropped down the stove pipe. Although the grenades detonated, the pipe was apparently blocked. The explosion only resulted in the destruction of a section of the pipe. The occupants were unharmed.

Next… phosphorous grenades were dropped through the ventilator in order to smoke the rear of the box. Thus screened, Capt Schmidt crossed to the entrance of the pillbox accompanied by two riflemen firing at the range of 10 feet, into the slits, Schmidt tossed an 18 pound charge into the doorway, but little damage resulted. In the depression housing the door, the riflemen momentarily ceased firing. Immediately the enemy fired several [sic] bursts with a Schmeisser, but nobody was injured. The riflemen continued to shoot [sic] their M-1. The captain placed a 30 pound satchel charge in the [sic] embrasure. Before it was necessary to ignite the charge, muffled cries from within indicated a desire to surrender. Six enlisted men and one sergeant were captured."[216]

This operation led to the capture of a second pillbox connected to the first pillbox by a communication trench. Knowing that the first pillbox was breached, the men in the second pillbox became amenable to surrendering as well, and an additional 22 enlisted men and one officer were captured.

The American troops then set up guards on the pillboxes to prevent re-infiltration by the Germans.[217]

Other elements of the 417th Regiment were also engaged in capturing a pillbox at Ernzerhof with the help of mortars fired from the 91st Chemical Battalion and an hour of friendly artillery pounding the area of the Ernzerhof pillbox. The Germans quickly surrendered.[218] This capture also led to additional Germans surrendering at nearby pillboxes.

Despite this success, the 1st Battalion of the 417th Regiment had multiple problems. The lack of radio communication, not yet set up in the bridgehead in Germany, resulted in a lack of supplies, made worse by the loss of the mortars and a shortage of bazooka ammunition. Food and water were scarce, and men resorted to drinking muddy water out of foxholes just to avoid dehydration. Because bridges were not yet installed, all resupply had to be dropped in by plane, and poor weather conditions caused the planes to be erratic in their airdrops. One after-action report noted, "Many times, it was necessary to crawl out close to the enemy lines to secure the supplies… Many fell into enemy hands."[219]

Most impactful, however, was the condition of the men themselves. The wet conditions and tiring work the men endured while crossing the river and reducing the pillboxes were starting to weigh on the troops' morale. They were hungry and drinking dirty rainwater, and the number of casualties in the 1st Battalion was starting to mount. 22 members of the 417th Regiment lay on litter badly in need of medical care and evacuation.[220]

At dusk, the remainder of the 3rd Battalion began the last crossing of the Sauer River. The weather was still rainy, and the river was still swollen from the thaw, but the crossing went ahead without any mistakes. The commanding officer of the 3rd Battalion crossed the river at 7:30 PM; the remainder of the troops followed.

On February 10th, the battalions and individual companies began to function as coordinated units. The regimental executive officer, Lieutenant Colonel R. TD. Boerem, crossed the river before daylight that morning. By the middle of the day, the 2nd Battalion was heading east in the direction of Echternacherbruck toward the high ground that was their final battalion objective, and the 3rd Battalion was organizing to move toward its own final regimental objective.[221] They continued to neutralize pillboxes during their advance.

The 417th Regiment reverted to the total control of the 76th Infantry Division on February 11th, and the regiment continued to advance in their zone.[222] The 1st Battalion and the Heavy Weapons Company of the 901st Field Artillery Battalion engineered a joint strike against a troublesome pillbox they had been trying to capture since the day before. The assault called for a 25-man, 3-pronged attack with a mixture of weaponry, including M-1s, M-3s, bazookas, BARs, and satchel charges carried by a demolitionist. First, the mortars and artillery bombarded the enemy and forced them to "button up," which would allow the assault team to safely approach the box. Then, supporting troops fired bazookas from the woods nearby. The fire was so strong that the Germans in the pillbox were completely prevented from firing back.[223] The assault team, including the demolition specialist, then moved in with satchel charges and grenades. As the men threw grenades into the passageway, the Germans inside finally surrendered. The operation, lasting a total of 1 hour and 15 minutes, ended with the capture of 15 Germans.

In taking out the pillbox, the 1st Battalion had essentially accomplished its goals for the Sauer River crossing. A and B Companies were located on the high ground they were ordered to take, and the reduction of the pillbox in the area helped secure the surrounding area. The men received a serious beating from the Germans, however, and needed to be relieved of their position. By the time the 3rd Battalion of the 385th Regiment arrived on the evening of February 11th to assume control over the zone established by the 1st Battalion of the 417th Regiment, the latter's fighting force had suffered significant casualties, the number of which is unclear.

According to the regiment's Commanding Officer, Lieutenant Colonel Boerem, 28 men from the 1st Battalion were killed in action during the river crossing, and an additional 78 men were missing in action.[224] Besides losing these 100 men, there were wounded men classified as additional casualties. These numbers may better explain why the 1st Battalion was relieved so quickly after it was first put into combat.

While the 1st Battalion was relieved of duty on February 11th, the rest of the 417th Regiment remained in combat until February 16th, when they reached their objectives. During the next few days, the 2nd and 3rd Battalions spent their time attempting to move toward their objective points on high ground while removing German resistance along the way. The sheer number of bunkers, pillboxes, and other fortifications in the area, combined with the terrain, made the general procedure for advancing unique compared to standard movement in the war. They soon developed guidelines for how to overcome some of the obstacles. Lieutenant Colonel Boerem highlighted the general procedure established to clear a pillbox:

> "The attacks during the period were unlike the regular infantry attack, where the units advance more or less in a line. The points of resistance, the pillboxes, determined the place of attack and altered the routine procedure. Assault teams of approximately 12 men were organized

and assigned specific pillboxes to eliminate. In the assault team there was usually a BAR team, a MG Section, some riflemen and personnel carrying satchel charges. While fire from the BARs and MGs kept the embrasures of the pillboxes buttoned up the riflemen and men carrying the satchel charges would advance on the pillboxes from the blind approaches. The satchel charge (18 to 36 lbs) would be placed in a port and detonated [sic] If that didn't bring the Germans out, smoke and fragmentation grenades put down the ventilator would sometimes do the trick. It was often possible to take a prisoner from a reduced pillbox and use him to induce his comrades in nearby boxes to surrender."[225]

The engineers in the 1103 Engr C Group finally completed two bridges in their sector over the Sauer River on February 11th. The 204th Engr C Bn completed a treadway bridge with a span of 204 feet over the Sauer River during the morning. It was located between Bollendorf and Echternach near the town of Weilerbach. The 282nd Engr C Bn completed a treadway bridge measuring 180 feet near Echternach. Troops, supplies, food, and equipment could now easily move across the river.

In the 5th Infantry Division sector, the 10th Regiment was well behind in its mission on February 9th. While the 417th Regiment had successfully crossed the river to the south and was proceeding toward its initial objectives, the lack of progress by the 5th Infantry threatened the 417th Regiment's flank and could cause the assault on the West Wall to fail. February 9th, however, became a turning point for the 5th Infantry Division.

As dawn broke, so did the Siegfried Line's outer defenses along the 10th Regiment's front. By 10 AM, almost the entire F Company followed E Company across the river, and at 4:40 PM, the entire battalion, excluding a single mortar unit, was on German soil. The 10th Regiment finally had a large enough group of men to allow them to attack toward their objectives and establish a bridgehead. Within an hour, F Company sent a patrol toward their first objective in Diesburgerhof, where they encountered fire from nearby Ferschweiler.[226]

Meanwhile, the troops in the 3rd Battalion failed to make headway in their struggle to cross the Sauer River using a single boat early in the morning; and then a shakeup in leadership occurred. The lieutenant colonel in charge of the entire 3rd Battalion was removed from duty at 6:50 AM, and one of his majors was ordered to replace him.[227] There was no written reason given for the change, but the 3rd Battalion was disorganized, with half the troops lagging behind others attempting to cross. Lieutenant Louis J. Merlino of L Company recalled that on the night of February 8th, his company was ordered to move across the river, but the men were "too tired and the night was too dark" for the men to make a crossing.

They waited instead until the following night to start the assault.[228] The men had been notified that morning that they would be making the attack, meaning that everyone participating should have been well prepared to follow orders. Darkness should not have been a detriment to the men crossing the river, as it meant that they were less likely to be targeted by enemy fire.

The change in command, however, was beneficial for the 3rd Battalion. Under the command of Major Haughey, the battalion launched an attack later that day, with I Company reaching the opposite shore, but the attack stalled from that point onwards as the engineers were unable to get a cable across the shore.[229] Nevertheless, the two battalions of the 10th Regiment now had hundreds of men on the German (north) side of the river. It was the first day in which the men felt they had a working foothold in German territory.

In the 11th Regiment, the 3rd Battalion launched a special mission consisting only of the commanders of K and M Companies at 2:15 AM on February 9th. Together in a single boat with only a handful of other men assisting them, the two men crossed the river to meet up with the 24 men occupying a small bridgehead on the German side of the river. The two officers' presence provided a morale boost after a series of unsuccessful crossings left them waiting for reinforcements.

The commanders helped distribute rations, evacuate the wounded, and resupply ammunition for the 24 men.[230]

At the other crossing site for the 11th Regiment, the 2nd Battalion launched another attack across the Sauer River at 8 AM. By 10 AM, as many as 200 men and additional munitions crossed, and the troops began to make their way toward their objectives. Troops immediately attacked a pillbox that was firing on both the roads on the far shore and the crossing site. The pillbox was blown by the assault squads and captured at 10:30 with 10 officers and 8 men inside. This reduced enemy fire and eliminated small arms fire on the crossing site. Additional troops were now able to cross over the river safely.[231]

The strategy was now beginning to take place. More and more US soldiers were setting foot in Germany.

The assault by the 11th Regiment continued during the afternoon. Two companies overran another key pillbox without opposition. When the observer was captured, enemy artillery fire lost effectiveness. The clearing of the observation post, which took direct observation off the bridge site, occurred at approximately 3 PM on February 9th.[232] Two hours later, the entire 2nd battalion of the 11th Infantry Regiment was across, and the 1st Battalion began to follow suit.[233] They now had a clear pathway for the Allied armies to move into Germany in that sector.

The crossing of the Sauer River, while significant, was only the beginning of the operation. The 11th Regiment began to establish a secure, relatively safe area of control that could be used by headquarters as a new command center. The knockout of the enemy's observation point over the Sauer River allowed the engineers to finally complete a treadway bridge, and the 1st Battalion, whose mission was to capture the German town of Ernzen, was able to cross. It had taken 2 days for a single company to cross the Sauer River amidst the maelstrom of German fire, swift Sauer River currents, and heavy downpour. Now, with enemy fire focused instead on the 2nd Battalion troops already in German territory and a bridge installed, three companies of perhaps 180 to 200 men each were able to cross within 2 hours.[234]

The assault by the 5th Infantry Division now turned toward the German inland defenses known as the Siegfried Line and the terrain on the German side of the river. One after-action report described this action as "crossing the Sauer River into the steep, pillbox-infested hills."[235] The obstacles now were heavily forested woods on hills with limited roads and limited visibility through the trees. The pillboxes, often located on the cliffs and bluffs, had to be neutralized to eliminate the strong artillery and mortar firings impeding American advancement. There were other obstacles as well, such as minefields, trenches, machine gun nests, and barbed wire to move through. After assembling on the other side of the river, different units were disbursed in different directions - up hills, along the bluffs, and downstream - toward their specific objectives.

The major goal now was capturing the town of Ernzen, a stronghold with a concentration of artillery. It was also a collection point for Germans trying to avoid capture."[236] It was strongly defended by a full regiment trying to provide cover for the German troops withdrawing to the other side of the Prum River. Later that day, the 1st Battalion methodically advanced toward Ernzen under the cover of darkness and settled in an area on the west slope of a bluff. By 9 PM on February 9th, they captured a group of pillboxes southeast of the crossing site.[237]

The engineers in support of the 5th Infantry division were still facing severe casualties, and the bridges they were working on were in shambles early on February 9th. They requested additional men in the 133rd Engineers and new materials, but headquarters responded that the road for resupplies was blocked.[238] The next day, the engineers were still under fire from the Germans, and the troops of the 10th Regiment still in

Luxembourg were ordered to move up the river toward Bollendorf to cross at the 11th Regiment's crossing site instead. It was a longer but safer route into Germany. The 3rd Battalion was able to cross all of its men into Germany by 4:45 PM.[239] The 1st Battalion soon joined them, and by 9:40 PM, the entire regiment was across.[240] The 11th Regiment's 3rd Battalion also crossed their remaining troops into Germany at that site. The engineers immediately went to work constructing a footbridge and, later, a pontoon bridge.

The cost of getting the men across the river was catastrophic for the 10th Regiment. Colonel Breckinridge stated that 100 rubber boats were lost in the assault, while the 133rd Engineers reported that the battalion lost 100 wooden assault boats and 20 rubber recon boats.[241] As the week-long battle ended, Breckinridge estimated that the 10th Regiment suffered 300 casualties, most of whom were lost in assaults across the river.[242] Additionally, the 133rd Engineers suffered severe casualties of their own. In the middle of the action on February 10th, an entire company of men from the 204th Engineer Battalion was brought in to relieve one of the 133rd Engineers' companies.[243]

With the entire regiment across on February 10th, the troops of the 10th Regiment began to clear out the German defenses. They moved north and began reducing pillboxes or scaring the Germans into abandoning them. Several pillboxes on cliffs overlooking Bollendorf were taken, and minefields were cleared as the American troops advanced toward their objective.[244] The 11th Regiment also advanced toward its own objectives.

On February 11th, the 10th Regiment moved toward the German town of Bollendorf. They cleared several pillboxes along the way and found others already abandoned. A patrol sent into the town of Bollendorf reported it deserted, and prisoners of war taken by the Americans informed them that the German soldiers in the area had either fled or remained in the vicinity because they could not escape before the American troops arrived.[245] The 11th Regiment reported less German opposition on that day as they cleared additional pillboxes and reached a strategically important location between Ernzen and Fershweiler.

In the 80th Infantry Division zone, the weather turned better on February 9th, the third day of action. The 318th Regiment reported "slightly less enemy fire"[246] at their crossing site near Dillingen. XII US Corps provided additional artillery support for the assault across the river and for efforts to enlarge the bridgehead.[247]

Elements of the 318th Regiment sector continued to mop up and expand the Dillingen bridgehead west of Bollendorf and south of Wallendorf. The 1st Battalion began crossing at 3:30 in the dark. The crossings began slowly, but the battalion completed the crossing late on that day. According to the 1st Battalion's after-action report, their plan was to attack northward in the hope that the engineers would have more room to work on the construction of a bridge over the river.[248] There are contradictory accounts in the official records as to exactly what happened in this regiment during this day. One historical record said the 1st Battalion moved northward and gained approximately 1000 yards before dark on February 9th.[249] Another record said they were forced to repulse an enemy counter-attack. There was a fire fight "all day of the 9th but gained no ground."[250] Divisional records indicate that the 1st Battalion gained one mile and moved through heavy woods.[251] On a positive note, they found a jeep abandoned by the 2nd Battalion and made it operational. The jeep was transported across the river on the ferry's only successful crossing. The ferry was later broken and was washed down stream.[252] Several accounts noted that by nightfall, the 1st Battalion did make some gains and was in a defensive position to the north of the peninsula.[253]

The 2nd and 3rd Battalions of the 318th Regiment continued to clear the peninsula between Dillingen and Bollendorf and advanced 1000 yards east of the bridgehead despite strong enemy resistance. By the end of the day, the northern half of the peninsula was in American hands,[254] and they managed to seize the strategically important high ground.[255] All of the 318th Regiment was finally on the German side of the river, and a CP for the battalion was established in a log bunker on high ground near the river. Late that night, the 317th Regiment, which had been in reserve, relieved the 318th Regiment of responsibility for the river crossings. Divisional and regimental records indicate that the Germans brought additional troops to the Dillingen crossing site area as reinforcements in an unsuccessful effort to force the regiment back across the river.[256] The 80th Infantry Division G-3 report noted that, "Machine gun fire on this bridgehead slackened during the day but continued on the Wallendorf crossing site."[257]

The 319th Regiment also attempted to cross their remaining troops on the third day, but they were less successful.[258] One company in the 2nd Battalion succeeded in crossing under cover of darkness; however, the crossing by the 3rd Battalion in Wallendorf met with heavy mortar and artillery fire. The first boat attempting to cross took a direct hit from enemy artillery fire, sinking the boat and killing the boat's eight occupants. The company then abandoned any additional attempts to cross the Our River.[259]

Troops of the 319th Regiment already across the river continued to attack and advance, but not without some difficulty. One company of the 2nd Battalion repulsed a counter-attack by the Germans in the morning.[260] The 1st Battalion was busy reducing pillboxes in the area overlooking Wallendorf during the day, and the 2nd Battalion reportedly advanced in the afternoon northward to expand the bridgehead in that direction. The regiment then advanced along a road near the river toward Wallendorf. As they approached the town, they occupied positions on the north on a steep slope of a hill, another location left of them and a third position on high ground above the others and to the right.[261] During the day, American artillery and tanks assisted in attacking and destroying pillboxes. The Germans answered with their own heavy concentrations of their own artillery and nebelwerfer fire.

As the 319th Regiment worked to destroy the pillboxes in their sector, they also gained experience and knowledge of the complex organization of the pillbox structure itself. The 2nd Battalion recorded their understanding of how the pillboxes were designed:

> "The primary pillboxes were strongly built and located to give each other mutual support. They were usually found three in a group, each of which housed about eight men. A command pillbox in the rear completed the setup and formed more or less the outline of a kite on the ground … Adjacent to the command pillbox was a bunker for personnel, having from 18 to

20 men. In rear of the primary command pillbox was a secondary row of pillboxes, less strongly reinforced, and behind these was still another command pillbox. Underground communications connected the defensive pillboxes to the command pillbox. The command pillboxes were connected for control purposes. Round about the pillboxes were communication trenches and other field installations."[262]

They also became more adept at capturing the pillboxes as they gained experience. They developed their own system to clear a pillbox, which required a combination of pole charges, satchel charges, bazookas, and smoke generators.[263] They began by surrounding the pillbox area with artillery. Their fire would drive the Germans into the fortifications around the pillbox. Then mortars and tank fire would be used to button them up. At that point,

"Machine gun and small arms accomplished the rest. Once the box was buttoned up the assault squad would move in on the rear. Few boxes had to be taken by use of the explosive charges placed therein. Of the first twenty taken satchel charges were used only on the first one. Thereafter once the initial phases of the reduction had taken place, a representative talking to the German occupants usually was successful in bringing about their surrender. …. The boxes which held out were in almost every case controlled by an officer."[264]

Like the 5th Infantry Division, troops over the river in the 80th Division had supply problems; ammunition was low, and the one-day food rations the troops received prior to their crossings into Germany were gone. American planes dropped food, war supplies, and medical supplies for them, 80% of which reached the American troops. The 1st Battalion of the 319th Regiment reported that the strength of the fighting units had decreased to an average strength of 80 men per company, which would be less than half of the normal strength of an army company.[265]

Engineers working on the boat crossings discontinued ferrying operations across the river in the Wallendorf area and concentrated on crossings in the Hoesdorf area northwest of Wallendorf. At the same time, the engineers continued to build a treadway bridge in the area of Wallendorf and another bridge in the Dillingen area. Due to the strong German artillery fire, the engineers made little progress in building these bridges.[266]

By the end of the third day, the 80th Infantry Division bridgehead in Germany enlarged to a depth of one mile, and a width of approximately one-half mile, and many pillboxes were captured or demolished. Planes reportedly flew 35 missions to supply the troops in Germany with medical supplies, food, and ammunition.[267] And one-third of the 319th Regiment was still trying to cross in boats. On both sides of the river, American and German artillery units continued to fire at each other. Interrogations of prisoners revealed many Germans had little interest in continued fighting.[268]

On February 9th, SHAEF and the New York Times reported that the US Third Army under General George Patton had breached the Siegfried Line. One headline was titled "U.S. 3D Army Invades Reich at 10 Points." Another story described how "Four Divisions Cross Our and Sauer at Night to Hack Westwall," and a third story described "Americans in Assault Boats Beat Torrents and Nazi Fire."

On February 10th, the 1st and 2nd battalions of the 318th Regiment advanced northwest of Wallendorf toward Biesdorf. They encountered many enemy troops fighting from dugouts, fox holes, and even stone bunkers; there were heavy casualties. Despite an injured commander, troops still managed to reach their high ground objective by evening after a lieutenant stepped forward to take command. That night, the 1st Battalion dug in on high ground at the edge of the woods north of Wallendorf, east of the town of Biesdorf, and about 1500 yards southeast of Biesdorf, which was protected by a series of pillboxes on the north and west sides of the town. The 2nd Battalion also encountered well-defended pillboxes on their way to Biesdorf. There was heroism here, too, as individual American soldiers crawled or charged the Germans for 150 yards during the fighting and artillery fire to kill, wound, and capture enemy troops. The 2nd Battalion finally captured Biesdorf after darkness set in by bypassing certain enemy strongholds.[269]

The 3rd Battalion of the 318th Regiment remained farther south, clearing the peninsula to the south between Dillingen and Bollendorf.[270] The regiment's history noted that with the capture of Biesdorf, the Sauer River bridgehead "was the largest in the [XII] Corps sector."[271] However, the price for the 318th Regiment was reported to be over 100 casualties on February 10th.[272] One wounded American was captured and then repatriated the same day after the infantry captured the German position where he was taken.

In the 319th Regiment, the 1st and 2nd Battalions continued to expand their bridgehead across the Our River on February 10th by clearing German fortifications. Records for the regiment do not mention much activity; enemy fire appears to have slackened off to some degree. By the end of the day, the battalion advanced to high ground northwest of Wallendorf. The regiment still required that supplies be airdropped and was able to evacuate their wounded men during the night.[273] The Third Army reported that the bridgehead for the 80th Infantry Division was now four miles wide and two miles deep. Two objectives had been met: the town of Biesdorf in Germany was cleared, and the 318th and 319th Regiments made contact with each other, merging the two bridgeheads.[274]

In Dillingen, the engineers continued to construct a treadway bridge but, once again, were harassed by enemy fire. Rising flood waters threatened the partially built bridge and increased the required length of the bridge as the swollen river grew even wider. The bridge would not be completed for several more days.[275]

Operations became easier for the 80th Division on February 11th despite the cold and heavy rain that drenched the area. The newly-attached 2nd Battalion of the 317th Regiment relieved the 3rd Battalion of the 318th Regiment of some of their positions on the peninsula so that the 3rd Battalion was free to advance to the high ground overlooking Bollendorf, the town west of Dillingen. They then captured and cleared the town.

The 318th Regiment was north of Wallendorf. After capturing the town of Biesdorf, they moved to secure the well-fortified town by mopping up areas not yet cleared of Germans opposition. Other troops in the 318th Regiment advanced to a location southeast of Biesdorf near the formidable Huehnenkopf Hill. Troops that entered the densely wooded area were met with opposition from embedded and patrolling enemy troops in the woods. They were fired on by machine guns, mortar, and artillery fire, all of which pinned them down.

The battle for Huehnenkopf Hill lasted for several days. It resulted in high casualties and included the loss of officers on both sides. Troops also met heavy German opposition at a strategic roadway intersection as they headed east.

Pillboxes, which were described as "defended fanatically,"[276] continued to be reduced by the 319th Regiment in their sector of the Siegfried Line. The 1st and 2nd Battalions were able to drive out the Germans from their observation points overlooking the river.[277] According to the 1st Battalion report, Wallendorf was cleared of Germans for the third time after the enemy infiltrated back into town after the Americans had cleared it. This time, the Americans also cleared the high ground and the ridge above the town in the hope of finally settling the problem.[278]

The engineers continued to construct two bridges over the river at Dillingen and at Wallendorf to transport equipment over to the German side.[279] Progress was slow because the Germans continued to periodically send artillery fire on the crossing sites. The swollen river had widened so much that it was estimated that the length of the one bridge would require an additional 75 feet, and there would be more work than expected to the approaches of the bridge to make it operational due to the current conditions.[280] In the Wallendorf area, the bridge under construction was still short by 30 feet, but the 3rd

Battalion learned to cross the river on the unfinished ponton bridge and then wade through water three feet deep to reach the other side of the river.[281]

Several days into this assault on the Siegfried Line, the raging currents of the swollen rivers continued to capsize boats, and delivering supplies to the troops in action was still a challenge. German prisoners reported that the Germans continued to bring reinforcements into this sector to provide additional resistance against the American advance.[282] Lt. Col. Paul Bandy, CO of the 2nd Battalion of the 319th Regiment, crossed the river to his troops on that day. He observed the troops, who had been continuously fighting since the crossings began on February 7th, and noted that "he had never seen troops so weary."[283] The operations by the XII US Corps had now changed from an assault over the Sauer and Our Rivers to establishing and enlarging a bridgehead in Germany. They had mastered the art of capturing pillboxes and destroying the formidable defenses of the Siegfried Line. They were advancing on key objectives and capturing German towns and territory.

General Patton wrote his wife about the Sauer River crossing on February 14th:

> "Sometimes I get so mad with the troops for
> not fighting better and then they do something
> superb. The forcing of the crossing of the

Sauer and Our Rivers…was an Homeric feat…. The Siegfried line runs right along the river with hundreds of pill boxes and submerged barbed wire. The river was in flood, running at ten to twelve miles an hour, and yet they crossed…. "One day we lost 136 boats but not all the men. We built bridges under [enemy] fire, and even when I crossed they still had to keep them covered with smoke."[284]

Truth and Significance: What Were the Casualties?

Official records do not entirely corroborate the numbers given to Roland Hartman. I decided to determine how many men attempted to cross over the Sauer and Our Rivers that first night and how many died or became casualties. Unfortunately, these numbers can only be estimated for some sources recorded crossings by the number of boats sent over, others by the number of companies or troops sent over, and others used percentages of battalions and not the number of troops. One group of engineers did estimate the number of troops sent over, but only for one group. Besides the number who tried to cross, there are the questions about how many found themselves in the water, and if so, how many managed to reach the German shore, how many found a way back to the Luxembourg side, and how many died in the river.

There are no records for this. Another complication is there are no estimates regarding how many successfully made the crossing and then died during the assault on the German side of the river. A final problem in any calculation is that many boats were guided by engineers who were supposed to return the boats to the Luxembourg shore after depositing the infantry troops in Germany; this leads to other questions, such as how many engineers were involved in the action, and how many of those engineers successfully made the crossing, how many returned to Luxembourg, and how many boats made more than one trip. These questions are not easily answered. For me, an accountant who likes simple numeric solutions with a single answer, there is no easy way to solve the question of how many attempted to cross the rivers or died or became casualties and when and how it all happened.

It turned out that the number of troops attempting to cross the rivers could only be estimated. Even so, being curious, I tried to approximate the number of troops sent over by the XII US Corps and how many troops became casualties. According to the regimental and divisional records, which somewhat differ in exactly what happened, the 417th Regiment sent approximately two and one-half battalions over the Sauer River in the early morning hours of February 7th in forty assault boats that can hold ten to twelve people. An additional fourteen boats were found to cross the remaining elements of the 1ˢᵗ Battalion and some of the 2ⁿᵈ Battalion over later in the day. Given that a battalion had approximately 900 men, it is not hard to guess that well over 1500 men might have tried to cross the Sauer River that night.

Alternatively, engineers estimated that approximately 350 to 400 troops were ferried over during the night. That would be close to the number calculated if 40 boats went over with an estimated ten men each (not counting the engineers who would return to the other side). Similarly, one could estimate that another 140 troops tried to cross the Sauer River later in the day, bringing the total of the 417ᵗʰ Regiment troops who attempted to cross on the first day to approximately 540 men. This, of course, assumes no boat made more than one trip across the river, and all available boats made the attempt.

In the 5ᵗʰ Division, two different attempts were made in approximately 25 boats, which would translate to approximately 250 troops trying to cross the river farther north. On the left flank, the 80ᵗʰ Division reports rarely talked about the number of boats used or the number of men sent over during the crossing; they reported four battalions attacking the river from multiple locations and some companies making it across with attacks continuing into the daylight hours. Elements of six different companies made attempts to cross, which could have involved as many as 900 additional troops, but that means only some of the troops may have made the attempt. This does not include estimates of engineers who crossed during the operations. Using these numbers, it is not hard to estimate that as many as 1,700 troops may have crossed in the XII US Corps sector on the first day of operations, although it is also possible that only portions of some of these companies made it into a boat, that each boat held only ten men each, and each boat made only one attempt to cross, which may not be correct. My conclusion at this point is that the numbers given to Roland were possible.

Casualties from crossing during the crossings and after arrival on the German side of the rivers is also a hard question to address. After the first wave of crossings by the 417th Regiment, the journal reports indicate that the strength across the river was approximately 133 men, significantly less than the estimated 400 men that may have crossed initially. Heavy losses were corroborated in the after-action reports.[285] For example, Company A recorded 20% casualties in the regimental journal in the first few hours of the operation on February 7th. An after-action report for the first day reported the fighting strength for Company A was 56 enlisted men, and for Company B, it was 52 enlisted men. Given the fact that each company routinely had between 190 and 200 men, there were large casualties involved in this action. That same report listed at least 28 men killed in the 1st Battalion and 78 men missing in action, more than half of the company. Company C's effective strength went down to 78 men.[286]

Another clue to the number of losses is that of the 40 boats sent over the river by the 417th Regiment, only one was reportedly able to return. This indicates hundreds of men tried to cross, but only a few were able to move into action upon landing. It was not much easier in the 5th Infantry Regiment's sector. Reportedly, only eight men made it across the river in the 5th Division after two attempts utilizing approximately 25 boats. In the 80th Division where as many as five regiments tried to cross, two companies reported they lost 40 men, and two other companies reported that only 120 men (perhaps less than half) successfully crossed over the river. Almost all boats used in the initial crossing attempts were reported sunk, hit, or destroyed by enemy fire, lost to the currents, or abandoned on the other side. Clearly, the difference between the number that attempted to cross and the estimated troop strength after the crossing points suggests numerous casualties.

XII US Corps personnel records (which include Third Army G-1 daily records) are available for that time with their own numbers. They reported casualties for the first day of the operation, February 7th, of approximately 565 men, including 131 in the 5th Division, 155 in the 76th Division (where the 417th records reside), and 245 in the 80th Division. The majority were wounded, but there were 38 listed as killed and 74 missing in the three divisions.[287]

These statistics do not include how many were in the water and how many managed to swim to safety, perhaps to make a second attempt later. Additionally, there are no complete reports that indicate how many engineers attempted to cross and how many of them survived, although at least one engineering unit was taken out of service after only a few days due to high casualties. It is also possible that some men who reached the German side of the river were killed in action later that day.

The number of men lost in the campaign to cross the Sauer River was high for the 417th Regiment. Two battalions of the regiment—the 1st and 3rd—were forced into relief before securing their objectives, as enemy fire was too hot and the casualties were too high. Lieutenant Colonel Boerem stated that the 417th Regiment suffered 86 deaths (including 8 officers) related to the Sauer River crossing and action beyond the river, with 421 wounded, 156 men missing, and 224 men lost from non-combat injuries.[288] Together, this totals 887 men out of approximately 3000 men in the regiment at the start of the battle. Additionally, the 160th Engineers were so decimated during the river crossing that they were relieved before they could even start building the bridges assigned to them.

Although the men successfully smashed through the most dangerous part of the Siegfried Line, it is clear to me that it came at a great cost. But this is true of all war initiatives.

After the Crossing: February 12-20

In the Third US Army, the G3 section of the XII US Corps referred to operations at this time as "for the purpose of enlarging and consolidating bridgehead."[289] Some reorganization of troops occurred as overworked units were relieved by rested units previously in reserve. The XII US Corps transitioned to a ground war that required capturing specified towns and objectives, and all three divisions responded by advancing daily in multiple directions. They continued to destroy Siegfried Line defenses and enlarge the bridgehead even as the First US Army to the north and the Sixth US Army Group to the south were forced to slow down their action due to flooding in their zones. The Eifel Campaign continued with objectives that included the cities of Bitburg and Trier. Elements of the 6th Armored Division, which had not been active during the Sauer and Our River crossings, relieved the 284th Engineers of their zone and participated in the operations.

The XII US Corps issued another directive on February 14th. The divisions were ordered to "advance in zones on the line of Prum River, consolidate and defend west of the Prum River, and to prepare for further advance to the east and northeast."[290]

The weather was still cloudy and cold during the middle of February but was beginning to moderate toward warmer weather. Nevertheless, the roads remained in very poor condition; many had craters in them. Streams continued to rise, and visibility was still listed as poor, thereby hampering some operations. On February 14th, VIII US Corps reported that the sun was out for the first time in two weeks, which allowed some air operations to proceed.

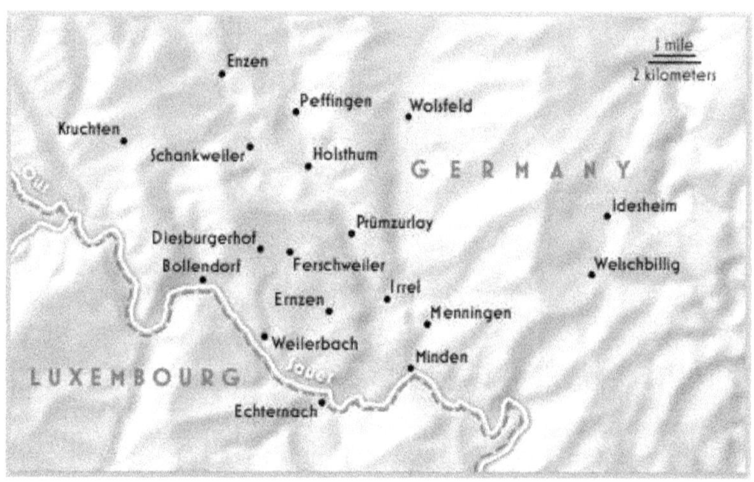

Area of 5th Division and 417th Regiment Bridgehead

In the 76th Infantry Division sector, the 2nd and 3rd Battalions of the 417th Regiment were augmented with an attachment of self-propelled tank destroyers that remained active with the objective of capturing the town of Minden on February 12th. The 385th Regiment was located on the high ground southeast of Ernzen. The treadway bridge recently completed by engineers at Echternach was being utilized by both the 76th and 5th Divisions.

In the next few days, the 76th Infantry Division continued to advance toward their objectives in their sector despite continued German resistance from pillboxes in the area. On February 13th, the troops from the 385th Regiment reached one of their objectives, a hill 300 meters southwest of the town of Ernzen. During the morning, elements of the 417th Regiment cleared the town of Echternacherbruck, the German town across the Sauer River facing Echternach, Luxembourg.

The next day, the 2nd Battalion of the 417th Regiment reached its final objective, the strategic high ground between Echternacherbruck and the town of Irrel.[291] Later that night, the battalion was relieved by the 385th Regiment.[292]

This left the 3rd Battalion as the last remaining unit in the 417th Regiment still active. They captured one objective point called Hill 259.1 and also linked up with the men of the 2nd Battalion, which helped to bridge a gap in the American front. The next objective, Hill 292, was located just southwest of the Prum River, overlooking the nearby German towns of Irrel,

Menningen, and Minden. Control over this hill would provide the Americans with an impressive vantage point for crossing the Prum River. The Germans, however, resisted the attack. The 3rd Battalion encountered a minefield resulting in several casualties,[293] strong opposition from intense mortar fire, and intense German defenses along the way. After taking one pillbox, the men occupied it, but the Germans prevented them from leaving."[294] The attack stalled for the next 36 hours until the men were released. The troops required reinforcements, which arrived the next day from the 385th Regiment. After the entrapped men were freed, the 1st Battalion from the 385th Regiment relieved the men of the 417th Infantry on the night of February 16th.[295] The 385th Regiment, now the only active regiment in the 76th Infantry Division sector, took over the assignment to secure Hill 292.

The 385th Regiment was now committed to action. Along with elements of the 417th Regiment, they captured one hill and then swung around to the road connecting Echternacherbruck and Irrel to capture another hill. By February 15th, they were located on high ground southeast of Ernzen. They continued to clear high ground southeast of the town of Ernzen and a hill southwest of the town of Minden, which allowed them to expand and consolidate the bridgehead.[296] At the same time, the 2nd Cavalry Group, also part of the XII US Corps, crossed the Moselle River near Ehnen, Luxembourg (west of Saarburg) to capture a road intersection east of Luxembourg City in Wincheringen. On February 20th, they made contact with the XX US Corps on the east side of the Moselle River, thereby merging their bridgeheads.

In the 5th Infantry Division zone, the 10th Regiment entered Bollendorf on February 12th without resistance, and the town was cleared by 9 AM.[297] At that time, the 5th Infantry Division was located southeast of the large, forested area with no roads and a sparse population. The 80th Infantry Division troops were still on the other side of this forested area. The new objectives for the 5th Infantry Division included reaching Ferschweiler and then heading northwest toward Schankweiler. Assuming the 80th Infantry Division simultaneously drove northeast from Biesdorf and then moved toward Nusbaum and then Schankweiler, the two divisions would connect to establish a unified front.

Unfortunately, engineers in the 5th Infantry Division still faced serious problems and encountered only limited success. They ultimately determined that it was impractical to build a Bailey bridge at the 10th Regiment's crossing site opposite Bollendorf and instead shifted efforts to building one at the 11th Regiment's site in Weilerbach. Therefore, troops waiting to move into Germany were delayed because they could not take a direct path to Bollendorf. While the 10th Regiment troops were ordered to take the town of Ferschweiler, the 11th Regiment was told to hold until artillery and TDs could move forward into position to aid in the attack.[298]

On February 13th, some units of the 10th Regiment successfully assaulted Diesburgerhof while other elements of the regiment attacked Ferschweiler. The 10th Regiment reported the capture of Ferschweiler at 10 AM:[299] This proved to be the last major objective that the 10th Regiment was a part of in breaching the Siegfried Line. They made contact with the troops of the 80th Infantry Division earlier in the day and remained in their position for the next two days monitoring troop movement in the Schankweiler vicinity and waiting for other 80th Infantry Division troops to take particular objectives.[300] Most of the 10th Regiment was relieved of their positions on February 15th by the 2nd Infantry Regiment and some elements of the 11th Regiment. Some elements of the 10th Regiment, however, pressed forward northward toward Schankweiler. When that town was finally captured, a new front connecting all the troops in the XII Corps was finally established.

The 2nd Infantry Regiment moved into several locations around the town of Schankweiler on February 16th. The next day, they advanced into part of Schankweiler, the immediate objective of the regiment, and secured two intact bridges over the Erz River. One company then crossed a log bridge and began to establish a bridgehead. The regiment also advanced to the east of Schankweiler to high ground overlooking the Prum River. On February 18th, the 2nd Regiment was close to the northeast edge of the town of Peffingen, north of Schankweiler and Holsthum, and established themselves along the Prum River west of that town. Other elements fanned out in different directions to clear the area near the Prum River. After capturing Schankweiler, they moved eastward toward the towns of Enzen, Peffingen, and Stockem (Stuckem). By February 20th, the 2nd Regiment was situated on the west bank of the Prum River, conducting mop-up operations and moving farther north of Enzen on the west bank of the river.

While the 10th Regiment moved on Ferschweiler, the 11th Regiment advanced toward Ernzen. The 3rd Battalion's attack began early, but troops came under fire from enemy artillery, mortars, and SP, impeding any further advance. Despite suffering many casualties and one company losing its commanding officer,[301] the men continued to assault pillboxes until they were ordered to dig in for the night. They were now in a position to attack Ernzen early the next day. At the same time, other units of the 11th Regiment unsuccessfully attempted, without tank support, to push farther toward Ernzen,[302] but failed to make progress.[303] Fortunately, the American troops learned that most German soldiers had orders to withdraw that night and flee across the Prum River north of Ernzen and Ferschweiler.[304]

The next day, the 11th Regiment, with armored support, moved into Ernzen in a coordinated attack from both the east and the south sides of the town.[305] The attack began at 6:15 AM the next morning.[306] The men swept in silently, and no shots were fired as they captured the outposts.[307] The entire town was cleared by 8:55 without much resistance.[308] The capture of Ernzen was a major victory because of the importance of its location relative to the Sauer and Prum Rivers. As the easternmost town south of the Prum River, Ernzen was the last refuge for Germans in the area. After taking Ernzen, the 11th Regiment moved north toward the Prum River to establish control of the southern side of the river in their sector. They successfully reached the high ground late in the morning. Troops then sent out patrols toward the river near the town of Holsthum. They saw limited enemy movement in the area but noted that the bridge across the Prum River had been blown.[309]

Regrettably, there was still some work to be done to clear the entire area of German opposition. Elements of the 11th Regiment, sent to relieve part of the 10th Regiment north of Ferschweiler, discovered a patch of woods in the sector that was not yet cleared of Germans. The patrols were unable to determine the strength of the enemy therein.[310] The woods in this location proved to be an obstacle nearly as deadly as the Sauer River itself and would take several days to clear. The Germans simply concealed themselves within the woods and opened fire on American outposts, forcing the Americans to withdraw. Artillery and armor support were then brought in to help clear the woods of the enemy.[311]

Throughout the next day, the 3rd Battalion of the 11th Regiment faced even more artillery fire from the Germans across the river near the town of Prumzurlay, and American artillery began dueling with German artillery and nebelwerfers. The American artillery knocked out at least two machine guns, set fire to a tank, and eliminated any opposing pieces of artillery.[312] Still, the woods itself remained under German control for several more days.

On February 16th, elements of the 11th Regiment were east of Ferschweiler and southeast of Schankweiler, scouting out the area around Prumzurley while other elements continued fighting in the unsecured wooded area west of the Prum River. The woods was the only known foothold still held by the Germans south of the Prum River and was the last objective left for the regiment. A tank division was brought in to help and fired 120 rockets into the woods. This was followed by machine gun fire and an assault by American troops into the woods, but the Germans still remained in control.[313] The frequent skirmishes with the German troops within the woods, artillery fire from Holsthum, and the sniper fire that commenced on the morning of February 17th caused many casualties among the troops, which were already reeling from losses sustained during the crossing of the Sauer River itself. Some battered companies were forced out of battle.[314]

The battle went back and forth. The Germans re-infiltrated cleared areas overnight. And the American troops were pelted with machine guns, burp guns, and rifle fire.[315] The stiff resistance forced the 11th Regiment into retreat. The regiment, however, persevered, and by February 18th, the 11th Regiment was close to its final objective with only one small sector to clear out. The tank division fired on various parts of the woods for a full 30 minutes,[316] and then the 11th Regiment swept once again into the woods. Outposts were established in the wooded area to eliminate the last pocket of resistance in the sector.[317] On February 18th, the regiment was located as far north as Prumzurley. They were relieved by the 358th Infantry Regiment of the 90th Infantry Division on February 19th.[318]

General Patton visited the area of the Sauer River crossings on February 13th. He and Lt. General Manton Eddy crossed an American-built bridge over the Sauer River into Germany and drove along the German bank. They also inspected several pillboxes on the German side of the river. He wrote about his visit: "The men were quite surprised to see me. However, the chance of getting hit was small and worth the risk due to the effect it had on the troops…"[319] Regarding the pillboxes, Patton wrote: "The amazing thing about all these defenses is that they produced no results."[320]

Area of 80ᵗʰ Division Bridgehead

In the 80ᵗʰ Infantry Division of the XII US Corps, the cold and heavy rains did not prevent the division from once again enlarging its bridgehead on February 12ᵗʰ.[321] For the next few days, troops continued with their efforts to clear the pillboxes in their sector of the bridgehead.[322] Many of these pillboxes were isolated or bypassed in the initial action and were now being reduced. At the same time, the division was now attacking further north and east of their established bridgehead. The Germans, however, continued to resist and sent heavy artillery fire into the sector.[323]

During the morning of February 12th, elements of the 318th and 319th Regiments made contact to the east of Wallendorf, thereby merging the two bridgeheads. Contact was also made with the 5th Division to the south of the 80th Division near Bollendorf, thereby linking the three divisions of the XII US Army Corps involved in the assault across the Siegfried Line. A treadway bridge over the Our River at Wallendorf was also completed that morning. Five tanks and 3 TDs immediately crossed over the river, but the bridge was temporarily closed midday as the rising waters caused the approaches to the bridge to go underwater.[324]

The 317th Regiment was located near Rohrbach (north of Bollendorf and southeast of Kruchten) on the right (southern) flank of the 80th Infantry Division next to the 5th Infantry Division. They patrolled the area north of the town and generally maintained their position.[325] On February 14th, the 1st and 3rd Battalions joined the 2nd Battalion south of Rohrbach. The regiment then drove northward to clear pillboxes along the way and then seized high ground east of the town of Rohrbach during the next few days.[326] The regiment occupied the town of Schwarzen, just south of Rohrbach,[327] and then moved to a location two kilometers southwest of Krutchen.[328]

The advance continued with the capture of the town of Rohrbach,[329] then the town of Stockigt,[330] and then secured high ground south of Nusbaum. Next, they drove to the Enz River and a wooded area south of Enzen.[331] By February 20th, the regiment was situated on high ground north of the town of Nusbaum. They crossed the Enz River on a bridge found intact and then captured the town of Enzen nearby. Regimental records indicate the troops traveled four miles on that day alone.[332] Some troops moved north of Nusbaum and then captured the town of Freilingen to block Germans trying to leave the area.

The 318th Regiment was situated near Biesdorf on February 12th, consolidating their bridgehead. They gained control over Biesdorf and made contact with the 319th Regiment farther south in Wallendorf. At the same time, they received strong enemy fire from a heavily wooded location called Huehnenkopf Hill, which was also known as Hill 380 in military records.[333] Some units, however, were still located in the Bollendorf area participating in several firefights with enemy troops in that area. The battalion completed the clearing of the peninsula southeast of Dillingen on February 12th and then moved north to high ground southeast of the 318th Regiment, linking the two battalions.

During the period between February 12th and 15th, the 318th Regiment fought to secure the hills around Biesdorf and capture the formidable Huehnenkopf Hill to the east of Biesdorf. The hill itself was a dominating feature in that area of their sector due to its heights and heavily forested features. The hill was strategically important to the Germans because it guarded the roads leading to the east and west of that area. For the Americans, therefore, the hill had to be taken to allow their advance to move forward. Unfortunately, they encountered strong enemy resistance that lasted for several days.

On February 12th, efforts to clear Huehnenkopf Hill were underway. During the next few days, American troops met stiff resistance and periodic heavy artillery fire. At one point, some troops cleared a wooded area and were able to reach their objective, but they were then cut off from contact with other American companies. The link was restored, but the gains were erased. There were several casualties and little progress that day.[334]

On February 14th, the regiment slowly advanced to Hill 380. The 1st Battalion was now located on the hill, the 2nd Battalion was located in and around the town of Biesdorf, and the 3rd Battalion was located near the bottom of the hill. As the battle continued, the Americans were forced to withdraw to where they began with no gains after a significant number of casualties.[335] The following day, one company, under the cover of darkness, moved forward and quietly bypassed enemy guns protecting the hill. They reached their objective by 0800 but were surrounded by the Germans. Other troops kept attacking to free the men but were repeatedly repulsed. Eventually, other troops effectively bypassed the enemy strongholds and successfully reached the encircled company. Both companies dug in on the hill during the night.[336] Huehnenkopf Hill was now partially under American control.

The 318th Regiment shifted its strategy the next day on Hill #380, also known as Huehnenkopf Hill. Attacks on the enemy occurred during the hours of darkness, and mopping-up activity occurred during the day.[337] They successfully cleared several pillboxes in their zone and "destroyed" small groups of enemy troops that had "infiltrated their location."[338] They were aided by a communication system installed after those already on the hill managed to slip a mile-long telephone wire past the Germans. It took two additional days to neutralize the enemy fire in that area and mop up the remaining enemy resistance.[339]

On February 18th, the 318th Regiment, in concert with the 317th Regiment, drove northward to capture Krutchen, but one battered battalion was forced into a regimental reserve to recover from the many casualties incurred during these operations.[340] The remaining troops then advanced northward to seize Hommerdingen.[341] They then moved to high ground southeast of the town of Huttingen. By February 20th, the regiment advanced to a location close to the town of Mettendorf, a key position because of the intersection of several roads located there. All three battalions then moved toward a high ground called Hasslich Hill. By the end of the day, the three battalions were strategically located close to each other, with a good vantage point overlooking Mettendorf.[342]

The 319th Regiment continued to reduce the German fortifications on the left flank of the division, south of the Our River, on February 12th. One battalion cleared the wooded area near the river, another advanced toward Ammeldingen, and the third moved to seize the high ground east of Ammeldingen and north of Wallendorf. [343] Between February 13th and 15th, the regiment, accompanied by tanks and TDs from the 51st Armored Infantry Battalion,[344] advanced northwest along the Our River and captured the town of Ammeldingen, northwest of Wallendorf and north of Hoesdorf. They found the town unoccupied. Troops then fanned out in multiple directions along ridges and over hills to clear pillboxes and to advance in a "slow and exacting operation."[345] The regiment continued to clear the area near Ammeldingen for several days. They found that some pillboxes gave up while others fanatically opposed the Americans.[346] The 3rd Battalion of the 319th Regiment went into reserve on the evening of February 16th after a failed attack against the enemy resulted in many additional casualties.[347] Nevertheless, the 319th Infantry Regiment was now located to the northeast of Niedersgegen and north of Ammeldingen and Wallendorf.[348]

During this period, the Germans unsuccessfully launched three counter-attacks against the 80th Infantry Division in the 319th Regimental zone. Each attack was repulsed by the 319th Regiment with the help of artillery firings from the XII US Corps and VIII US Corps to the north.

On February 18th, the 319th Regiment drove northeast toward Niedersgegen and reached the high ground at Biesdorf, southwest of Kruchten. The next day, the 314th Field Artillery relocated from Luxembourg across the Our River and then traveled 7 miles to the high ground at Biesdorf. They now held a commanding view of the German landscape in that region.[349] The next day, the regiment captured the town of Niedersgegen during the afternoon and cleared enemy troops from various pockets of resistance in the regimental sector.[350] They attacked to the south and seized the town of Obersgegen and the high ground southwest of that town on February 20th. They also captured the town of Seimerich, cleared several pillboxes in the area southwest of Niedersgegen, and moved close to the town of Huttigen to the west of Obersgegen.[351]

By the middle of February, the 150th Engineer Combat Battalion reported that they completed the construction of a treadway bridge at Dillingen. The construction took four days during which the engineers endured bad currents, rising waters, the need to provide ferrying operations across the river via boats, and continuing enemy artillery fire. The length of the completed bridge was 288 feet long, at least 75 feet longer than originally envisioned due to the flooded river's widened banks. The demand for additional bridges was still high, and the engineers immediately turned their attention to the construction of other bridges of various types in additional locations.[352] By February 18th, bridging the rivers became less challenging as the raging currents weakened and enemy opposition abated. Both the Sauer and the Our Rivers now had operational bridges. Tanks and other heavy equipment could now be routinely transported over to support the troops fighting in Germany, thereby changing the battlefield logistics.

The 80th Regiment reported that most of the German defenses along the Siegfried Line in their sector were eliminated by February 20th. They also noted that their success during their operations thus far occurred largely without the use of tanks, which were not able to cross the rivers until the construction of the bridges was completed.[353]

On February 20th, Generals Patton and Eddy once again visited the XII US Corps sector together. Patton was especially pleased to see the newly completed bridge built by the 1303d General Service Engineer Regiment and named in his honor.

Other Allied Activity Along the Allied Front

The operations in Luxembourg were not the only activities in Europe during the crossing of the Sauer and Our Rivers. There were also operations in progress north and south of the XII US Corps. This fit with Eisenhower's broad front strategy, which would prevent the Germans from concentrating their troops in one place and force them to distribute forces along a longer front. Given that they were fighting a two-front war with the Soviet forces attacking from the east of Germany, these actions strained Germany's available manpower. At the same time, the long front, with multiple actions at the same time, was able to keep the pressure on the Germans when unexpected events altered Allied plans.

North of the Twelfth US Army Group, the 21st British Army Group's Canadian First Army launched Operation Veritable on February 8th. Their mission was to clear the region between the Maas and Rhine Rivers in the Netherlands near the German border. The Canadians launched an amphibious attack over flooded terrain in support of the ground operations, but there was no rapid breakthrough as they had hoped. According to Eisenhower, "the fighting soon developed into a bitter slugging match in which the enemy had to be forced back yard by yard."[354]

Despite the same bad weather as farther south, muddy roads, and flooded terrain, they did achieve many of the objectives on the first day of the operation. By February 11th, the troops were close to the canal near Kleve and controlled much of the traffic flowing in that area, but the fighting in the Reischwald Forest continued. Unfortunately, the Germans blew the dykes in the Alter-Rhine Canal area, which flooded that area near Kleve.

In the First US Army, north of the Third US Army, only the V US Corps was in action during this period. They attacked the Schwammenauel Dam to gain control of the dam before the Ninth US Army began operations on February 10th. After capturing the towns of Kommerscheidt and Schmidt, they advanced to the north shore of the Roer River and captured the northern end of the Schwammenauel Dam and its control house. Farther south, other troops were clearing the northern shore of Urft Lake.

The Germans, however, retained partial control of the dam from a different end. They destroyed the discharge valves and blew the gates at the Schwammenauel Dam as they began withdrawing from the area, allowing water from the dam to flood the surrounding territory. The impact was immediate and extensive to the region. The water levels in the V US Corps sector continued to rise for days. The Roer River rose to its peak level on the morning of February 10th. North of Duren and the dams, the river's width enlarged to approximately 400 yards wide.[355] To the north, the Ninth US Army also watched the Roer River overflowing its banks. The water level increased by five feet, and the velocity of the river grew to over six miles per hour. The width of the river now averaged 400 yards along its length and was 2000 yards wide in the area near Linnich.[356]

After clearing all areas west of the Roer River and capturing the remainder of the Schwammenauel Dam, the First US Army postponed operations.[357] The Ninth US Army was forced to delay the long-anticipated Operation Grenade.[358] Air operations and artillery fire were left alone to wage war against the Germans in this area, and they continued to harass transportation locations such as roads, rail lines, and rail bridges and tactical locations such as pillboxes and road junctions.[359] The loss of operations in this sector affected other operations along the Allied front. Eisenhower needed to keep the pressure on the Germans along the entire front. Fortunately, operations such as those in the Third US Army sector kept the Germans busy.

The VIII US Corps of the Third US Army, located to the north of the XII US Corps, continued their assault eastward towards Prum despite what they termed "tenacious opposition"[360] from many pillboxes in the area. By the end of February 7th, troops were closing in on Prum and the Prum River. They recorded that they encountered flooding from thawing snow and damaged roads in need of repair. There was concern that this could endanger the supply chain.[361] Troops secured a bridge over the Prum River north of Prum and advanced to a position within five miles to the west of Prum when a field directive on February 10th ordered the corps to "organize and defend in zone."[362] As they prepared to go on the defensive with no immediate plan to take Prum, troops patrolling the area determined that Prum was not heavily defended. Despite being officially on the defensive, the VIII US Corps entered Prum the next day and captured a portion of the town on the west side.

The XX US Corps on the southern flank of the Third US Army continued their aggressive defense and maintained contact with the XII US Corps but saw little action during this time.[363]

The Ninth US Army finally commenced Operation Grenade on February 23rd after the flooding from the Schwammenauel Dam receded. Three American corps crossed the Roer River in multiple locations near Julich and Linnich. By the end of February, they had cleared the area and began a rapid 50-mile advance in two directions: eastward toward Dusseldorf and northward to link up with the 21st British Army Group's First Canadian Army and British 30 Corps, which were advancing southward from the Nijmegen area. At the end of February, the Ninth US Army was approximately five miles from the city of Neuss (next to Dusseldorf) and six miles from the Rhine River. The quick advance was partially attributed to a reduction in German opposition.

At the same time, the First US Army began an attack across the Roer River to the south of Julich, not far from the town of Duren (Deuren). They then drove toward the northeast, with the major objective being the Erft River. In the next few days, they rapidly advanced and watched the Germans destroy bridges as they withdrew from the area. Enemy resistance was listed as "crumbling."[364] On February 27th, the First US Army established a bridgehead over the Erft River.

In the Third US Army's VIII US Corps sector, troops remained inactive until February 18th when they began a drive from Prum southward along the Prum River's west bank and along the Our River to join up with the XII US Corps, who were moving northward.[365] They linked with the 80th Infantry Division near Neuerburg (south of Ammeldingen) on

February 24th, having cleared the area west of the Prum River as they moved southward. The next day, the corps reported that there was "a total collapse of enemy defenses west of the Prum River."[366] The planned crossing over the Prum River was launched on February 28th.[367]

South of the XII US Corps, the XX US Corps fought to clear German troops from the area known as the Saar-Moselle Triangle. By February 22nd, they had gained control of most of that area and reached the Saar River and the town of Saarburg. They then continued across the Saar River and advanced farther northward. On February 28th, they were approximately ten miles south of the city of Trier. South of them, the Sixth US Army Group was mostly quiet during the last half of February.

Roland's Trip Into Germany and Processing

I will now break from the theater of action in the war to discuss the life of the prisoners of war, such as my father, and the prison camps throughout Germany. My father preferred not to talk about this part of his story; he spent the remainder of his World War II experience as a prisoner of war in Germany. Roland did indicate that several days after his capture, he left the Sauer River area and was sent to Dietz Castle, where he was interrogated. Dietz, also known as Diez an der Lahn, is a town approximately four miles southwest of the city of Limburg and is also approximately 30 miles east of Koblenz and 35 miles northwest of Frankfurt. It is situated in the Lahn Valley and overlooks the Lahn River, where it merges with the Aar River. The town was settled in ancient times and included a large castle dating back to the Middle Ages. The earliest portion of the castle was constructed in the eleventh century. The castle belonged to the Count of Nassau-Dillenburg in the 16th Century and later became part of the house of Orange-Nassau, relatives of the Dutch Royal family. It was abandoned as a residence during the 18th century and is now used as a youth hostel and a museum.

The first time I visited the National Archives in College Park, I unexpectedly came across the original records that contained the handwritten alphabetical listing of American prisoners of war in Europe. Roland was listed as being in Stalag IX-B in Bad Orb. His name was not recorded in some of the listings of prisoners at Bad Orb made during the war, but a listing of the men in each barracks at Stalag IX-B found later noted "R Hartman, #27608," was in Barracks 23.[368]

To journey into Germany to reach that area, Roland would have had to travel from Echternach to Limburg, approximately 120 miles to the northeast of where he was captured. He did not talk or write about how he did this transfer, but most newly captured American prisoners at that time were moved by a combination of a forced march into Germany to a train station and then by rail to the area of the POW camp. The trek to the train station was often long and arduous. Many accounts by Americans captured at that time mention marching to Gerolstein, Germany, which is approximately 40 miles to the north of Echternach. The weather was still cold and possibly snowing; there were several inches of snow and mud on the ground to trudge through. Many of the prisoners were not adequately dressed for such a long march, as they were missing their warm winter coats and boots. This was the result of the Germans often confiscating warm clothing - as well as cigarettes, watches, money, and anything valuable - for themselves. Some prisoners were sick or injured, making the long walk even more difficult. They spent their nights in unheated barns, an abandoned farm, or some minimal shelter. The march itself may have lasted several days since the location of the Allied front was at a distance from the camps located inside Germany. At that time, this required a march by the prisoners, first into Germany and then to the location of the train station. Only a few weeks later, the Third US Army would also be making the trek eastward and taking control of this territory. During their march, the Germans supplied the new POWs with little or nothing to eat. Sometimes the prisoners were allowed to pick up food found by the side of the road to eat, but at other times they were not allowed to stop. They drank water from the snow on the ground. Some prisoners reported they were jeered or even physically assaulted as they moved through the towns of Germany.[369] It was not unusual to force the prisoners to walk 25 miles each day despite the cold winter weather, the snow on the ground, and the lack of food.[370]

After arriving at the train station, the prisoners were loaded into boxcars for the trip to Limburg, the town next to Dietz. There were often sixty to eighty men in a car - sometimes even more - leading to overcrowded conditions such that not everyone could lie down at the same time. The cars were unheated and often had small, slotted side openings.

The floor was often covered with straw, dirt, and manure. There was a stench from previous passengers and their own conditions. The boxcars had no bathroom, only a small bucket shared by all and emptied perhaps once a day. The prisoners may or may not have received food during the trip, but often food was thrown into each car once a day. On many trips, the prisoners were not allowed out of the car until they arrived at their destination, which often took several days. By then, it was not unusual for some to have died in transit.

> "It is painful and impossible to move, with 80 men in an area 10 by 66 feet. We sit back-to-back, knees under chins, in three rows in the middle of the boxcar. Clothing is frozen to the floor, and, if we lean back, to the sides of the car. Cloth rips and ice cracks each time someone moves. We are nothing but crappy garments over bones, covered with loose-hanging skin. Not enough meat on all of us combined to fill one can of Campbell's soup. Cattle in such condition would be ignored at the Chicago stockyards."[371]

Many of these trains traveled primarily at night and sat on the tracks during the day. While waiting in the rail yards, they were at risk from bombings by Allied planes trying to disable the rail system in Germany, unaware there were Americans in the boxcars. In December 1944, the Allies unknowingly bombed boxcars containing POWs and killed or injured several American POWs. These trips often took five to eight days to cover the 110-mile trip between Gerolstein and Limburg.

The American prisoners of war captured at the beginning of the Ardennes Offensive (Battle of the Bulge) were often transported directly to a permanent POW camp and were processed and interrogated there. In February, many new prisoners were first sent to a transit camp where they were registered, interrogated, sorted by rank and military service, and then sent to the appropriate permanent camp. One of these transit camps, Stalag XII-A, was located in Limburg Germany. Roland, however, said he went to Dietz Castle, which is near Limburg. I have found no evidence to determine where he was sent after the trip into Germany.

In Limburg, a town near Dietz, there was a POW camp called Stalag XII-A, which was predominantly a transit camp for processing and interrogating the newly captured prisoners of war. Most new POWs were sent there, especially if the Germans felt the prisoner had little intelligence to offer. There is some evidence, however, that the castle in Deitz was used for special interrogations during World War II. An American socialite named Gertrude Sanford Legendre, who was a spy for the OSS, was held there and interrogated in late 1944, according to her 2000 obituary.[372] I do not know whether

Roland was sent to Stalag XII-A after his time at Dietz Castle, but it was the usual route for new prisoners. At this stage, however, the purpose of the initial stay was for processing and interrogation.

Processing involved documenting each prisoner and giving them a unique prisoner identification number. The POWs had their pictures taken and were finger-printed. They received German dog tags with their number. Some interrogations were more intense than others. For some, the prisoners supplied their name, rank, and serial number - all that was required by the Geneva Convention treaty - and the interrogation was complete. For others, the Germans sought additional information, leading to periodic and intense interrogations that could last for days.

This was a difficult time for the new prisoners. How they were treated and what they said determined their next stop. It was important to be identified as an air corps officer or enlisted man and not as a spy who could be held and segregated for special interrogations. Being identified as a Jew could also lead to segregation. The wounded might be removed and taken to hospitals or denied treatment altogether. Unfortunately, until a POW was taken to a permanent camp, he might not be documented and protected by the rules of the Geneva Convention. A transit prisoner did not receive mail or Red

Cross packages until he was in a permanent camp. One person defined this time as a "judicial no man's land."[373] The goal for POWs was to get to the right permanent POW camp safely.

Roland said he underwent an interrogation "by an Oxford-speaking German SS man."[374] His interrogation, however, appears to have been more brutal than many. He wrote he was "very upset when I was interrogated by a German SS Colonel." The interrogator spoke English well, he noted. Roland refused to answer any question except to provide his name, rank, and serial number. "I was sent out of the room with a guard who made me stand at attention with my nose touching the wall. And I started to fade a little bit and he hit me in the back with a butt of a rifle." Roland noted that the hit left pain in his back that he felt for the rest of his life.[375]

Other than that, Roland noted, "I was treated reasonably. As a matter of fact, no different than any other GI." He never did indicate whether he was still wearing his dog tags at the time of the interrogation, which would have indicated that he was Jewish, or whether the Germans knew he was Jewish. If he lacked the dog tags, the Germans might not have been able to label him a Jew; at the same time, it would have also made it harder to classify him as an enlisted man (which he was) and not a spy.

Stalag XII-A was built at the beginning of the war in Europe just outside the town of Limburg. By July of 1944, the camp housed approximately 6,000 American prisoners plus some British and Indian men. It was unclear at that time whether the camp was to serve as a transit or permanent camp for prisoners, and it functioned in both capacities at the beginning of 1945. Prisoners included commissioned officers, non-commission officers, and enlisted men. The camp contained clusters of barracks in seven sections, separated by barbed-wired fences and policed by guard posts. Each nationality was segregated into different sections.[376]

An inspection of the camp in November 1944 indicated that British and American officers held there were separated in barracks nearby the seven sections as if they were in their own "dulag." The total population of the camp was listed as 1,600 prisoners, most of whom were Americans. German high command notified the camp to expect 4,000 more "in transit" prisoners in the camp in the future. The inspectors called conditions at that time satisfactory but noted that there were some small sanitary issues, an insufficient number of latrines, no clothing reserves, and they were running out of Red Cross packages. The Germans also promised to fix leaking roofs and improve lighting and heating deficiencies at that time.[377]

The camp was bombed on December 23, 1944. Many roofs, the recreation hall, and the infirmary sustained damage. The officer barracks took a direct hit. At least 39 prisoners were killed, and 10 men were injured.[378] Since winter had already set in, no repairs were yet made, leading to leaky roofs, a damaged infirmary facility with no delousing equipment, and reduced shower facilities.

New prisoners entering Stalag XII-A in February 1945 saw a camp surrounded by tall, barbed wire. Inside, they saw a series of large barracks which sometimes contained three levels of bunks on the wall and sometimes only a floor to sleep on. The POWs who remained at Stalag XII-A were assigned to specific unheated barracks. There were substandard daily food rations consisting of coffee in the morning, watery soup later in the day, and a portion of a loaf of bread (shared with other men).

One American soldier noted that many German soldiers in Stalag XII-A "spoke almost perfect English" and tried to engage the American prisoners in conversations about the United States and American sports.[379] According to one POW named Hoffman, his warm clothing was taken away and replaced with clothing inadequate for winter, the building he stayed in had three levels of bunks, and the food was inadequate. He stated that "We were cold, hungry, and miserable." He was eventually transferred to Stalag III-A. There, he recorded receiving bed boards, blankets, and Red Cross packages.[380]

Other former residents of Stalag XII-A noted the camp was crowded and they slept on the floor. They also mentioned they encountered unsanitary conditions and starvation rations. There was no heating during the harsh winter and the camp was filled with lice and dysentery.

For most prisoners at Stalag XII-A, the camp was a temporary stop on a journey to their permanent camp. This was their introduction to understanding the daily routines and poor conditions of a POW camp, as well as the rules and penalties for disobedience. The second purpose of Stalag XII-A was as a transfer center to sort the different prisoners, assign them to the proper camp, and send them out to that camp. Where they went from there was partially dependent on rank and military service. The nationality of the prisoner was also taken into consideration. Roland's assignment, for example, should have been to a stalag for enlisted Americans.

A prisoner's stay at Stalag XII-A, or any other transit camp, would last for anywhere from two days to weeks or months. It was here that the new prisoners learned the rules of being a POW and were allowed to send a postcard to family back home. In February 1945, conditions at these camps were deteriorating. There had been a large influx of new prisoners arriving as a result of the Battle of the Bulge (Ardennes Offensive) since the middle of December, and the population of the camp increased to over 3,000 men. New arrivals were processed, situated, and then maintained. Once the processing and interrogation concluded, most prisoners were transferred to other POW camps within a few days or weeks. When they left, unfortunately, the good uniforms and shoes were replaced by clothing and shoes of "inferior quality." A report of the camp in February 1945 noted that "No Britisher or American has been able to carry away his [sic] overcoat."[381]

A few prisoners, however, remained permanently at Stalag XII-A. Most of these permanent residents were British and Indian. They lived in wood or brick buildings or tents and sometimes slept on the floor.

According to an inspection in February 1945, Stalag XII-A had not fixed the leaky roofs, the infirmary, and the recreation building following the December bombardment of the camp. The report referenced the use of tents to house some prisoners. Other problems included unsanitary conditions, lack of clothing for the prisoners, and overcrowded living quarters. The population of the camp had increased to over 35,000 prisoners, including over 3,000 Americans and 16,000 French prisoners. Food rations at the camp were reduced and prisoners voiced discontent with the changes. The report labeled the infirmary as "particularly defective" and badly in need of medical supplies. On a more positive note, mail was being delivered.[382]

The conditions in Deitz Castle, which Roland mentioned, are unknown. One can imagine that any prisoners there would not have been treated much better than at the Stalag XII-A facility. There are few references about the use of Dietz Castle as an interrogation center during World War II. It was not listed as a POW camp. What I do know is that Roland's interrogation was more severe than many infantrymen's interrogations and that could have occurred at either location. Why my father would have been diverted to Dietz Castle, which my father mentioned on two occasions as a location on his POW tour, can only be speculation. Maybe it was because he was captured at the onset of an unexpected offensive in a location the Germans never expected and needed to gain intelligence as fast as possible. Maybe it was just luck. I still do not know why he was there, but I can still believe it happened, as he said. And because he said he was at more than one location before Stalag IX-B, I believe that he may have been at both Dietz Castle and the transit camp.

Following processing and interrogations at a transit camp, the transfers to a permanent POW camp were once again accomplished by marches and railcars. The Germans established hundreds of camps throughout Germany and its territories during the war.

The Geneva Convention of 1929 defined the rights of many prisoners during World War II. The rules and code were written into an agreement signed by the United States, Germany, and forty other nations. The code included the right of prisoners of war to the same amount and quality of food that was being provided to the soldiers of the country holding the prisoners. Prisoners were also entitled to send and receive mail, receive adequate medical care, and receive decent clothing and footwear. Tobacco and books were also mentioned in the guidelines for POW camps. The facilities for housing the prisoners should include water, heat, and sanitary conditions. There should be an exercise area, and a canteen for the purchase of incidental items. The code also included monthly medical inspections.

During World War II, the International Red Cross was designated as the group to make inspections. They also distributed Red Cross food packages prepared by the prisoners' countries for the camps and collected and distributed mail. There were approximately 94,000 American prisoners of war in Europe in World War II. Prisoners often referred to themselves as Kriegies, a shortened version of the

German word "kriegesgefangenen," which means prisoner of war. Treatment should have been guided by the principles set forth by the Geneva Convention, but by February 1945, many of the camps were not adhering to these guidelines.

There were different German POW camps in Europe for officers, air force personnel, and enlisted men. The names of the camps reflected these differences. Many camps housed a variety of nationalities, but members of each of these groups were segregated together within those camps.

Commissioned officers were usually separated from the privates and sent to their own camps, named Oflags. Air corps prisoners of war were also segregated into their own camps known as Dulags or Luftstalags. Non-commissioned officers (NCOs) and enlisted men were sent to Stalags. Most camps were the responsibility of the German army during the war, although the camps housing the Allied Air Corps prisoners were run by the German Luftwaffe, the air force branch of the German military. There were also a series of medical facilities in Germany, known as lazarettes, to house sick or injured prisoners. Civilian prisoners were housed in facilities known as ilags.[383]

The numerical designation of the camps (usually in Roman numerals) related to the region in which the camp was located. There were approximately twenty military districts in the

German system, including some in Poland and Lithuania (often designated using regular numbers). If there was more than one camp of a certain type in a district, a letter was attached after the number.

As an example of how descriptive the names were, we can look at the name of Stalag XII-A. The use of stalag means that the camp was designated to house privates and non-commissioned officers. It was located in the twelfth (Wiesbaden) district, which was in western Germany, not far from Frankfurt. The A indicates that it was the first of more than one stalag in that area. In fact, there were four stalags in Wiesbaden. There were also two Oflags in the twelfth district.

Roland's Experience as a Prisoner of War

Roland's Entry into Stalag IX-B

Roland said he was ultimately transferred to a camp known as Stalag IX-B in Bad Orb, Germany, after a brief stay at a transit camp. He noted that "I was in several places up until that time." Roland barely talked about his experience in Stalag IX-B, except that "the Germans at that time had no food anyway. They had no food to feed themselves. They couldn't feed the prisoners that they had so I can't blame them for that as much as I might. Not a happy time." He estimated that he was at the camp for about three to four months.[384]

By my calculations, given the multiple stops on the way to the camp and the customary combination of marches and boxcars for transportation, he probably arrived at the camp around the end of February. At that time, additional prisoners were arriving at the camp at the rate of about 200 men per day. One prisoner later described walking into Stalag IX-B:

> "…vast, dismal expanse of one-story wooden barracks, divided by parade areas and surrounded by a barbed-wire fence and guard towers. One of a constellation of prisoner-of-

war camps in Germany, where conditions had grown steadily worse, Stalag IX-B was ill-equipped for a massive influx of new prisoners. When the Americans arrived, it already housed large numbers of Russian prisoners, some there since 1941. The Russians were so mistreated that more than fourteen hundred died at the camp of cold, hunger, and untreated illness."[385]

Stalag IX-B was located in Bad Orb in the Hesse district of Germany. It was approximately 165 miles northeast of Echternach and 35 miles northeast of Frankfurt. The camp was used for German troops during World War I and then as a children's camp between the wars. At the beginning of World War II, the camp was renamed Stalag IX-B and was used initially for Soviet prisoners captured by the Germans. By the end of 1941, there were over 18,000 prisoners held there.

Early on, the French and Soviet prisoners held in the camp were used as laborers on farms, in the local forests, or in factories nearby. Reports indicate that during these early years, the French and Belgian prisoners in the camp were treated according to the provisions of the Geneva Convention. The Soviets, however, did not sign the treaty developed at the Geneva Convention and were not treated as well as the French and Belgians. Some reports indicate that during the period between the end of 1941 into the beginning of 1942, Soviet POWs may have been dying at Stalag IX-B at the rate of about

20 per day, largely due to starvation, exhaustion from their work, exposure to elements, disease (such as typhoid fever), and perhaps actual murder. This was not uncommon, for the treatment of Soviet soldiers in many camps was considered especially harsh during World War II, and the overall death rate for Soviet prisoners during the war surpassed 50% of those captured by the Germans. This was significantly higher than the death rate for American prisoners in Germany, which was under 3%. The number of Soviets who died while prisoners in Stalag IX-B was never determined, but records indicate at least 356 Soviet prisoners died between December 5, 1941, and January 22, 1942. After that date, deaths at the camp were no longer recorded.[386] There is a Russian soldier's cemetery just outside of Stalag IX-B with over 1,400 dead Soviet POWs. Some records estimate that over half of the Soviet prisoners of war held by Germany died by February 1942.

Over time, prisoners from other countries, such as France, Great Britain, Serbia, Slovakia, and Italy, were also sent there. In 1944, prior to the arrival of the Americans, there were over 25,000 prisoners located in the camp. At the end of December 1944, following the German offensive's Battle of the Bulge, over 4,000 American POWs were sent there, many from the 106th and 28th Infantry Divisions that were heavily battered in the initial days of the Ardennes Offensive.

By the end of January 1944, there were approximately 4,700 American prisoners in Stalag IX-B, and the total population of the camp was approximately 25,000. This sudden explosion of additional Allied prisoners of war taxed the German prisoner-of-war camps. Estimates indicate that about 17,000 Americans were captured or went missing in the first two weeks of the German offensive, and an additional 6,300 Americans were captured or listed as missing during January.[387] This sudden influx of prisoners saw them transported to transit camps, processed, and then moved to permanent camps. The Germans became responsible for housing and providing for the enlarged captive population. Over time, conditions at most camps deteriorated even more, partially because of the increase in the prison population, partially because of the German military's own eroding situation, and partially because of shortages and disruptions to the German economy and infrastructure of roads and railways. By the end of 1944, when the first prisoners from the offensive arrived in Stalag IX-B, the system was not functioning as it had in the past, nor was it functioning according to the Geneva Convention's expectations. Starvation, dysentery, lice, illnesses, and other health problems were rampant throughout the camp. Deteriorating conditions were apparent at other prisoner-of-war camps as well.

New prisoners to Stalag IX-B usually arrived by train at the train station in the village of Bad Orb. To get there, they probably spent several days in overcrowded boxcars without heat or adequate bathroom facilities. Many received little or no food during that period and arrived already starving. When they reached the train station in the village, they saw a German village located in a valley surrounded by tall hills and mountains. The village consisted of stone buildings with gabled roofs, cobblestone roads, and many local families with children who were still living there. The town itself was surrounded by a wall built centuries ago to protect the citizens living there.[388]

After disembarking from the train, the prisoners were marched up the mountain to the actual prison camp several kilometers from the train station. The camp itself was located on a mountain, beginning with the luxurious administration building toward the bottom of the mountain and ending on the top of the mountain where the barracks were located. It was surrounded by barbed wire and contained a series of high posts and towers with guards surveilling the camp and the surrounding area.

The camp consisted of several areas designated for different nationalities. The barracks within these areas were one-story wooden structures. The mostly enlisted American men were housed in approximately 16 buildings in their sector of the camp, the officers having been directed to other camps. The barracks in Stalag IX-B contained two large rooms, and each room housed approximately 250 prisoners. There was a stove in each room, but the stove only received enough wood to supply heat to the room for one hour per day. Some barracks had bunks (usually triple-deckers), and some did not. Mattresses were scarce, as were blankets. Between the two rooms was a washroom that contained one cold water tap, without a drainpipe, that emptied into a hole in the floor and one latrine hole that emptied into a cesspool next door. There were outdoor toilets nearby, but they were not convenient during the cold winter and not available at night. The buildings themselves were in disrepair; there were leaky roofs, broken windows, and little or no electricity. There were few tables or chairs in the barracks. Every building suffered from infestations of lice, fleas, and bedbugs. There was often a putrid smell in the buildings due to a lack of sanitation, and the ceilings and walls were damp.

The starving new prisoners arrived at the camp, already shocked by the strenuous march into Germany, the crowded boxcar rides to Bad Orb, and sometimes a bombing attack on the railcars they were in. They discovered a camp with too many prisoners and not enough food. The space was not adequate to house all the prisoners. In some barracks, men shared beds or mattresses, and in other barracks, men slept on the bare floor. Not everyone had their own blanket, so men shared the blankets available. Due to the lack of heat during the winter and inadequate clothing, there was sometimes ice inside the buildings or even on prisoners' clothing. To keep warm, men would huddle together.

> "The floor is cold. My clothes are damp and crackle from the ice that has formed on them. My whole body aches. I wiggle my toes to stop the searing pain. I turn from one side to the other. I can feel pebbles roll from the top of my knee to the bottom. More pain. To put one knee on the other causes both to ache. My back has a constant dull pain. ..."[389]

Each barracks was locked during the night so that prisoners could not leave the building. This left many men in the dark.

> "Every night is both miserable and frightening. We are locked up like caged animals. The claustrophobia begins when the doors and windows are locked, made even more unbearable when I have to contend with the pungent odor of cigarettes, the smells of filthy garments, vomit, runny bowels, and endless farts..."[390]

There were other buildings in the complex to house religious services and church studies. There were no dining rooms, so men ate in their barracks. Within the POW population, the Americans had one doctor and one dentist as well as two clergy men, the only American officers left in camp. Medical visits were limited to emergencies, as there were limited medical supplies available.

Stalag IX-B did not have outside recreation fields or indoor recreation facilities. The French developed a library during the early years of the camp, but the Americans never had one. The camp had centralized kitchen facilities to prepare the meals for the camp, but the food was sent to the barracks.

Many prisoner-of-war camps were multi-national in their composition, and the Germans segregated the different nationalities within each camp. Stalag IX-B, for example, contained Soviets, Serbians, Italians, Asians, British, and South Africans in addition to Americans in 1945. Fencing often separated the areas, and these partitions within the camp allowed each group to be treated differently. From the prisoner's point of view, each group could approach their captivity differently and create different activities within their group. For example, the Serbians at Stalag IX-B liked to sing and dance and would entertain prisoners in the camp with their musical performances. Additionally, certain activities, such as education, recreational activities, lectures, and Red Cross packages, were developed around their national origin. Other activities, such as trading and bartering, engaged the entire camp, even if it meant the goods were going over the fences.[391]

The German administration of Stalag IX-B was headed by a commandant named Oberst Karl Sieber. His staff included an officer concerned with security, intelligence, and preventing escapes, a welfare officer, a mess officer, guards, and an interpreter. Guards were assigned to different areas of the camp and manned the towers surrounding the camp.

POWs also had their own administration in the camps. The Americans at Stalag IX-B were guided by their own distinct organization. It was led by the Man of Confidence (MOC), who was chosen by the Americans. He spoke German and interacted directly with the German commandant as well as the American prisoners of the camp. He had two assistants. Each of the American barracks selected a barracks leader who coordinated with the Man of Confidence. The original MOC was named J. C. F. (Hans) Kasten. When he left the camp in early February, he was replaced by Edmund Phannenstiel, who also spoke fluent German. This American structure was not unusual in the German prisoner-of-war camp system, for it helped create support systems and its own self-discipline structure within the camps as well as a link to German administration. In some camps, the American structure included other committees, such as an escape committee, which was not present at Stalag IX-B. The duties of the MOC included discussions with the German commandant regarding various problems with the prisoners, negotiating work schedules, and meeting with Red Cross officials during their inspections.

Some guards spoke English and understood American culture and baseball. Others did not. Many were older Germans who served in World War I. Several were compassionate towards the POWs; a couple of German guards even risked their own safety by sharing food with the prisoners. The discipline at the camp was strict, and the punishments were often harsh when there was an infraction. Among the offenses were stealing personal possessions or food, trying to get seconds on food, and trading with the Russian and British POWs. The guards manning the towers around the camp would kill a prisoner if he went too close to the fence. Falling down when working could also bring harsh punishment. At times, men were hit just for talking.

Every day, the Germans had a roll call. Some were longer than others. The prisoners were counted, and announcements were made. Sometimes punishments were meted out at these roll calls.

The daily routine at Stalag IX-B was repetitive and uneventful. It began with the unlocking of the barracks doors in the morning. Prisoners were given a cup of ersatz coffee (perhaps made from some type of organic matter). Roll calls occurred in the morning. Periodically, the American POWs were given a work detail, which could be chopping wood for their stove or cleaning out the latrine.[392] Since the barracks were unlocked during the day, prisoners could go outside from about 6:30 in the morning to about 5:00 in the evening. During the cold winter weather, when there was slow starvation (which reduced energy levels) and no outdoor activities, POWs were less likely to go outside. Later in the day, the prisoners were given soup, and in the evening, they received black bread and tea. At night, the prisoners were locked in their barracks.

There was a significant amount of time during the day with little to do, and the days became monotonous, frustrating, wearisome, and sometimes challenging.

> "Camp life was tedium, broken by work details to gather firewood for the potbellied stove in the barracks. Joe received one shower in 80 days, near the end, cold and quick. He sent two pieces of mail and received exactly none back…. Occasionally, a dozen POWs got to divvy up a Red Cross package; some men, sad to say, begged for more than their share."[393]

The ability to send and receive mail, a service that was made possible by the International Red Cross, was important to prisoners of war. It provided an important bridge between family and the outside world. Representatives from the Red Cross periodically visited Stalag IX-B and distributed postcards the prisoners could use to write to family back home. They would then be collected and sent home subject to censorship. Postcards were sent out of the camp on January 23rd and again on January 30th. Only a portion of these letters made it back home, and it sometimes took weeks or months to get there. Interviews with former prisoners at Stalag IX-B indicate that they never received mail back. This was not the normal standard at other camps where mail was sent and received via the Red Cross system.

Living conditions at Stalag IX-B were horrendous. Overcrowding, dirty clothing coupled with no showering, and no effort to clean or maintain the buildings contributed to an extremely unhealthy environment. It was nearly impossible to clean a building if the men were constantly packed into it, and limited access to lavatories, little water to wash in, and lack of cleaning products only contributed to the problem. Despite the rules of the Geneva Conference, confiscated coats and shoes were never replaced, making it difficult to survive in unheated buildings. One military report estimated one-fifth of the POWs had no coat.[394]

Stalag IX-B was visited by Red Cross inspectors several times during the war, and the reports' findings changed during the duration of the war. In 1943, inspectors arrived to evaluate the welfare of the Serbians and French. They noted that clothing was ordered and received for the Serbians, and there was a library and sports equipment for the French. There was a review in August 1944 of a hospital related to Stalag IX-B. Everything seemed to be in order, and it was recorded that "The general impression of the camp is good. There appeared to be adequate food supplies, and there was even a library in the building.[395]

The situation shifted in January 1945 after the Americans arrived at the camp. The Red Cross arrived on Jan 17, 1945, to identify the Americans; the inspectors revisited on January 24th to examine the conditions for Americans at the camp. The report listed over 4,000 American prisoners already in a camp "unprepared for their reception." They also noted that 1,300 men were sleeping on bare floors in crowded buildings with missing windows, inadequate heating, with little or no lights or washing facilities, and minimal indoor latrines that "left much to be desired." There were no laundry facilities, no canteen, and no recreation or exercise areas for the prisoners either. In addition, there was no Red Cross food found, and "German rations alone are scarcely sufficient." The Delegate of the Protecting Power, as the inspector was called, labeled the accommodations "untenable." When told that this was supposed to be a transit camp and not a permanent camp, the delegate indicated that this was unlikely and demanded that improvements be made. The report ended with the statement that "this camp makes a rather depressing and poverty-stricken impression."[396]

A telegram sent to the American Secretary of State on February 15th, 1945, highlighted and reinforced the problems at Stalag IX-B previously stated in the report in January. It also noted that the camp was not prepared to receive the American prisoners, and conditions were "most inferior," especially with respect to sleeping accommodations, food, clothing, and sanitation issues. The report indicated that the inspector demanded improvements and the POWs were in "urgent need."[397]

One of the alarming issues was that the prisoners' diet at Stalag IX-B did not include enough calories for survival. Breakfast was nothing more than a cup of ersatz coffee, which was alternatively described as tea made from acorns or bark. Lunch consisted of a small amount of watery soup. Some thought the soup was made with grass. Occasionally there might be a small scrap of meat, potato, or vegetable in the soup. Dinner was a portion of a loaf of black bread with a cup of tea. The black bread was made with sawdust. In February, six men split one loaf of bread. By April, there were as many as nine men to a loaf. On occasion, there was butter or marmalade with the bread. The November 1945 prisoner of war report noted that "A thousand men lacked eating utensils of any kind - either spoons, forks, or bowls. They ate out of their helmets or old tin cans or pails - anything on which they could put their hands."[398] It was estimated that this diet contained under 1000 calories each day.

> "The German rations had a paper value of 1,400 calories. Actually, the caloric content was even further lowered by the waste in using products of inferior quality. Since a completely inactive man needs at least 1,700 calories to live, it is apparent that PWs were slowly starving to death."[399]

Another function of the International Red Cross was the delivery of food parcels to German POW camps. These parcels were prepared by various nations to be delivered to each prisoner of that nationality on a routine basis. This was to supplement the prisoner's diet, which was important in those camps which only provided a limited amount of food. The parcels contained everything from meats and fish to vegetables and fruit. There were cigarettes, cheese, and crackers, and also some chocolate, milk, and sugar. The added nutrition made a major difference in the ability to function and the survival rates of the prisoners. At Stalag IX-B, these parcels were rarely delivered to the Americans. One reason for this was that Allied bombings and advancements had disrupted the supply chain infrastructure after the destruction of the railways and the train cars. A second reason was the theft of some of the parcels by the Germans. One prisoner recorded receipt of these food parcels at the beginning of February by Czech POWs in camp, who were kind enough to share some of their own parcels with the Americans. One box was shared by four to six Americans.[400] It was not until March that American Red Cross packages were located and distributed to the American POWs. When the parcels did appear, six to ten men would share the contents of one package. According to one report, many of the undelivered Red Cross packages designated for the Americans were found in the town of Bad Orb after liberation.

The Americans in Stalag IX-B suffered extreme weight loss, estimated to be between 50 and 100 pounds for each soldier. Many men who were prisoners of the camp for several months saw their weight plummet to under 100 pounds. Some died.

> "Starvation blunted every other concern, made men hard. When it was his turn to cut the daily loaf of bread, to be evenly divided between 15 POWs, Joe remembers "those 14 faces looking at me like they wanted to kill me if I made a mistake."[401]

Without the body fat, facial expression changed and it was more difficult to sit or lean back. Eyes became cloudy, and the men stared around them. The very act of walking to chop or gather wood became an enormous task for some. After one foray out of camp for work detail, one prisoner wrote: "Chopped wood for three hours; was so weak could hardly walk. All of us were - couldn't lift a log two inches in diameter and two feet long; didn't know I was so weak."[402] He later recorded:

> "The lousy food keeps me alive, but barely. I can count my ribs through the dirty shirt and smelly jacket. My waist measures about 15 inches - on the outside of my clothing. It hurts to sit, as there is no fat on the cheeks of my butt. Both hips are black from lying on one side, then the other."[403]

There were emotional changes as well. They became jittery, nervous, and depressed. Moods changed, complaints were numerous, and men snapped and argued with each other and even pushed and fought with good friends. Desperation even led to stealing other people's food.

> "Hope, then despair. Up, down, up, down. Accompanying these emotional ups and downs is the fighting, bitching, screaming, snarling, and stealing. I have to retain my sanity, none of us have training in how to survive as a prisoner of war; how to cope with the demeaning physical and psychological conditions…"[404]

As the starvation continued over the weeks, some men constantly discussed food and starvation. "Only talk—about anything—will keep my mind active," said one prisoner.[405] They argued about menus and recipes and talked about their favorite meals. Many dreamed about food. "The dreams were terrible. We always dreamed of food."[406]

Unfortunately, the act of eating could also be a problem. After weeks of starvation diet, eating large amounts of food was too much to handle and could make them uncomfortable and sick. Spicy food also created problems. Although Red Cross parcels eaten too quickly had side effects, the hungry prisoners gratefully ate everything they could find as quickly as they could and willingly accepted the consequences later. After repatriation, the soldiers had to be trained on how to eat moderately to prevent these side effects.

Diseases were rampant throughout Stalag IX-B. This was not unexpected given the overcrowding, unsanitary conditions, and the reduced immunity created by the starvation. Dysentery, a malady of the gastrointestinal tract, was common among the prisoners, probably due to the unsanitary conditions of the camp and the poor quality of the food. Many prisoners had nagging coughs and other illnesses, some of which persisted for weeks. Due to the cold, frostbite was a frequent problem. Pneumonia was also not unusual. There was a doctor and a dentist in the prisoner population, but there were few medical supplies to help fight the illnesses or wounds around the camp. As a result, wounds became infected, and coughs would not go away. As the health of many prisoners continued to decline, there was fear that an epidemic - such as the flu - could lead to deaths. This, fortunately, did not happen, but some dangerous diseases, such as meningitis and diphtheria did occur and proved deadly due to a lack of available medication. By March, the camp hospital was full with pneumonia cases. Deaths increased as the men had no more energy reserves to fight the illnesses.[407]

At night, there was a cacophony of sound related to these illnesses, and this affected their sleep. One prisoner wrote: "The moans, groans, wheezes, hacking coughs, plus all sorts of unidentified weird sounds, mingle with the dank and pungent smelly clothing of over 200 men crowded together, creating a strangling frustration."[408] These problems were compounded by other issues during the night: "There were electric lights from 7 to 9 PM, but after that time, men continually stepped on one another. Arguments were many, and the discomfort increased every night."[409]

Pest infestation at Stalag IX-B was another problem for the prisoners. The camp was plagued with lice, fleas, bedbugs, and other vermin. They were everywhere, and little was done to reduce the unsanitary conditions supporting them. The men were occasionally allowed to shower and be deloused, but their infected clothing (unlaundered and worn for the duration of their stay), blankets, and barracks still contained the bugs, leading to reinfection.

Unfortunately, death from starvation, disease, and other causes was part of camp life. Officially, there were 32 American deaths between February 28 and April 1, 1945, in the camp, but prisoners questioned that number.

> "The official count of deaths at Stalag IX-B was 32. Those of us who were there believe that was the number the Germans bothered to document and that the actual count was at least four times that number. The doctors and the medics had no medicine, no bandages, nothing to treat us. We saw men stagger to the dispensary and then we never saw them again. When a doctor was interviewed the day we were liberated, he was asked if the deaths were due to natural causes. His answer was "Yes, if malnutrition, exposure, cruelty and disease are natural causes." Some men had meningitis, some diphtheria, others had tuberculosis. Some gave up the will to live."[410]

When deaths occurred, there were burials. As the soldier was carried out for the burial, the men would stand and salute out of respect for the fallen soldier. The occurrence of deaths increased during the last weeks of incarceration. One American later noted that burials seemed to be a daily occurrence.[411] On March 4th alone, three soldiers were buried.[412] The dead were often stripped of their clothing and the items were given to other prisoners in need of additional clothes. The dead were wrapped in a blanket instead.[413]

> "It was almost a daily routine to line up along the kitchen street and pay our last respects to another American soldier. Funeral processions were taking place regularly, it seemed. Malnutrition, or "German pneumonia," was taking its toll. Those who made the supreme sacrifice in a PW camp took their last ride on a two-wheeled cart. No casket was provided - blankets covered the body. Burial was made in a small cemetery outside of camp."[414]

Unfortunately, even burying their dead presented difficulties for the prisoners. The POWs on such details were weak and unable to perform the duties easily. Additionally, the camp's burial ground was situated on the ground containing shale and had to be broken down with a pick. The task could sometimes take two days to perform properly.[415]

Daytime activities for all enlisted men in POW camps required them to work. Some prisoners, such as the Soviets in the camp, were assigned to a daily work detail. The jobs for American prisoners were sporadic and more centered on themselves, such as shoveling out the local cesspool, hauling water, and cutting and transporting wood for the stoves inside the barracks. As men died, the Americans were also asked to dig graves for their soldiers. Most of these tasks became difficult for the men.

> "Went to the woods today to cut wood. Two men fell out, but we had to carry them anyway. We are so weak that we can hardly move; the guard was rough and worked the hell out of us. Guard hit two men and drew his gun on one; we were ready to kill him. It was too rough for me."[416]

Still, the Americans had an easier existence than the Soviet prisoners had at Stalag IX-B, who were used as forced laborers outside of the camp, mistreated by the Germans, and also received minimal food and inadequate living conditions. One POW noted that "Stalag IX-B was not considered a work camp by the Germans."[417]

Despite the harsh conditions, there were American POWs who volunteered to work in the hopes of getting extra food. Sometimes they received extra rations for some work, and other times, they did not receive anything.

Otherwise, for much of the day, there was little to do. Prisoners were allowed to walk around outside the barracks during the day, if they were strong enough to do so. In bad weather conditions and in winter, it was difficult to get outside. On many days, the prisoners just remained inside with their small network of friends and perhaps just talked with each other. It was often these close relationships that sustained them and encouraged them to survive.

Religious services and bible study occurred several times each week and provided an avenue for passing time for many prisoners, even for those who were less religious.[418] There was a separate barracks used as a chapel and it was warmer and cleaner than other barracks. As one chaplain said, "Try to attend, regardless of your religious preference. Not only will it be good for you, it will help kill time."[419] Rev Samuel Neel and Father Edward Hurley were the camp chaplains. On Sundays, Catholics attended church services first; this was followed by Protestant services. Services were often crowded. Bible study occurred during the week. Some men became more religious in the camp, others did not. Some men sought mental stimulation and spiritual peace, while others found it a way to keep busy, stay warm and keep their minds from thinking about their circumstances. One prisoner wrote, "Religious involvement helps me keep my sanity."[420]

Different nationalities sponsored different activities. Former prisoners of Stalag IX-B remembered various forms of entertainment. The stalag itself was given some instruments and thus formed an orchestra. There was also a choir and a theater group who performed musicals and plays. A few

Americans, with the help of violin, guitar and harmonica, performed for the American prisoners.[421] A group of singers from the 28th Division performed concerts; among the songs was the Stalag IX-B theme song, sung to the tune of The Battle Hymn of the Republic. It began with the "We're a bunch of prisoners living deep in Germany" and ended with "Come and get us, Georgie Patton, So we can ramble home."[422]

An American newspaperman gave a series of 21 lectures on American history. From 50 to 500 men attended the lectures. He also organized a weekly quiz show event that drew as many as 1,000 men at once.[423] A single issue of a camp newspaper was published in the camp, but no more.

One ex-POW at Stalag IX-B remembered that a recreation hall was opened in February in the barracks that also contained the chapel. There were a few musical instruments there as well as playing cards, maybe a few books, checkers, and games. He noted that tables, benches, and a ping pong table were added later. Men used the facilities to help pass the time.[424] However, due to the poor health of the POWs, limited recreational activities occurred.

Unlike other camps, planning and executing escapes was not a major pastime at Stalag IX-B. The soldiers were too weak and the location of the camp was not optimal for escape. The prisoners could not dedicate themselves to such a task.

After the doors were locked, some barracks sought their own activities. Entertainment at night was often arranged to keep morale up.[425] There were discussions, praying and sometimes even singing in the dark. In some places, people told stories or developed other types of entertainment.[426]

Discussions were an important vehicle for breaking the monotony of the time and taking the prisoners' minds off their situation. One prisoner at Stalag IX-B wrote 'The major topics of discussion are the extreme cold, deteriorating health, home, war news, and food, food, food. Oh boy! Do we talk about food! That is my salvation. I make every attempt to retain an attitude of sarcasm and a sense of flippancy.'[427] News of the war was also important to the prisoners. Rumors about the news- right and wrong moved quickly through the camp and were discussed and interpreted in detail. Even the trivial discussions had meaning to them. The POW wrote, "And so it goes. At least the discussions fill idle time, and keep our minds off the miserable conditions in Stalag IXB."[428]

Buying, trading, and bartering was an ongoing preoccupation at the camp, and cigarettes were the main currency. German rules forbid trading with other nationals in the camp but it was done discreetly over the fences separating the groups. When various groups in camp received Red Cross packages, there was an increase in trading for the food and cigarettes as the men now had something with which to trade. Morale would increase along with the intake of additional food.

By January, men looked to trade for food to ease their hunger. However, there was also a great addiction to cigarettes such that some men traded food, clothing or watches away for them. "Cigarettes especially became valuable units of exchange for those of us who didn't smoke. Even under conditions of semi-starvation, many smokers traded us food for cigarettes…"[429] The going rate in January was one watch for five cigarettes.[430] Another prisoner noted that for ten cigarettes he could get his hair cut. In the middle of February, the French in the camp received Red Cross packages, creating a large amount of trading.[431] This happened again in March when the Americans received their packages. There were even a few "big-time operators" known for their bartering skills.[432]

> "The cigarette situation was critical. Cigarettes cost 1000 francs or $23 each. 1/6 of a loaf of bread sold for 500 francs. Watches were worth $200 and good fountain pens brought $100. One young man who was fortunate enough to bring along an ample supply of tobacco made a young fortune. G.I.s would take their jewelry to the Russians and French and trade for American Red Cross cigarettes. Potatoes would sell for $1 each and a half-ration of soup went for $5. Inflation in America would be no problem after this."[433]

Changes & Events at Stalag IX-B in January and February

Life in Stalag IX-B remained one of routine and sameness through February 1945, and the prisoners remained generally inside their barracks due to the poor weather.[434] However, the prisoners were aware that the Americans were advancing into Germany.

> "For the remainder of February, our existence remained about the same. Because of transportation difficulties, our scant meat did not come in regularly. A group from the camp at Gerolstein marched eight days [to get there]. Americans were getting close in that area. Our spirits were raised by the sound of artillery in the distance."[435]

At the same time, there were events that strongly affected life for the Americans in the camp. Almost all commissioned officers were relocated to other camps on January 10th. Then, over 1,200 non-commissioned officers were moved out of the camp to Stalag IX-A nearby on January 25th. This temporarily reduced some of the crowding in the camp. Stalag IX-B was mostly occupied by enlisted men after January 1945.

Another more ominous change also occurred at the camp in February. In response to instructions issued by Hitler, the camp began a campaign to identify and segregate the Jews in

Stalag IX-B. First, incoming American prisoners were asked via questionnaire to identify their religion as well as their name, rank and serial number, although only the last three factors were required to be provided by the prisoners.[436] At a roll call on January 19th, Jewish prisoners were then asked to identify themselves by stepping forward. Some did and some did not. All identified Jews were then moved to separate barracks.

The Germans tried again to identify American Jews later in February. At least one man was repeatedly interrogated in the hope of proving he was Jewish. Then, during the first week of February, approximately 350 men were sent from Stalag-IX-B to a forced labor camp at Berga, a subcamp of the Buchenwald concentration camp. Many believe that the soldiers selected were chosen because the Germans believed they were Jews or of Jewish descent, were thought to have Jewish names, or looked like Jews. Among those chosen for this transfer were the 80 men known to be Jewish.[437] Others selected to go were considered troublemakers in the camp. Of the 350 soldiers requested for transfer, approximately 20% were actually Jewish.[438] This may be the only instance of POWs being sent to a slave labor work camp. Berga was identified as a German concentration camp, not a POW camp. The men were subjected to long, strenuous work hours digging tunnels underground and were given a less than subsistence diet. Within ten weeks, over 70 of the 350 men were dead.[439] At least

25 additional men died. Then, on April 5th, the men still alive were forced into a march eastward, where 50 additional undernourished and starved men died.[440]

The list included Hans Kasten, a medic and the American Man of Confidence, and his assistant Joe Littell. Kasten had refused the commandant's demand to identify all the Jews in the camp, stating that "We are all Americans, we don't differentiate by religion."[441] He also defied the commandant by revealing the problems at the camp to the Red Cross inspectors. He received several beatings by the Germans for his actions.[442] Kasten was replaced by Edmund (Eddie) Pfannenstiel who also spoke fluent German.[443] He provided the Americans at Stalag IX-B with leadership until the liberation of that camp.

This was not the only resistance to identifying Jews in the stalags during World War II. It also happened at a sister camp. Master Sgt. Roddie Edmonds was a non-commissioned officer who was a prisoner at Stalag IX-A nearby. On January 27th, 1945, the Germans at that camp asked all Jews to step forward and identify themselves. Edmonds, as the highest-ranking NCO there, asked the more than 1,000 American POWs there to step forward together, and he announced that they were all Jewish. He then told the Nazi officer who was aiming a gun at his head that the Germans would have to shoot everyone there because the Americans all knew who the Germans there were. The Germans then backed down. This action prevented the Jews from being segregated and may have saved their lives. Edmonds is now listed as a Righteous Jew at Yad Vashem in Israel.[444]

On January 28th, two starving Americans at Stalag IX-B attempted to steal food from the camp kitchen during the night. They were startled to find a guard there and responded by beating him and stabbing him multiple times. The reaction by the Germans was swift. When none of the Americans would give up the guilty men, all Americans were brought outside and forced at gunpoint to stand in the cold weather for hours until the two assailants were identified. After ten hours, the attackers were found and taken into custody.[445]

At the end of February, there was an influx of new prisoners. Over a period of several days, approximately 200 new prisoners arrived at the camp each day. This may have been the period when Roland Hartman arrived at Stalag IX-B.

On the positive side, on several occasions during February, the prisoners heard about and witnessed Allied forces moving closer to Bad Orb, bringing a celebratory atmosphere to the camp. They saw Allied planes overhead and heard the guns and bombings not far away. In one incident on February 7th, an Allied plane inadvertently strafed the camp during a dog fight with the Germans above Stalag IX-B. Everyone was shaken and over a dozen prisoners were killed or injured, but the prisoners were encouraged by the sight of American planes in their area. As the Allied front moved eastward and the weather improved for air action, planes were often visible from Stalag IX-B. Sam Higgins wrote on February 21st that: "All afternoon the skies have been filled with B-17s; I hear the Yanks are on Corregidor. Hope they bomb tonight, as it is pretty…"[446]

Stalag IX-B in March

The tedious routine continued into March at Stalag IX-B. Barracks 42A was pitted against Barracks 29 in a "Take it or Like It" Quiz.[447] The Germans cut down on rations around March 11th and men continued to die from starvation and diseases. Yet, the prisoners sensed that things were about to change. There were rumors around camp that the Americans were advancing toward the camp; by March 8th, they could hear bombing and artillery from Patton's Third Army drive.

The weather improved at the beginning of March. The days were warmer and sunnier than in February. Prisoners began to go outside to spend time in the sun. For a few days, some men even began to wander around the prison complex. After a few days of warmer weather, it snowed again, but then spring reappeared. By the middle of the month, the warmer weather was drawing the men outside and the days in the sun began to help morale. The Germans adopted a new rule requiring that everyone walk around outside during the day. "A beach atmosphere prevailed as everyone lay on their blankets with their shirts off," said one prisoner.[448]

March was a month of increasing optimism as the camp continued to hear good news about the Allied front advancing into Germany. The hope of liberation hung in the air. The news filtered into the camp through several sources and prisoners at Stalag IX-B followed the news about the Allied front closely. There were at least two illegal radios in the camp - one Serbian and the other British - and news from the BBC was routinely shared with other prisoners.[449] Additionally, new prisoners were a source of war news. Some guards also supplied the prisoners with what was happening outside the camp. Another news source was the Man of Confidence, Eddy Pfannenstiel, who learned about war news from the daily meetings he had with the German commandant of the camp. He then disseminated the news through the camp by relaying the news to the barracks leaders, who in turn passed the information on to other POWs in their barracks. "Rumors about the war spread like wildfire through the prison camp... The news is embellished, interpreted, expanded, and twisted as it passes from one mouth to another."[450] Pfannenstiel also followed the action by marking a map he had secretly obtained.

"There was a young G. I. in camp who spoke perfect German, named Pvt. Pfannenstiel. He was able to smooth the way in many different ways. He became friendly with two of the Germans who helped us secretly. A Pvt. Wolfgang Dathe, a mess guard, stole some potatoes for us even though he knew it would be his life if he were caught. Gefrete Weiss worked in the headquarters building as an interpreter. At great personal risk, he informed Pfannenstiel of the progress of the war. He had smuggled a map in to the Americans and daily he would locate the position of the advancing Allies."[451]

In March, the prisoners frequently talked about the big push by the Americans. They knew almost in real time that the Americans crossed the Rhine River in March and were getting closer to their camp. By March 8th, the prisoners could hear bombings and artillery fire from Patton's Third Army located near Koblenz which was just over 100 miles to their west. On March 12th, the Americans knew that Patton's troops were driving eastward. One prisoner wrote:

"I hear that Patton has crossed the Rhine 25 miles north of Koblenz, so we pray for the best. Some say two weeks. From the cut in rations and news, it seems like a matter of time. This is truly a day for thanksgiving. Everyone has all hope in Patton. He is the main person around here."[452]

The prisoners had conflicting thoughts about the war. "The constant rumbling of the distant artillery was a reminder of the war. The sounds of war are an unsettling backdrop to a daily routine of maneuvers to survive," wrote one prisoner.[453] At the same time, these sounds brought hope of liberation to the men.

When asked about whether he knew during his imprisonment what was going on in the war and how close the Allies were to winning the war in Europe, Roland answered that "the only thing that we could see was the planes going over to bomb Germany and return and how the Germans were knocking them out with the new jet fighters. And we saw many, many bombers destroyed….We did hear some of the mortar fire and other fire….We did hear the bombardments that were going on." He did not know until his release that the war was almost over in Europe.[454]

Where once food was the main discussion, news and rumors became the main topic in the camp. By March, every rumor was discussed, dissected, and analyzed. The Americans began to focus on General George Patton and his Third US Army, looking to him for liberation.

> "The name Patton creates excitement in Stalag
> IXB. A group of about 15 men gather on the
> hill behind our barracks and bellow the chorus
> to the camp theme song as if his troop could
> hear the off-key singing vibrating among the

mountains….'come and get us, Georgie Patton…"[455]

Prisoners began tracking the location of Patton's troops. One POW wrote: "The news is good; Patton has nine bridgeheads 31 miles from here. By the first, we hope to be freed; I sure am praying so."[456]

The sense that the liberation of Stalag IX-B could happen sometime soon created optimism and hope. Men began to alter routines, wash their clothing and walk around smiling and laughing. Trading amongst prisoners increased as they bought personal products to improve their appearance. They talked about the future and attended classes on how to find a job. There was more gossiping about the war. And the prisoners stood outside and cheered as the planes flew above them.

> "Prisoners walk with more spring—almost on their toes. Feet don't drag the ground. Shoulders are straighter, as if a heavy weight has been lifted. I am hearing humming songs now and then, even "…the halls of Montezuma…" and there aren't any Marines in Stalag IXB. Men begin to trim their beards, brush sticky, stringy hair. The barber's business picks up."[457]

The men were busy and optimistic: "Trading, eating, washing clothes, gossiping about the war, more eating, vomiting, crapping, running up and down the streets of the camp. Lying around picking lice from body and clothing. Only the sick stay inside. It is a great day to be alive."[458]

Other things were also happening at Stalag IX-B. On March 15th, men, not the performers, started gathering outside to sing the camp song, sung to the "Battle Hymn of the Republic" with lyrics by Chaplain Neal:

"We're a bunch of prisoners living deep in Germany.
Eating soup and black bread and a beverage they call tea.
And we'll keep on singing 'til Patton sets us free
And we go rambling home.

Come and get us, Georgie Patton,
Come and get us, Georgie Patton,
Come and get us, Georgie Patton,
So we can ramble home."[459]

On March 16th, Red Cross parcels arrived for the Americans. It was reported that the ratio was down to three Americans to a box. As usual, the packages sparked another trading frenzy among the prisoners around the camp.

"It looks like a Sunday School picnic— everyone lying around eating, washing, and so on. Huge crap games in process for cigarettes. I got a toothbrush and powder from a Limey. It sure felt good to brush my teeth after three months. My gums bled, but I feel better. I took a good bird bath and washed some clothes; I feel tired now. The news sounds good. The sun and Red Cross packages improved our morale."[460]

"The prison camp is a maelstrom of activity. card games, wherever you find a clean area, bazaars selling or trading clothes, pots, pieces of uniforms, watches, even food and cigarettes. Barkers hawk their wares like a carnival sideshow."[461]

On March 19th, the Americans finally caught the camp thief. He had been victimizing the prisoners by stealing their meager food holdings for weeks. He was hauled to a latrine amid screaming and threats from other prisoners. Eventually, the guards broke up the disturbance and hauled him away.[462]

At this point, the men at Stalag IX-B were luckier than many other POWs in many areas of Germany. The Germans were marching prisoners of war out of their camps and relocating them to camps farther from the front lines before they could be liberated. If a camp could not be found, prisoners were just continuously marched around Germany. It was estimated that on March 13th, there were 30,000 prisoners walking around Germany looking for a POW camp.[463] On March 20th, the Soviet POWs in Stalag IX-B were marched out of camp and 400 new British prisoners arrived. The British had walked for six weeks and traveled over 400 miles. Other prisoners also entered the camp.[464] There were rumors circulating in the camp that additional Stalag IX-B prisoners would soon be moving out of the camp. The march never occurred, however, after the Man of Confidence convinced the Germans that the prisoners were too weak to march:

> "During around the third week of March, the Americans were told that about 1000 prisoners were to be marched out of Stalag 9B for another camp. But Pfennenstiel realized that many were too weak and the American military was getting close. He protested and convinced the doctors that there were diseases in the camp (diphtheria and typhus perhaps) that could be passed to the Germans if they left camp. The doctor put a ten day quarantine on the camp so no one could leave and that lasted until the camp was liberated."[465]

On March 23rd, a Red Cross inspector arrived at Stalag IX-B to look for the promised improvements to the bad living conditions found to exist in January. He once again found overcrowding, men sleeping on the floor, men suffering from undernourishment, a lack of Red Cross parcels, and a cut in food rations. There were no improvements, he was told, due to a lack of materials. The Swiss representative also visited Stalags IX-A and IX-C at that time. In the report that followed, he wrote:

> "The situation may be considered very serious. The personal impression which one gets from an inspection tour of these camps cannot be

described. One discovers distress and famine in their most terrible forms. Most of the prisoners who have come here from the territories of the East, and those who still continue to come, are nothing but skin and bones. Very many of them are suffering from acute diarrhea with bloody phlegm due to their complete exhaustion. Pneumonia, dorsal and bronchial cases are very common."[466]

Roland's Liberation and Repatriation

On March 23rd, the prisoners in Stalag IX-B saw artillery smoke on the horizon.[467] Rescue, it appeared, was nearby. The prisoners were already excited with the receipt of the Red Cross boxes and the resulting bartering frenzy. Now, American planes began to circle the camp and wave to the prisoners.

> "Oh joy! Liberation seemed almost at hand. Souvenir hunters started working, and on March 27th, we again received American Red Cross packages. Rumors had placed the number of boxes sufficient for one per man. Cigarettes sold like hotcakes for $23 a pack. About noon we watched 20 fighter planes mostly P-47s, continually circle the camp. On the Plaza near the hospital, a huge white PW had been painted with lime. One pilot had swooped down, tipped his wings and waved with his hand...."[468]

The Americans began to prepare for the arrival of liberation. Eddy Pfannenstiel, the Man of Confidence, started planning how to keep the prisoners safe during the period of transition. He organized a group of Americans to be a "military force" with the goal of maintaining order within the camp and negotiated with the commandant on how to handle the transition. The commandant ordered Pfannenstiel, accompanied by unarmed German soldiers as escorts, to go down to the village of Bad Orb and meet with American forces to arrange the surrender of the town.[469]

On April 1st, Easter Sunday, the Americans shelled the town of Bad Orb. The Germans quietly departed the camp later in the day under cover of darkness, and the American and British prisoners took control of Stalag IX-B. Prisoners manned the towers, controlled the perimeter of the camp, and guarded the gates. Everyone waited for the Americans to arrive as they heard American artillery, mortar, machine guns, and rifles. That night, the prisoners sang to the accompaniment of an accordion.[470] The camp theme song that night was still the Battle Hymn of the Republic but had different words:

'We're a bunch of Yankee soldiers
And we're leaving Germany.
We're a bunch of hungry Yankees
Butt [sic] happy as can be
Georgie Patton came around today
And set the whole camp free

Three American tanks arrived at 8:00 AM the next morning at the camp's gate to liberate Stalag IX-B. They were the forward reconnaissance party of the Third US Army's 2nd Cavalry Group. One prisoner wrote: "The mob of prisoners went wild as they fought for "K" rations, souvenirs, ammunition and autographs… What a sight! Everyone happy, cheering, waving, shaking hands, crowding the tanks."[472] The American troops from the Sixth US Army's 114th Infantry Regiment of the 44th Infantry Division were approximately 60 miles behind and arrived later. Many placed the time of liberation on that date, although some sources placed it as the day before.

By the next day, the former prisoners were protected by the 44th Infantry Division and were being supplied with as much food as they could eat. The American troops emptied their own PX stores to feed the starving prisoners.[473] There was celebration all over the camp, but some were so weak they could hardly move. For a while, overeating caused the men to suffer gastrointestinal issues since their stomachs had shrunk, but the effects of overeating did not matter to the liberated POWs at that time.[474]

The National Archives has a film made by American troops approximately two days after the liberation of Stalag IX-B. It includes a segment of Commandant Karl Sieber surrendering to Lt Walter Fettery (from the 114th Regiment) and includes the Man of Confidence Eddie Pfannenstiel. There are sequences of the freed prisoners gleefully smoking and eating and of American soldiers carrying provisions for the men. Troops carry a coffin out of the camp and there are trucks beginning the process of transporting men out of the camp. Knowing what happened at that camp made it difficult for me to watch. The original version of the film is hours long, but there is a short version available. It took years for me to watch even a portion of the movie and I could not find my father.[475] Members of the 44th Division and the medical group that liberated the camp also took pictures of the camp. Their pictures include shots of the crowded barracks stocked with multi-level bunk beds, gaunt prisoners, men too weak to get off their beds, and a display of crosses with the names of men on them.[476]

The Process of Repatriation Begins

In February 1945, as the XII US Corps was crossing over the Sauer and Our Rivers and advancing into German, SHAEF began to examine the plight of the Allied prisoners of war in Germany and how to effectively repatriate liberated prisoners. At that time, the Allies and the International Red Cross knew that prisoners in camps located in eastern Europe were being evacuated from their camps and being marched westward and southward "under conditions imposing great hardship and likely to result in considerable loss of life."[477] The Soviet/German front was located near several POW camps, putting the prisoners in those camps in a war zone. The Allies determined that there was less risk in leaving the prisoners in their camps with supplies rather than an arduous march through a war zone. The Allies attempted to reach an agreement in February with the Germans to stop the evacuations and keep the prisoners in concentrated safer locations.[478] General Eisenhower even proposed that motor caravans be employed via the International Red Cross to transport supplies to the prisoners.[479] The marches, unfortunately, continued.

Between the end of March and the month of April, many of the German camps that contained American prisoners of war were liberated. The Germans, however, had already evacuated some of the camps and sent their prisoners to other camps or forced them into one of these perilous marches. In

February 1945, estimates suggested that there were 100,000 POWs marching westward on a northern line near the German coast and another 60,000 POWs moving westward farther south in the area of Berlin, Dresden and Leipzig. There were other smaller groups in the south of Germany also marching. Food rations were limited for these men, but the Germans did try to deliver some food to them. The International Red Cross was monitoring the situation and tracking the movements and conditions of the men. This information was reported to SHAEF, who was made aware of the locations, transfers, movements, and conditions of the POWs, both in the camps and on the march.[480] The Black March, as this forced march was called, lasted for weeks and covered hundreds of miles. Many POWs died enroute. It was not until the middle of April that the Germans agreed to leave all prisoners of war in camps and stop evacuations as the Allies and the Soviets advanced through Germany. It was also agreed that the recovered prisoners would not be allowed back into combat against Germany and German guards at the camps would be allowed to leave the camps.

At the end of March and beginning of April, SHAEF were aware of approximately 97,000 American and British prisoners in the SHAEF sector (Germany's western front) and there were approximately another 70,000 prisoners marching toward that sector as the Soviets continued their advance from the east. The Allies began formulating plans and protocols to help and evacuate the prisoners. Understanding the starvation and unsanitary conditions many of the prisoners were being subjected to in the camps, they tried to coordinate the transport of supplies to liberated camps until evacuation could safely occur. The stated goal was for liberated prisoners to be transported to safety in Le Havre, France, by air if possible.[481]

The Americans and British examined the issue of repatriating prisoners held by Germany in Europe as early as 1944. They issued guidelines covering the transport, treatment, and administration of liberated prisoners and continued to refine the process involved well into 1945. The problems were complex, and there was a range of issues to consider, including the logistical issues of safely evacuating the prisoners, concerns over each prisoner's mental and physical health, the rehabilitation and care that would be required, the disposition of the prisoners once the prisoners were ready to be released from that care, and the administration and logistical systems to guide the whole process.

There were different groups of prisoners liberated during the war. The guidelines issued by SHAEF only covered the British and Americans; the French, Soviets, and other nationalities came under different rules and procedures after the camps were captured, including how those prisoners were released from the camps. Non-military personnel, including civilians, generally did not fall under the jurisdiction of the army rules for evacuation and care. American soldiers who were detained by Germany for under 60 days often passed through a different set of procedures under these rules.

By April 1945, several documents were issued detailing procedures for the liberation and repatriation, evacuation, reception, rehabilitation, administration, and disposition of Allied (American and British) prisoners of war, then called Recovered Allied Military Personnel (RAMP). Administrative Memorandum #48 was issued in February to define the procedures for the hospitalization and evacuation of RAMPs. The initial response upon liberation was to provide immediate medical care and food for the men and then evacuate the liberated camp as quickly as possible to an Allied camp or hospital.[482] SHAEF issued Standard Operating Procedures (SOP) #58 on April 3rd, 1945, just after the liberation of Stalag IX-B, to guide processing RAMPs after they were evacuated.[483]

The act of the Allied military taking control of a prisoner-of-war camp and its prisoners after liberation was called repatriation. At the time the military gained control of the camp, the policy was for the prisoners to "stay-put." This policy was adopted to give everyone time to organize the various groups in the camp, identify and record those prisoners who were actually American and British military and who fell under the classification of RAMPs, determine plans for evacuation by the Allies or other nations, determine what the supply requirements were for the prisoners (for example, food and clothing), provide medical care for those in immediate need, determine any restrictions related to the camp from contagious diseases and pest infestations, and ensure the security of the prisoners. There were often concerns about spreading diseases, the need for disinfection, documentation of prisoners, and the military situation outside the camp. Those people found outside of camps were considered "displaced persons" and were investigated to determine whether they fell under the rules for RAMPs. Overall, command of the camp at that time was under the control of SHAEF, and responsibility for the prisoners rested with the American military commanders of that area.[484]

Although the stalag was now in Allied hands, it took days for the Americans to organize Stalag IX-B and arrange for the evacuation of the camp. At first, the prisoners were locked up again with British and American guards. Typhus was rampant amongst the Germans in that area and the Allies did not want the ex-POWs infected by it. American troops set up a type of commissary to hand out food; K rations and C-rations were distributed, and there was an unlimited amount of cans. The prisoners were advised, however, to not eat too much at first to avoid additional gastrointestinal distress, but this turned out to be difficult for men who had been deprived of adequate food for many weeks. For those too weak to move, they were fed at their beds. Another consideration at that time was that the camp was infected by lice and fleas and the men were filthy. They needed to be deloused, cleaned up, and supplied with new clothes before they could be moved. For some, there was an immediate need for medical attention; the administration identified and provided care for these men.

During the next few days, the prisoners of Stalag IX-B ate GI food and celebrated their freedom. Soviet soldiers arrived to take their own soldiers back. The Italians and French prisoners were released from the camp to return home on their own. Some ex-POWs went down the mountain to Bad Orb to find GI food, but they were sent back up to the camp to avoid interfering with the war. Some prisoners hunted ducks, geese, rabbits, and other animals for food. At some point, a large quantity of Red Cross packages that had not been distributed to the American prisoners was found in the town and sent to the camp.[485] Eventually, the British and American prisoners were told of the plan for evacuation. Approximately twenty-five men per hour were sent to be showered, deloused, and redressed in clean clothing and then were evacuated.

> "I am one of 24 selected to leave for the delousing tent. Pet, Huck, Strubinger,

Tutherow, and Mahoney are among the group. This eliminates any sad goodbyes. We gather our meager belongings and walk to the main gate.... I am so frail and weak I am pushed and pulled into the covered army truck. My body aches with every move. Cries of anguish and barely audible moans come with every breath. Even the joy of leaving prison camp can't blot out the pain that consumes my body. I don't dare go to the hospital or stay behind, so I don't complain out loud.... Since my bones are meatless the ride is hell."[486]

The next stop for the ex-prisoners was Camp Lucky Strike, a transit camp in a safer location better prepared to deal with the many needs and maladies suffered by the ex-prisoners.

Where They All Went

As the war progressed, priorities and needs shifted, and the military units changed to meet these needs. Within weeks of the crossing of the Sauer and Our Rivers, the XII US Corps was reconfigured, and the 80th, 5th, and 76th Divisions advanced in different directions.

Advance to the Rhine

At the beginning of March, the Allies were attacking eastward toward the Rhine River, and by the middle of March, all army groups in Europe had reached Eisenhower's goal, the west bank of the Rhine River. As the month progressed, the Allies reported that German resistance to the Allied drive was significantly decreasing and the German troops were disorganized as they withdrew eastward.

North of the Third Army, the 21st British Army Group captured Xanten, the last major German stronghold west of the Rhine River in their zone, on March 9th. The Ninth US Army reached the west bank of the Rhine River in several locations, including capturing Neuss, a suburb of Dusseldorf located on the Rhine River, on March 2nd, and the Canadians linked with the Ninth US Army near Geldern (south of Goch) the next day.[487] The Germans offered little resistance in their retreat, but they took down every bridge they could find across the Rhine River before they left. Operation Blockbuster concluded on March 10th. The 21st British Army Group, including the Ninth US Army, now occupied positions along the Rhine River from Arnhem in the north to Dusseldorf in the south, a distance of approximately 75 miles.

In the Twelfth US Army Group, the First and Third US Armies jointly launched Operation Lumberjack at the beginning of March. The First US Army drove through the industrial Munchen – Gladbach area eastward toward Dusseldorf on the Rhine River on March 2nd. Two days later, they reached the Rhine River north of Cologne in Worringen on March 4th and captured much of Cologne within three days. Farther south, troops cleared the city of Bonn on March 10th. There were only a few pockets of resistance left in the First US Army zone, and by March 12th, the First US Army was sitting on the Rhine River.

Unexpectedly, troops in the 9th Armored Division in the First US Army reached the Rhine River south of Bonn and discovered the Ludendorff Bridge across the Rhine River at Remagen still intact, an oddity since the Germans had destroyed almost every other bridge over the rivers they crossed while fleeing back to Germany. With Eisenhower's backing, Bradley ordered at least five divisions to move across the river to establish a bridgehead on the eastern side of the river, an unanticipated opportunity to advance easily and reach beyond the Rhine River itself.[488] Despite strong efforts by the Germans to reclaim the bridgehead on the eastern side of the river, the III US Corps strongly defended the bridge and enlarged their bridgehead. It became the first bridgehead established by the Allied forces east of the Rhine River. When the original bridge at Remagen finally collapsed on March 17th, six divisions had moved across the bridge and established a bridgehead nine miles deep and 25 miles long. The Americans had already built two other bridges nearby.

Meanwhile, the Third US Army drove toward the Trier area and northeast through the Eifel region toward the Rhine River. They met the First US Army at the intersection of the Rhine and Ahr Rivers. The VIII US Corps reached the Rhine River, their final objective, near the city of Andernach, approximately ten miles north of Koblenz, on March 9th.[489] In the XII US Corps, the 80th Infantry Division began north of Bitburg between the Prum and Nims Rivers, and the 5th Infantry Division, farther south, began on the west bank of the Kyll River, which runs north and east. They crossed the Kyll River at the beginning of March and then advanced to the Rhine River between Andernach and Koblenz.

The XX Corps, with the support of the 76th Infantry Division, remained in the Trier area to complete the capture of that region. They advanced toward Trier and the Kyll and Moselle Rivers. After crossing and bridging the Kyll River, they established a bridgehead and linked with the 5th Infantry Division. The XX US Corps had cleared the old city of Trier on March 2nd. The objective of Sweich, which is where the Moselle and Rhine Rivers meet, was reached on March 6th. The entire area west of the Kyll River was now cleared. On March 7th (the same day the First US Army captured the intact bridge at Remagen), they advanced to high ground overlooking the Rhine River not far from Koblenz. By March 11th, the Third US Army operation was reduced to clearing a few isolated pockets on the western side of the river.

The west side of the Rhine River was now occupied by the Allied forces from Nigmegen to Koblenz. The Allied front, north to south, was approximately 250 miles long. All German resistance west of the Rhine reportedly stopped on March 25th. Bradley wrote about the operation, which took under one week: "Lumberjack was very nearly flawless, the kind of campaign generals dream about but seldom see. All five corps of both armies advanced according to plan, with dazzling speed and elan. The German armies opposing us were utterly routed, the men falling back in confusion and disarray, leaving a trail of weapons and equipment behind."[490]

For the POWs located in Stalag IX-B, this was exciting news. Koblenz is approximately 120 miles west of Bad Orb, where their camp was located.

The Breakup of the XII US Corp

The XII US Corps remained part of the Third US Army during the remainder of the war in Europe and the 5th Infantry Division remained in that corps. They ended the war in Czechoslovakia with the rest of the Third US Army. Both the 76th and 80th Infantry Divisions were reassigned to other corps in the last few months of operations. The 80th Infantry Division left the XII US Corps on March 10th - at the time they reached the Rhine River - when they were reassigned to the XX US Corps to the south of the XII US Corps. They remained with that corps in the Third US Army until the end of the war and were also located in Czechoslovakia. At the beginning of April, the 76th Division was briefly assigned to the XX US Corps and then reassigned to the VIII US Corps a few days later. In April, the VIII US Corps was reassigned to the First US Army. The 76th Division remained in the VIII Corps and in the First US Army until the end of the war in Europe.

The 417th Regiment, along with the 304th and 385th Regiments, remained active in the 76th US Division until the end of the war. Beginning February 27th, the regiment drove to the southeast toward Trier from the area of Gilzen. The 417th Regiment was briefly attached to the 10th Armored Division from March 4th through March 12th, which was when the XX US Corps' was active to the northeast of Trier. During this period, the regiment once again encountered extremely high casualties - especially in the 1st Battalion- after the Germans mounted strong opposition near the town of Kordel near the Kyll River. According to an after-action report in March 1945, the strength of the 1st Battalion had been reduced on March 5th to approximately 273 men and 4 officers, compared to the 2nd Battalion, which had about 450 men and 13 officers. Troop strength for companies B and C in the 417th Regiment was under 100 men, and Company A had only 120 men, not close to the normal 180 to 200 per company.[491] The report did not specify the exact date of the action or what happened, although it may have been at the same time as the Kyll River crossing and may have involved an unexpected German counter-attack. As in February, the regiment required replacements to continue in battle.

Given the requirements for additional troop replacements in both early February and the following month, I believe the 417th Infantry Regiment in April was composed of many troops who never saw action at the Sauer River. It is even possible that the regiment never regained its full strength. Towards the end of the war in Europe, elements of individual battalions of the 76th Infantry Division were briefly attached to other units during the remainder of the war in Europe; for example, elements of the 385th Regiment were attached to the 6th Armored Division for two days in late March, portions of the 304th Infantry Regiment were attached to the 6th Cavalry Group at the end of March for several days, and later in April parts of the 304th Infantry Regiment were attached to the 87th Infantry Division for two days. The 76th Infantry Division ended the war at the Mulde River in Germany. On May 7th, 1945, the division was part of the VIII US Corps in the First US Army.

Roland's Last Stop: Camp Lucky Strike and Home

After liberation, American prisoners from Stalag IX-B were transported out of the camp by truck to a landing strip nearby. They were then flown by C-47 planes to Le Havre, France, the only northern port then open that could accommodate large transatlantic ships. From there, they were transported to Camp Lucky Strike, one of several transit camps for recovered personnel, before they returned to the United States. The camp was situated on over 1,500 acres near the coast of France. Originally established as a transit camp for Americans arriving in Europe before they went to the front, it now provided shelter and recovery services for liberated POWs and other soldiers departing the European theater.

Camp Lucky Strike, the largest of the "cigarette camps," was now busy processing most of the liberated POWs in the European theater. In December 1944, it housed American engineers arriving to make repairs and make the camp ready for its new activity. Red Cross workers were assigned to the hospital in March 1945. In that same month, liberated prisoners started to arrive in larger numbers as Soviet soldiers began liberating prison camps in eastern Europe and eastern Germany.

Containing more than 12,000 tents and huts, Camp Lucky Strike housed as many as 100,000 soldiers at one time. There were four sub-camps at Lucky Strike, each with its own small town that contained housing, messes, a hospital, a chapel, a post office, a police station, a barber shop, a theater, and a store to purchase groceries, personal items, and gifts.[492] In each sub-camp, the messes were dining areas that catered to the special dietary needs of the soldiers at various stages of recovery, and there were special nutritional bars with supplemental drinks for between meals. There was also plenty of ice cream available. The 77th Field Hospital was located in that area for those men in need of additional medical attention.

Upon arrival at Camp Lucky Strike, each solider was interviewed. He was asked his name, rank, serial number, his unit, where he was captured, and where he was held after capture. He was then assigned to a specific tent in a specific sub-area of the camp. The ex-prisoners were examined for any medical issues. At times, Camp Lucky Strike welcomed as many as 20,000 new ex-prisoners of war on a single day. Depending on health and other recovery issues, liberated soldiers remained at Camp Lucky Strike for anywhere from a few days to several months.[493]

I can envision my father arriving for his interview after liberation. He supplies his name, his unit, and other information. Roland later remembered the man's reaction, "This man was surprised to see me" because his unit "was completely wiped out." The man had only heard of another ten people known to have survived that action, and now Roland is listed as the eleventh survivor.[494] They discuss his injuries: shrapnel in the head, the phosphorus in the wrist, a limited amount of feeling in some of his fingers, and back pain caused during the German interrogation. After his medical evaluation, he is sent to recover from his injuries. According to Roland, he spent several weeks recuperating in the cigarette camps before he was returned to the United States.

The camp was designed to help repatriated soldiers regain their health and re-acclimate to their liberated status. There were special diets to guide them through the process of expanding their ability to eat a normal diet. It began with eating small meals of bland food at first and then eventually increasing the amounts and types of food they could safely eat.

As a RAMP's health improved, he was moved to another area of the camp that provided care more in line with his point in the recovery process and provided additional food choices with larger portions. When he reached the third level, he was transferred from the custody of the RAMP camp to the direct control of Camp Lucky Strike and was eligible for the journey back to the United States.[495] If a man had been a prisoner of war for less than 60 days, RAMP rules specified that he could be kept in Europe and reassigned to other duties.

One of the first prisoner-of-war camps to be liberated by the Americans was Stalag IX-B in the western regions of Germany. Stalag IX-A in Ziegenhain, not far from Bad Orb, was liberated at approximately the same time. It held many of the non-commissioned officers taken out of Stalag IX-B in January. In Camp Lucky Strike, many men from the two camps were able to reconnect with old friends. Also in the camp at that time were prisoners from Stalag XII-A in Limburg, the transit camp Roland may have passed through after his capture in February.

Early in the recovery process, many men slept, relaxed, and tried to recover their health and strength. Their health was monitored and they were reminded about how to eat. If they were hungry between meals, eggnog and cocoa were always available. At the same time, they were free to roam the camp. Each prisoner was given some back pay which could be used to buy personal items, including toothbrushes, chocolate, watches, and cigarettes. Also available at the PX were gifts for their relatives, such as perfume, lace, and jewelry.[496] There was a post office in the sub-camp, and they were encouraged to write home.

The soldiers were given new uniforms and other clothing to wear. If the uniforms did not fit correctly, there were tailors available to make necessary adjustments. Other supplies were also available.

The American Red Cross played a significant role in Camp Lucky Strike. They greeted the liberated men and distributed various toiletries and supplies when the men first arrived. Some were nurses in the hospital. Many visited the men during their recoveries, talked with them, listened to their stories, answered questions, helped write letters for them, and tracked down information about family members in the United States.

Sometimes they would serve the men food or eat with them. The Red Cross members also worked in the snack bars, ran an athletic program, and provided entertainment in the Red Cross Club. They also were involved in different forms of entertainment throughout the camp, including movies and live entertainment shows. The Red Cross workers also supplied news reports, encouraged the men to participate in the shows, and danced with them.[497]

As the men gained strength and walked around the camp, they discovered there were areas and tents for different activities.[498] There was an area with tables and chairs decorated like a café where men sat for refreshments with friends. There was a large tent with ping-pong tables and a piano. Another tent was set up as an information center with people to help them. There were desks with stationery to sit and write letters, and there were local people who could provide services such as mending clothing and sewing on patches. Another tent housed the nutrition bar, where men found eggnog, coffee, fruit juice and soup; sometimes, there were sandwiches. There were other tents as well.[499]

It is not known how long Roland was at Camp Lucky or what his experience there was. It is known that several days after ex-prisoners from Stalag IX-B began arriving at Camp Lucky Strike, a hospital ship set sail on April 13th for the United

States with approximately 500 of the sickest men. It arrived in New York on April 28th along with another ship containing 1,475 ex-prisoners from several other prisoner-of-war camps. Another ship departed Le Havre for New York with prisoners from Stalag IX-B on April 22nd. The New York Times documented the arrival of 1,975 liberated soldiers on April 29th, 1945.[500] Ships carrying the recovered prisoners continued to transport men home for the next few months. A dated photo with Roland indicates that he was back in the United States by the middle of July.

The United States and Great Britain liberated many of the prisoner-of-war camps in their sector during April and early May 1945. The Soviets also liberated Allied troops in their sector. When Stalag VII-A in Moosburg was liberated on April 29th, it held over 100.000 prisoners. Many of these prisoners were from other German POW camps who were forced to march through Germany after their other camps were evacuated. 30,000 of the prisoners in Mooseburg were Americans, which was one-third of the total Americans captured in the European theater. The last camp in Europe was liberated on May 9th, several days after the end of hostilities. Most of the American RAMPs were processed through Camp Lucky Strike, often taxing the systems in the camp. General Eisenhower ordered that the recovery process be expedited and over 64,000 of the recovered men were shipped back to the United States by June 6th. Another 20,000 were waiting for a ship to take them home at that time.

Back in the United States and Back to their Lives

Upon arriving in the United States, many former prisoners of war in Europe were given 60-day leaves and ventured home to visit with family. Roland had originally been listed as dead, but now the family knew it was not so. When Roland returned home, his brother Alan, four years younger than him, met him outside the door of their home. A large family reunion was waiting inside.

During their leave, the war in Europe ended, and many American POWs were discharged from the armed services without returning to Europe. A few soldiers were reassigned to other posts. My father, for example, was sent to Camp Landing in Florida to teach some of what he had learned. He also spent time typing discharge papers for others while waiting for his own. The return and re-entry into their previous lives were not always easy. Some returned to previous jobs, easily found a new job, or entered college and easily moved on. For others, there were health issues to consider and barriers to returning to the life they had before. Recovering from what they encountered on the battlefield and what they endured as prisoners took time. Each soldier experienced a unique road to recovery and found different degrees of help along the way.

Perhaps the most immediate need for many of the ex-prisoners was recovering from their starvation diets and other health issues resulting from their time in the camps. Their bodies needed to adjust to the larger and richer diets they should have. Since many were deficient in various nutrients and suffering from the effects of bad foods, they lacked the strength, endurance, and concentration to function well. Over time, many of these problems disappeared as they ate better, took supplemental vitamins, and regained the lost weight. Some ex-prisoners, however, had gastrointestinal problems that lasted for years or for the rest of their lives. Additionally, some never totally recovered from injuries sustained on the battlefield or during their time as prisoners and suffered from chronic pain, lost limbs, or disabling injuries.

Many returning POWs (as well as other soldiers) exhibited mental health or behavioral issues after their return to the United States. Many developed some form of post-traumatic stress. Some displayed changes in temperament, or their reactions changed. Others became anxious, depressed, or developed nightmares and other sleeping issues. Post-traumatic stress syndrome, once called battle fatigue or combat stress, was not well understood after World War II. Men often did not want to discuss their experiences. They tried to put it all behind them, or they did not wish to relive the bad memories of seeing friends die. Some ex-prisoners felt they failed when they were captured. Often the soldiers could not process their experiences, and they were not necessarily encouraged to do so. The incidence of alcoholism, divorce, and suicide was greater for returning POWs. As a result of these feelings, many waited decades to tell their stories or never shared their experiences at all. Today, help for mental health issues is more available than after World War II. Fortunately, many were able to gain control and move on. Some men joined organizations or support groups for ex-prisoners or went to a reunion and began the process of sharing their memories. These discussions with their old comrades often helped in finally processing their experiences and their feelings.

There is evidence that some returning ex-prisoners were forced to sign what was called a "security certificate" before they left the armed forces. The men sent to Berga, for example, signed forms promising not to reveal their experiences there. Anthony Acevedo, a prisoner in Berga, signed a security certificate after repatriation promising not to reveal information such as clandestine organizations in prison camps, intelligence activities, and escape attempts.[501] American POWs who worked for private Japanese companies as slave labor also signed forms.[502] Some Jews and former prisoners were also asked to sign the forms or verbally told not to discuss their experiences. Their stories remained secret for years and benefits were often denied as a result.[503] Eventually, decades later, ex-prisoners began to tell their stories and, in doing so, left us with a better understanding of what occurred. Stories, such as the prisoners from Stalag IX-B sent to Berga, surfaced decades later. So have the stories of life in the prisoner-of-war camps. Fathers, suddenly, became heroes later in life.

Roland Hartman eventually discussed some of his experiences with me. I heard about the crossing of the Sauer River, but he had a difficult time talking about his boat being torn apart by fire and refused to talk about a pillbox he said he helped capture. The POW experience, however, was a taboo subject. I was counseled by an expert on World War II many years ago not to press too hard because my father was probably still too traumatized by his experiences to talk about it, and I listened to the advice. The grandson of Roy Martin, another survivor of the first day of the crossing, also said his grandfather found some things too painful to discuss decades later. The one subject Roland never had a problem discussing was General George Patton. He hated the man and was more than willing to tell me so.

In 1993, Roland visited Luxembourg and his crossing site into Germany. He noticed that the Sauer River was more like a stream than a raging river and spoke with several Germans in the area; he called the Germans some of the nicest people in Europe, but he never resolved his hatred for Patton. He was also touched by the memorial to the 417th Infantry Regiment in Echternach. The US government eventually recognized his status as a POW and granted him additional benefits decades later for his service in World War II. We buried him in Arlington National Cemetery to make sure the prisoners' stories were remembered.

Understanding and Making Sense of My Father's Story

I began my research looking for an understanding of what my father's combat experience was and what it meant. Given Roland's story, I wondered why so little was known about the crossing of the Sauer and Our Rivers, why it was necessary for so many to die, and whether the casualty numbers he gave me were even accurate. As my research continued, I sought to give meaning and validation to these losses and tried to understand what it meant to be a POW in Europe in 1945. I also had to come to terms with the myths of Patton, a general who was both revered for his battlefield achievements and hated by others, including many men who served under him.

As a master's student of World War II studies, I felt it was important to provide context and perspective to this one small part of the war in Europe. I learned about the complexities involved in waging war, from the strategic decisions that set the priorities and defined battlefields to the supplies and logistics supporting operations. I learned about the uncontrollable variables that affect and can derail any operation and the incredible tenacity and bravery of those many soldiers who supported each other on the frontlines.

Each man, such as Roland Hartman, had his story and his own perspective that emanated from his own experience. I realized that there was the personal story, and then there was the part it played in an overall synchronized effort. Rarely did soldiers speak of that.

Context and Perspective

The crossing of the Sauer and Our Rivers in February 1945 was part of a larger, coordinated operation to move the entire Allied front located to the west of Germany into Germany itself and then to the western bank of the Rhine River. Eisenhower and his generals made the decision to fight through the brutal cold and snowy winter to keep the pressure on the retreating German army, which was also being pressed by Soviet troops advancing into Germany from the east. Unfortunately, the XII US Corp, which included the 76th, 5th, and 80th Infantry Divisions, was positioned along one of the most fortified sectors of that front with rivers, pillboxes, obstacles, mines, high hills, and forested areas. It was their task to overcome these challenges. Pragmatically, the question then became not if they would cross the raging rivers but when to cross these rivers and how to do it. My research indicates that the operation was authorized, and the results were reported to the commanders at the army, corps, and army group levels. It was front-page news when Patton's Third Army moved over the rivers and crossed into Germany. At the same time, there were other actions occurring along the American sectors in both the First and Third US Armies. It was a coordinated, planned effort. There is also evidence that the planning for this operation never anticipated the level of difficulty that occurred during the crossings. However, the strong opposition by the Germans and the obstacles encountered along the Siegfried Line were expected.

In the early part of 1945, different elements of the Allied front advanced toward the Rhine River. The main thrust of the Allies shifted along the front based on opportunities and problems which presented themselves. For example, when flooding occurred from the opening of the Schwammenauel Dam in early February, the Ninth Army was sidelined for two weeks, and other sectors of the front were ordered to continue their advances to maintain pressure on the enemy. Under this concept, it was probable that at some time during this period, the XII US Corps would be involved in operations in their sector. For the untested 417th Regiment, their zone, unfortunately, included the swollen Sauer River near Echternach and a heavily fortified, pillbox-infested area in Germany.

The exact timing of the beginning of this operation, however, is interesting. Operation Veritable, the British attack on the Reichswald Forest between the Meuse (Maas) and Rhine Rivers was due to commence the next day, February 8th. This would shift the emphasis away from the American sectors and toward the British sectors. Eisenhower's orders, however, did allow Patton's Third Army to continue their "probing attacks" that were already in progress.[504] The crossing of the Sauer and Our Rivers commenced one day before the British attack; therefore, it could be considered "in progress." Patton was known for his aggressiveness toward battles and his philosophy of continuous action, and it was no secret that there was a rivalry between Patton and Montgomery. There is no conclusive evidence that this was the motivation behind Patton's decision to cross the Sauer and Our Rivers on February 7th, but in his diary, Patton did allude to taking a chance with this operation.[505]

Leadership and Strategy: Military Questions Related to the Crossings

In many ways, the crossing of the Sauer River was inevitable. Under the concept of the broad front strategy, everyone was moving eastward toward the Rhine River, some faster than others and some advancing while others rested. This was just a continuation of military orders issued in the fall of 1944 and updated periodically by Eisenhower and his generals, and Patton found himself in Luxembourg facing the German frontier at what was arguably the most fortified portion of the German border. While Montgomery tried to support his Operations Grenade and Veritable, Patton was figuring out how to continue his operations. At the same time, Bradley collaborated with Patton and quietly sought permission to allow Patton to do what he wanted to do, which was to attack.[506] Eisenhower was aware of what was happening.

The Twelfth US Army Group, at the end of January, was ordered to be "defending aggressively" in their zone south of the Moselle River with the objective of "penetrating the Siegfried Line."[507] The term "aggressive defense" was used by Eisenhower again on February 1st in a letter to Montgomery and Bradley regarding the Third US Army.[508] The term continued to be used in other letters of instruction issued at that time by the Third US Army, the XII US Corps, and then by commanders under them. It never was precisely defined, but it appeared in several directives in January and February of 1945 from as high in the command as SHAEF and on down to the corps level:

> "Orders for the maintenance of an aggressive defense were given Twelfth US Army Group by SHAEF on 7 February, but an exception was made for Third US Army which was told to make probing attacks and single corps attacks toward critical objectives. Thus, the

attack toward PRUM continued, while elsewhere in zone the Army went on an aggressive defense which was intended to hold the enemy on the Army front, and to prevent the redeployment of units then on the Third Army attack toward the RHINE River."[509]

Bradley and Patton used the term "aggressive defense" to mean that any action that could enhance the troops' security and move them forward was allowed as long as they had the means to do so. Several February directives used a similar term, "probing attacks," without a definition attached. For Patton, the question of whether the crossings of the Sauer and Our Rivers were permitted was yes, especially if kept under the radar and it did not create problems with Montgomery. Patton believed he might have been taking a chance in doing so, but Bradley wrote that Patton was to advance through the German fortifications at the West Wall and "advance quietly to the Kyll…There he was to seize a bridgehead in anticipation of a full-scale advance to the Rhine."[510] Bradley further wrote that he and Patton were not disobeying Eisenhower's orders using aggressive defense. It appears that orders were given to move ahead quietly. It was predictable that Patton would react to the situation by continuing his operations to push ahead the best he could. Bradley, with reference to the Third US Army and its

Eifel campaign, understood this meant something else besides maintaining a position and standing still:

> "For Third Army viewed defensive warfare as something to be shunned at all costs. Now with Eisenhower's consent, I ordered Patton to mount an offensive in the Eifel. It was to be strong enough to keep the enemy from shifting his strength to the Roer but not so strong as to arouse the objections of Monty. Replacements for this limited offensive could be spared initially while the First and Ninth Armies fidgeted on the Roer….Rather than directly disobey SHAEF's written orders consigning him to the defensive, Patton termed his Third Army operations in the Eifel an "aggressive defense." His staff innocently believed that they were hoodwinking Ike's staff at Versailles. Moreover, it was rumored that I had joined Patton in this conspiratorial offensive. My insubordination however was purely make-believe, for without the knowledge of Patton's staff and mine, Eisenhower had agreed to it."[511]

Ralph Ingersoll, once a staff officer for General Bradley, defined the term "aggressive defense" as he understood it in his book, "Top Secret," as something else:

> "Patton's army, having finished straightening out the Ardennes bulge, was drawn up along a little river on the German border. Obviously it was consistent with an "aggressive defense" that they send a few patrols to the far bank of the river, just to stir up trouble. The patrols turned out to be battalions, making assault

crossings- in midwinter, across raging mountain streams that tore the pontons loose and swept the assault craft downstream. When they got across, they stuck there. Obviously it was consistent with an "aggressive defense" to consolidate such positions on the far shore. Patton ordered them consolidated, and heavy bridges were put in to take tanks across. But on the far shore there were hills overlooking these positions. So, still consistent with the idea of an "aggressive defense," Patton sent his troops up over the hills, simply to protect the crossing site from enemy fire. And beyond these hills there was another valley, with another stream, which you had first to go down to the edge of, and then to cross, and then to protect by getting to the next ridge line beyond."[512]

According to Charles McDonald in "The Last Offensive," Eisenhower informally modified the written directive for the Twelfth US Army Group by allowing probing attacks in the First US Army, although their primary mission was still to attack across the Roer River and to protect the right flank of the Ninth US Army. In the Third US Army, the probing attacks were even more brazen: "At headquarters of the Third Army, "probing attacks" were popularly known as the "defensive-offensive," which meant, in more widely understood terminology, a major attack. Bradley knew, too, that the Supreme Commander himself well understood General Patton's special lexicon."[513] The friendship between

Eisenhower and Patton dated back to the 1920s when both had a strong interest in the development of tank warfare. And everyone knew of Patton's philosophy of continuous action.

With respect to the question of whether Eisenhower knew what was happening in the XII US Corp, the quiet offense was not a secret for long as SHAEF issued daily communique to the press reporting actions on the European front. Within a day of the events near the Sauer River, the New York Times reported that the Third US Army had crossed the Sauer and Our Rivers and was close to Prum. On February 8th, the New York Times reported on the Third US Army action, with a headline that included "Four Divisions Cross Our and Sauer at Night to Hack Westwall."[514] There were even maps indicating multiple crossings between Echternach and Wallendorf. Although Eisenhower had to know what was happening in the Third US Army, he never acknowledged the Third US Army operations and never wrote about them in his autobiography or in his official biennial report.

Thus, at the beginning of February, it appears that Patton was quietly allowed, under Eisenhower's consent to continue his Eifel Offensive under the pretext of probing attacks, providing these attacks were a continuation of action already in progress and they kept the activity under the radar of Montgomery. Their objectives were actually Prum and Bitburg, and the number of troops involved may have been higher than officially directed. As I see it, everyone knew Patton would take on the challenge of the Sauer and Our Rivers, even if the rivers were in flood stage.

Another interesting part of the planning process was by the generals for the actual battle. Operational planning in the Third US Army was done at the divisional level in coordination with other generals. Each of the three divisions approached the crossings in different manners, which may have impacted the outcomes of the crossings. The 5th and 80th Infantry Divisions had been fighting in Europe since their landings in Normandy during the summer of 1944. They were veterans of various river crossings and survived the winter conditions. They knew how to plan and prepare for the upcoming operation. However, the Sauer River crossing was the first time the 417th Regiment was in battle. An observer's report recognized the problems with the terrain, river currents, German fortifications, and resistance but criticized the planning for the crossing and the lack of rehearsals for the operation. It noted the lack of experience of the 417th Regiment and labeled it the "toughest river crossing we have had." It also concluded that bridges cannot be built until an area is clear of enemy fire.[515]

No matter what happened, the operation may not have started out as intended, but the end result included successful crossings, the establishment of bridgeheads by all three divisions, and then an advance to reach all objectives of the operation. I was never a fan of studying how battles were fought, but I found persistence and ingenuity in how each group approached the challenges of subduing well-fortified pillboxes with the combination of BARs, bazookas, mortars, grenades, smoke, satchel charges, and other weaponry coupled with negotiation or threats. And I learned about heroism and cooperation in how infantry, engineers, medics, and artillery all supported each other on the frontlines.

What Were the Total Casualties?

Before we begin, there are several caveats to mention regarding the term casualties. Reported "casualties" also included illness and trench foot. Some men died from wounds days later and reports of deaths or casualties were sometimes delayed in the heat of a battle. In the case of the crossings of the Sauer and Our Rivers, some men survived crossing only to die or suffer injury during the intense battle to establish the bridgeheads and/ or during the advance towards their objectives. After the crossings, there were incidents where German tanks surrounded the Americans and there were battles in the forested areas and related to pillboxes. Records do not indicate exactly where the deaths occurred or when. This would explain why troop strength seemed to decrease over a period of time after the crossings. For example, two days after the original crossing, the troop strength of the 1st Battalion of the 417th Regiment had reportedly decreased to 57 in Company A, 51 in Company B, 85 in Company C, and 66 in Company D when a company is normally between 150 to 200 men This represents significant casualties in less than two days for these companies.[516]

The evacuation and casualty reports for the 301st Medical Battalion, attached to the 417th Infantry Combat Team, tell their own story by recording the number of casualties evacuated from their three collection companies each day. Between February 7th and 12th, dozens of men were evacuated daily, the worst being on February 10th (145 men) and February 12th (126 men). This seems to confirm that there were many battle casualties at the time of the initial crossings. One member of the 301st Medical Bn, 76th Division said, "We lost over 500 men in Luxembourg."[517]

Total casualties for the action itself are also not consistent in the different sources I found. The 417th Regiment reported 80 men killed in action and 156 men missing for the period between February 7th and February 17th. An after-action report for the same period listed 86 killed in action, 421 wounded, 156 missing in action, and 224 non-battle casualties.[518] A regimental history indicated that for the entire month of February, 108 men were killed, 415 men were wounded, and 121 were missing.[519] Perhaps part of the variance comes from the reclassification of some of the missing to dead later; many men who died in the raging waters were not discovered until days later, often farther down the river.

The XII US Corps recorded 2,425 casualties for the period of February 7th through February 11th, including 88 men killed, 1,406 wounded, and 20 missing. The American Cemetery in Luxembourg lists 206 military men buried there who were in the 5th Infantry Division, the 80th Infantry Division, and the 417th Regiment, with dates of death between February 7th and February 11th. Engineers would not be included in these figures, and not all men died on the same day they were wounded.

Troop strength and replacement reports also reflect the number of casualties. The army tracked each unit's effective strength daily. Regiments and divisions without enough strength to effectively fight were cycled out until they could recover their strength. Bringing in replacement troops was often required. At the end of January, the effective strength for the 417th Regiment numbered 3,116 troops, not far from the number expected to be in a regiment during World War II. The regiment listed 644 casualties for the month of February and then recorded 640 reinforcements to replace the shortfall in troop strength. There was a reduction in effective strength to 2,978 troops. In March, there was an even larger number of casualties, 720 in all, but the regiment was able to secure an additional 948 replacement troops, thereby increasing their effective strength to an almost normal 3,148 men.[520]

In the 5th Infantry Division, the after-action report for the month of February lists 69 men killed in action, 329 men wounded in action (including 11 officers), and 27 men missing in action.[521] The 3rd Battalion, in particular, was hammered, with the commanding officer estimating that I and L Companies fell to about 120 men each, while K was down to 90 men.[522] This means they lost anywhere from one-third to half of their strength by the time they were relieved. Additionally, the 7th Engineers experienced severe casualties. The battalion lost a total of 62 men (2 killed, 60 wounded) for the month of February, most during the intense fight along the Sauer River.[523]

The difficulties on the battlefield for the 80th Infantry Division also led to large losses, particularly in the second half of February when they waged a battle to capture Huehnenkopf Hill near Biesdorf starting around February 12th. According to records for the American Cemetery in Luxembourg, the number of deaths in the 80th Infantry Regiment increased between February 18th and February 22nd. XII US Corps records listed 118 men dead and over 350 men wounded in six days during that battle.

Were these losses significant? This was an important early question for me, and there was no direct way to determine the losses and whether the losses were significant within the context of the European Theater. The crossing of the Sauer River occurred under difficult conditions in one of the most fortified areas of the Siegfried Line. Lt Col Breckinridge of the 10th Regiment wrote about the level of difficulty in the crossings:

> "Of the seven river crossings made by the 10th Inf Lt Col Breckinridge termed the crossing of the Sauer "the toughest". He said a number of factors made it so: failure to achieve surprise, poor approaches to the river, swift current and swollen condition of the stream, inadequate reconnaissance, no rehearsal for crossing, and poor quality of officer and enlisted reinforcements."[524]

The casualties were high for this well-defended area, but other actions during the war also encountered major opposition and had similar or higher casualties. As already noted, the 80th Regiment found difficulties taking Huehnenkopf Hill toward the end of February and sustained significant casualties, and the 417th Regiment found themselves at the end of February or the beginning of March trying to cross the Kyll River under similar conditions as were encountered in the Echternach crossing and once again sustained large casualties.

There were other battles during the European campaign with unanticipated high casualty rates as well. Farther afield, the battle in the Huertgen Forest near Aachen lasted for months in 1944 and decimated several regiments in the First US Army. The casualties were estimated to be over 30,000 men. Operation Market Garden cost approximately 3,000 American lives in 1944.

Impact and Legacy: Results of the 417th Regiment's Sauer River Crossing

When the 417th Regiment crossed over the Sauer River, they were taking their first steps into Germany. That crossing was never expected to be so difficult, but they overcame the problems and moved on to the bigger challenge, which was conquering the Siegfried Line. As stated, they did their jobs and reached their objectives. The fact that the Regiment and its combat team worked through the obstacles was recognized and rewarded with commendations for their actions.

General George Patton wrote about the crossing of the Sauer and Our Rivers from his own perspective: "We are having a very funny battle right now. I am taking one of the longest chances of my chancy career; in fact, almost disobeying orders in order to attack, my theory being that if I win, nobody will say anything, and I am sure I will win."[525] Several days later, he visited the front and wrote: "Crossed the Sauer River into Germany and drove along the east bank…the men were quite surprised to see me. However, the chance of getting hit was small and worth the risk due to the effect it had on the troops…"[526] Patton also wrote about the troops crossing of the rivers in his book:

> "The crossing of the three divisions over these rivers was a magnificent feat of arms. The rivers were in flood to such an extent that the barbed wire along the Siegfried Line, which abutted on the rivers, was under water, and, when the men disembarked from the boats, they were caught in it. The whole hillside was covered with German pillboxes and barbed wire. A civilian observer told me afterward that he did not see how human beings could be brave enough to succeed in such an attack. Actually the audacity of the attack and the strength of the position materially aided in our success. However, weather conditions made progress at the time seem unnecessarily slow and both Eddy and I were considerably perturbed."[527]

The 417th Combat Team, comprised of the 417th Regiment, the 901st Field Artillery Battalion, Company C of the 301st Engineer Combat Battalion, Company C of the 301st Medical Battalion, and Company B of the 160th Engineer Combat Battalion, was awarded a Presidential Unit Citation (also referred to as the Distinguished Unit Citation) in February 1947 for their performance in February 1945.[528] The medical units associated with the 417th Regiment reportedly evacuated 145 troops on February 10th alone. Records indicate that the 417th Regiment also received a Meritorious Unit Commendation. This was not shared with the other divisions in the 76th Division. This particular award is given to acknowledge extraordinary heroism during an action. Words like gallantry, determination, and hazardous conditions are often attached to the award. I am not sure Roland ever knew about this honor or ever received the ribbon awarded to its recipients, as it was awarded two years after the war was over.

Other commendations also occurred. General Eddy, commander of the XII US Corps, in his commendation dated February 1945, wrote, "In its initial combat in the face of conditions which at times appeared prohibitive, the 417th Regiment showed its superior determination, dogged fighting qualities, and high spirit. It showed the mettle of which Infantrymen are made." He also noted that the combat team "instilled with an indomitable spirit to win, expertly and courageously executed their assigned mission in the face of seemingly insuperable obstacles."[529] He also issued a commendation to all engineers in the corps. Patton also issued commendations.

GO 19

GENERAL ORDERS}
No. 19   WAR DEPARTMENT
                              WASHINGTON 25, D. C., 10 February 1947

                                                              Section
TERRE HAUTE ORDNANCE DEPOT, TERRE HAUTE, INDIANA—Section V,
   WD General Orders 146, 1946, rescinded______________________________   I
BATTLE HONORS—Citation of unit____   II

   I..TERRE HAUTE ORDNANCE DEPOT, TERRE HAUTE, INDIANA.—Section V, WD General Orders 146, 1946, is rescinded.
   [AG 680.1 (26 Dec 46)]

   II..BATTLE HONORS.—As authorized by Executive Order 9396 (sec. I, WD Bul. 22, 1943), superseding Executive Order 9075 (sec. III, WD Bul. 11, 1942), the following unit is cited by the War Department under the provisions of section IV, WD Circular 333, 1943, in the name of the President of the United States as public evidence of deserved honor and distinction. The citation reads as follows:
   The 417th Regimental Combat Team, consisting of the 417th Infantry Regiment, 901st Field Artillery Battalion; Company C, 301st Engineer Combat Battalion; Company C, 301st Medical Battalion; and Company B, 160th Engineer Combat Battalion, is cited for outstanding performance of duty in action against the enemy from 7 to 12 February 1945 in the vicinity of Echternach, Luxembourg. Members of this combat team led an assault across the swollen Sauer River into one of the deepest portions of the Siegfried Line. The river was at flood stage, the current so swift that attempts by engineers to erect a footbridge proved futile, and the crossing had to be made in assault boats. The alerted enemy covered the area with heavy artillery, mortar, and machine-gun fire. Many of the boats were overturned before reaching the far shore and heavy casualties were suffered. Despite all difficulties, the major portion of the 1st Battalion, 417th Infantry Regiment, succeeded in making the crossing on the first night. Under heavy fire, members of this battalion scaled the muddy, steep, pillbox infested cliffs, whose every approach was heavily sown with mine fields, and succeeded in capturing the high wooded ground near the river bank. Two strong infantry counterattacks, supported by armor, were launched by the enemy, but both were repulsed after bitter encounters. Although this was the combat team's first engagement in combat, the 1st Battalion was the only unit in this vicinity to reach its objective on its initial assault and hold the ground gained. By similar aggressive action, the remainder of the 417th Infantry Regiment made the river crossing on the second and third nights and established contact with the initial force. The swiftly flowing river prevented supplies being crossed by boat and it became necessary to supply isolated groups by air. Despite violent enemy attempts to dislodge it, the combat team held tenaciously to the bridgehead it had wrested within the Siegfreid Line and secured a strong foothold, which facilitated the movement of other forces across the river and insured the success of an operation of major importance. In its initial appearance in combat and in the face of conditions which at times appeared prohibitive, the 417th Regimental Combat Team displayed outstanding heroism, determination, and an indomitable fighting spirit, which reflect great credit on all participants and are in keeping with the highest traditions of the armed forces of the United States.
   BY ORDER OF THE SECRETARY OF WAR:

OFFICIAL: DWIGHT D. EISENHOWER
   EDWARD F. WITSELL   Chief of Staff
   Major General
   The Adjutant General
AGO 1658B—Feb. 715118°—47

                              U. S. GOVERNMENT PRINTING OFFICE: 1947

417th Inf Regiment Presidential Unit Citation

Eisenhower never wrote about the crossings of the Sauer and Our Rivers in February 1945. Bradley wrote about the actions only to say that Patton's operations during that period were authorized by him, and he also noted that he and Eisenhower were both fully informed about what Patton's troops were doing. He later explained his attitude toward Patton during the crossing: "Too much limelight on Patton at this time could wound Monty's monumental ego, or, worse, again evoke charges from Monty that we were not going all out to help him."[530]

Perception and Motivation: The Patton Effect

General George Patton was one of the most complex commanders in World War II. I am not sure how I feel about Patton, but that is not an unusual stance to take on this complex man. To this day, he is loved by some and reviled by others. Roland Hartman, a member of the Third US Army, hated him. He slapped soldiers and made irresponsible statements to the press and others, but he also presided over some notable and decisive operations on the battlefields. He got things done. Is it fair, then, to claim Patton was responsible for the problems in crossing the Sauer and Our Rivers? Could he have anticipated or prevented some of the problems there?

Was the cost too high? Should the operations have been delayed? Who was this man, and how should he be remembered? It is hard not to respect Patton's achievements, but it is equally difficult to like the man. I have concluded that despite his flaws, he was dedicated to winning the war, and his achievements were important to the Allied victory. I think it best, at this point, to let the facts, experts, and biographers present their cases.

According to Eisenhower's plan for European operations, the entire Allied front would have to be on the west bank of the Rhine River before the Allies could move to cross the river and continue to advance eastward into Germany. All along the Allied front, the objective in February was to move towards the banks of the Rhine River in their zone. Patton was given the opportunity to continue in action by attacking a well-defended obstacle course which had to be tackled, and his army took on the challenge of the Siegfried Line.

Given the nature of his orders, Patton, Bradley, and Eisenhower knew Patton had until February 8th, the day the 21st British Army Group was set to begin action, to start his operation so that his underway operation could continue. It is also clear that there was at least a tacit agreement between Eisenhower and Bradley that this action could go forward. Both Eisenhower and Bradley were aware of Patton's aversion to standing still and his proclivity for continued activity, and neither appears to have stopped him. Bradley admitted that he and Eisenhower continued to monitor Patton's actions. Just keep it under the radar, perhaps, was the unstated order.

Many soldiers in Europe thought General Patton was a great general. Decades after the war ended, even those soldiers not under his command vividly remembered seeing him and considered it a memorable event. Norman Feitelson from the 11th Regiment said, "He was something to behold with his pearl handles, 45 pistols, his polished helmet, his shirt and tie, and the ETP Eisenhower jacket…. He took no nonsense."[531] Whether they heard one of his leadership speeches or came across him in the field, he was known for his foul language. Hank Sherr, from the First Army, remembered that every other word was a cuss word and mentioned the pearl handles, but he thought Patton was "terrific."[532]

His troops had mixed things to say about Patton. George Ketner, a medical technician in the 76th Division, did not think much of him and felt he was always showing off.[533] William Burrus, who joined the Third Army at Metz, remembered meeting Patton as he passed by him in a jeep. "He was a soldier's soldier. He was tough and he made damn sure you were tough." Arthur Staymates was in the 1st Infantry Division. He thought General Patton was "arrogant, self-loving, and only went to the front after the fight was over. He was an egomaniac."[534] After Patton slapped a soldier with battle fatigue, Stayates said, "The 1st Division had no love for him after that. Patton made a statement that he would rather lose 145 men than one tank. To the infantrymen in the 1st Infantry Division, that did not resonate well. That cinched the division's dislike for the general."[535] His troops also felt the pressure of Patton's insistence on constant action and battlefield strategies. Arthur Kramer said the spearhead formations Patton used with unprotected flanks cost extra lives.[536]

But his troops separated the man from his accomplishments. His troops remembered him for strict discipline and his visits to the troops. Engineers remembered Patton visiting them after the completion of bridges. He would commend them for their accomplishments and thank them for their efforts. Thomas Mano in the 5th Division called him "a tough character" but still preferred to serve under Patton.[537] Alan Moskin says that "Patton used to love to march with the enlisted men and he did it once with them. "He was tough on the officers." Moskin called him "a maverick."[538] Finally, Abraham Baum described the conflicted views of many: He did not wish to be related to Patton, but he respected him and his performance was outstanding. "When Patton gave an order, everyone listened. People did not like Patton's mentality."[539]

Most biographers of Patton describe him as one of the most complex generals in World War II. They generally describe him as an aggressive, ruthless and combative commander devoted to the study of warfare who believed in always being busy.[540] They recognized he was a flawed man. H. Essame, one of Patton's biographers, noted, "He had even less political sense than Montgomery."[541] Robert Allen, who served under Patton in the Third US Army, wrote that Patton had an "all-inclusive absorption in war coupled with his natural combativeness."[542] Patton's driver in Europe, Charles Codman, noted that Patton was "A real and literal enfant terrible—enfant…in his candor, intuitiveness, shrewdness, and unawareness; terrible in the intensity of his convictions, his self-discipline, and all the Spartan virtues."[543]

On a personal level, biographers noted Patton's deep religious faith, his responsibility to fight for his country, his traditional values, his ability to recite poetry and the Bible, and his all-consuming study of the history of warfare. Carlo D'Este, a biographer, wrote, "His old-fashioned virtues included the genuinely held belief that part of a citizen's responsibilities was to fight for his country when called on. To Patton, the "Duty, Honor, Country" of the West Point creed was a living thing."[544] Patton was elsewhere labelled as aloof and sometimes quick to anger, an image he worked to promote. General Eisenhower wrote to Marshall in August 1943 and alluded to Patton as having "unfortunate personal traits." He noted Patton's "habit of impulsive bawling out of subordinates, extending even to personal abuse of individuals, was noted in at least two specific cases...."[545] Eisenhower, however, believed that Patton suppressed these traits "because fundamentally he is so avid for recognition as a great military commander that he will ruthlessly suppress any habit of his own that will tend to jeopardize it." When faced with the possibility of removing Patton, Eisenhower recommended Patton remain because "he has qualities that we cannot afford to lose unless he ruins himself. So he can be classed as an army commander that you can use with certainty that the troops will not be stopped by ordinary obstacles."[546] "Very few of Patton's superiors liked him. All respected him professionally," wrote Allen.[547]

On the battlefield, Patton was resourceful when necessary. Patton reportedly detested immobility and defensive warfare and was very resourceful in response to allocation restrictions. He siphoned tanks to feed other vehicles,[548] repurposed German supplies and fuel found in the field, and developed a system called the "rock soup method" for supplies, which began by asking for water for soup and ended by asking for the remaining soup ingredients individually later. "In other words, in order to attack, we have first to pretend to reconnoiter and then reinforce the reconnaissance and then finally attack. It is a very sad method of making war."[549]

The Germans had a healthy respect for Patton. According to Harry Yeide, who wrote about Patton from the German perspective, the Germans were concerned about where Patton's army was located, but they tracked other Allied commanders as well.[550] Like the Germans, Patton subscribed to the concept of a speedy advance. Rundstedt considered him one of the best field commanders the Allies had. Rommel considered him a good tactician and called Patton's 1944 advance across Europe "the most astonishing achievement in mobile warfare." Kesselring recognized Patton's talent in tank warfare.[551] However, Yeide points out that the German army had many excellent commanders of tank warfare, many of whom had performed exceptionally well on the Eastern Front. The Allies only had a few who excelled with tank warfare and Patton lacked the ability for strategy that Montgomery had.[552] In the end, it was Patton's ability to conduct Panzer warfare that his peers respected.

Patton's relationship with his troops was complicated. "No commander ever dominated his command more effectively than Patton," Codman, his driver, wrote:

> "I have seen or heard of none, however, who can even remotely compare with General Patton in respect to his uncanny gift for sweeping men into doing things which they do not believe they are capable of doing, which they do not really want to do, which, in fact,

they would not do, unless directly exposed to the personality, the genius—call it what you will—of this unique soldier who not only knows his extraordinary job, but loves it. Here in France, as in Sicily, an entire army, from corps commander to rifleman, is galvanized into action by the dynamism of one man."[553]

Patton believed in strict adherence to discipline. He insisted troops wear heavy regulation clothing even in the heat of summer, and he would inspect the troops daily, even during a battle, to be sure that orders were carried out. Essame noted Patton was "kindly" toward those who had done well: "He was quick to praise where praise was due and quick to reward."[554] Those who were offenders saw "his irascibility was blistering and never forgotten."[555] Despite the strict discipline, Patton's troops generally believed him to be supportive, encouraging, and generally fair.

Patton appears to have infected troops with the spirit of teamwork and invincibility in battle. They believed in his loyalty to his men and aspired to be as courageous as he wanted them to be.[556] Martin Blumenson, who compiled Patton's letters, noted, "What endeared Patton to his men above all…was that he was fair and square."[557] Patton also expected his officers to be mindful of their troops. He, like Montgomery, believed that morale is the most important factor in war and emphasized to his officers their personal responsibility for their men.

Patton's relationship with his staff was also strong. Essame described Patton as "cordial and helpful, and he supported and trusted them. He often praised them. After he gave an order, he trusted them enough to leave them alone and rarely interfered with their work.[558] "He stood no nonsense from his subordinates: so far as he was concerned an order was an order and not a basis for discussion. … Nevertheless he had a happy headquarters."[559] During the Ardennes Offensive, Patton gave orders and let his staff do the rest: Farago believed that "So brilliant was the staff work backing him up that Patton was able to handle this enormously complex maneuver entirely by telephone…"[560]

When planning, Patton insisted on strict discipline and meticulous planning with an emphasis on unpredictability, speed and power. Allen, who served in the Third US Army, called Patton "ceaseless and meticulous" and also "deliberate and calculated."[561] He welcomed his commanders to participate in discussions on plans. His battle plans were described as "daring and unpredictable."[562] Codman, Patton's driver, wrote "Ninety per cent of the personal risks he takes are carefully calculated, from G.I. to divisional and corps commander."[563] His troops knew that "if the unexpected happens, he will find a solution…[564] Blumenson noted Patton "fused these combat arms- armor, motorized infantry, self-propelled artillery, and tactical air- into a fighting organization that fundamentally incorporated the mobility of the cavalry. Swift, surprising thrust and long, lightning strikes, reinforced and backed by power, became his battlefield trademark."[565] Essame noted Patton's "calculated audacity: better a good plan violently executed now than a perfect plan next week."[566]

Historians also wrote about Patton's legacy. Few of his biographers wrote about the crossing of the Sauer and Our Rivers by the Third US Army in February 1945. Essame noted that Bradley understood Patton well enough to know that Patton would not sit still and acknowledged that Eisenhower had given his tacit approval to the Eifel campaign.[567]

Several addressed his contributions to warfare, citing his appreciation of military history, his ability to use modern technology, and his attention to his troops. Codman wrote, "To him the concepts of duty, patriotism, fame, honor, glory are not mere abstractions, nor the shopworn ingredients of Memorial Day speeches. They are basic realities- self-evident, controlling."[568]

Others looked at Patton's legacy in terms of his battlefield planning and tactics. D'Este believed Patton should be remembered as a "trainer of troops" and for his tactical innovations and military writings."[569] Blumenson portrayed Patton's legacy as important for both his understanding of the soldiers and their weapons and equipment, how they could be best applied, and how he assessed a tactical situation. He noted Patton handled situations "like a fine surgeon's diagnostic perception and instant action."[570] And Essame recognized Patton for his ability to seize opportunities and optimally exploit them, how he ruthlessly went after opposition, and how he loved being unorthodox and unconventional. Patton, he said had "the will to win whatever the cost and, above all, in the shortest possible time."[571]

Others, however, were less forgiving of Patton's faults and his place in history. Farago believed that Patton's legacy is limited. He recognized him as "a skilled, imaginative and dynamic practitioner of his craft," who was "a complex and controversial man"[572] "who would always be remembered for slapping a soldier and then making up for it with conducting great battlefield campaigns."[573]

On a personal level, Roland always blamed Patton for the large number of casualties in the crossing of the Sauer and Our Rivers in February 1945. He believed the human cost was too high. He never stopped believing it was a suicide mission. The trauma of watching his own boat being destroyed by artillery fire and seeing so many fellow soldiers screaming and dying in the swirling waters of the river never really left him. He clearly remembered decades later reaching the German shore only to find two other men on the edge of the river and a deafening silence around him.

It is not unfair to consider whether Patton and his commanders could have anticipated or prevented some of the problems they encountered and whether they should have delayed the action. Patton and his generals knew about the terrain and Siegfried Line defenses from previous intelligence information, although the troops only learned how to clear a pillbox after making several attempts to actually take one. They also knew the condition of the rivers, but some have stated that they never encountered the level of difficulty they found during the February operations. Members of the 5th and 80th Divisions, who had already conducted river crossings in Europe, considered the Sauer and Our River crossings the most difficult river crossings they had experienced. Patton understood there would be problems but was certain they could meet the challenges. He knew there would be casualties, but he viewed it as a part of the war. However, he also chose to employ inexperienced soldiers- the 417th Regiment and the 76th Infantry Division- for this crossing. He was pragmatic about death and casualties in his speeches to the troops in 1944. "Death must not be feared. You are not all going to die.

Only two percent of you right here today would be killed in a major battle."[574]

While Patton may not have been responsible for the problems in crossing the Sauer and Our River, there have been assertions that he was reckless with his troops. Even when he was told to halt operations, such as in November 1944 when he was close to Metz, he continued to promote small probing attacks to keep his troops busy. His battlefield strategy was an aggressive defense. He was known for his strong belief in always remaining in action and continued pressure on the enemy. In the Luxembourg crossings in 1945, unfortunately, it is unclear whether he anticipated the degree of difficulty and number of casualties this operation encountered. He voiced concerns over the difficulties in the operation but also believed that his troops could prevail. However, as one after-action report noted, better planning, preparations, and test runs could have dealt with the dangers of this operation better. The troops were unprepared for the hazards of the river conditions, and the untested 417th Regiment sent hundreds of men over the river at the beginning without understanding these conditions, leading to many never making it to the other side of the raging river. The engineers only understood the level of difficulty in return trips during the action. More reconnaissance and test runs could have revealed these problems earlier.

To minimize the inevitable casualties, Patton tried to instill a feeling of teamwork, discipline, trust, strong training, and dedication to the cause and demanded his troops' best efforts. His battlefield philosophy was detailed in his letter of instruction #2, issued in April 1944 before the Normandy invasion and before he took control of the Third US Army. It was sent to the commanders of the corps, divisions, and other separate units soon to be under his control in the Third US Army. The letter outlined his principles for conduct in such areas of discipline, combat, training, leadership, and the use of weaponry and other firing equipment. In the area of discipline, Patton stated that "There is only one sort of discipline; perfect discipline." He instructed his officers to "assert themselves by example and by voice. They must be preeminent in courage, deportment, and dress." He believed that the purpose of strict discipline was to "produce alertness." It was important for commanders to set an example for their troops and to reinforce discipline by training, drills, and strictly enforcing rules because this would translate to better combat experiences for his men.[575]

With respect to tactical and combat rules, Patton also specified the overall guiding principle for his army: to use all means possible "to inflict the maximum amount of wounds, death, and destruction on the enemy in the minimum of time." He believed effective fire "reduces the effectiveness and volume of the enemy's fire, while rapidity of attack shortens the time of exposure." He suggested they "Hit hard soon…the idea being to develop your maximum force at once before the enemy can develop his." He noted that they should never yield ground to the enemy and mortars and artillery are "superb weapons, but "when silent, they are junk. See that they fire!" Tactically, Patton recorded rules for when and how to use various forms of artillery, mortar and other arms and discussed the importance of armor and reconnaissance. He defined how to fight in different types of terrain ("In mountain country secure the heights."), talked about the use of mines and wire and other battle tactics, and provided a guide for how officers should train and treat their troops… "An officer must be the last man to take shelter from fire, and the first to move forward." He concluded with, "The successful soldier wins his battles cheaply so far as his own casualties are concerned, but he must remember that violent attacks, although costly at the time, save lives in the end."[576]

Patton knew the operation to cross the Sauer and Our Rivers into the Siegfried Line would be difficult, and he believed in the probability of ultimate success. His training demanded each soldier make every effort to push forward. Patton believed his troops were prepared for battle and there was adequate planning for several days before the action began.

Sometimes, however, Patton did have a reputation for pushing his troops too hard.

In the end, despite the disaster of the first day of crossings, Patton's troops attacking the Siegfried Line learned from their problems, changed their approaches, and ultimately succeeded in moving the troops across the rivers in multiple locations, silencing the deadly German artillery, and disabling pillboxes and other obstacles on the Siegfried Line obstacle course. The Americans proved that the Siegfried Line could not stop their army, and perseverance worked. This was important because all Allied forces on the Western front were expected to advance to the Rhine River.

The persistence of the American troops forced the Germans to bring in additional troops from other conflicts, something Eisenhower hoped for in his multi-thrust, broad front strategy. Patton's Army did not give up the fight and outlasted the enemy. Roland never saw the objectives met and the meaning of this operation in the context of war. This was one of the multiple battles being fought along the broad Allied front to wear down the German opposition and force them to withdraw back into Germany.

The Brutality of the POW Experience

Roland Hartman never discussed his time as a prisoner of war. My grandmother gave me his medals when I was a teenager. Family members knew only a few facts regarding his military service. Stalag IX-B is often described as the worst POW camp in the German System. I am not surprised my father refused to talk about his POW experience.

A final report of POW camps was issued in November 1945, which noted that, "The personal impression which one gets from an inspection tour of these camps cannot be described. One discovers distress and famine in their most terrible forms...."[577] The report further noted, "The MCC considered it fortunate in light of the exposure, starvation and lack of medical facilities, that more PW did not die."[578]

This treatment by the Germans is a stark contrast to how the United States treated the German POWs captured in Europe. The Americans transported via their Liberty ships as many as 400,000 of their prisoners to the United States and kept them in over 500 camps around the country.[579] They were housed and fed according to the rules of the Geneva Convention. Their living quarters were close to the size of living quarters for American military buildings, and they ate rations comparable to the American soldiers, including some meat portions. They also received clothing, cigarettes, and beer rations. They were allowed to send and receive mail from their families in Germany and had access to libraries with books and newspapers, art supplies, and musical instruments. For entertainment, there were theatrical performances and cinema. There was also an education program.[580]

The German prisoners worked on farms, in canneries, and in factories with low-security risk. For security purposes, the camps were located away from urban and industrial locations in mostly rural parts of the country. As directed by the Geneva Convention, they were paid a small wage to be used at the local canteen for their efforts. They never took a job away from a local citizen; they only took jobs that were vacant, thereby alleviating part of the labor shortage on farms and in factories.[581] In accordance with the Geneva Convention, German officers were not forced to work.

There was some interaction with local Americans, and they generally were accepted by the local people around them. Due to a labor shortage in the United States, many of the German POWs continued to work after the war was over and did not return home until 1946.

It is clear that German POWs in American camps were fed and clothed appropriately under the guidelines of the Geneva Conventions, unlike American POWs in German camps. I found anecdotal evidence that some Germans even immigrated to the United States after the war was over.[582]

Summation - My Conclusions

417th Regiment Memorial in Luxembourg today

Many books have been written on World War II. Some are about the history of the war, some concentrate on specific battles and events or are about specific units or troops, and others are about specific people or leaders. Each attempts to demonstrate the courage, the brilliance, and the stories of that time. It allows us to not forget. However, understanding just one part of the war without understanding the context and impact of each person, action, or decision is often missing. For those who went through the war as participants and their families, there are often questions of how and why did a particular action happen and what does it mean. The crossing of the Sauer and Our Rivers in February 1945, with the obstacles presented and casualties involved, was no different for the men involved in that operation, and it was very personal to them. They may have come home with their stories, but what did it all mean?

Roland Hartman of the 417th Regiment crossed over the Sauer River on his nineteenth birthday in one of the first waves of troops crossing the river on February 7th. Not long after his arrival in Germany, he was captured and spent the remainder of his time in Europe as a prisoner of war. It is not difficult to locate his name in the enrollment records at the National Archives. The record of his POW status can be found in handwritten books recording the prisoners of war in Europe at the National Archives and in the barracks listing for Stalag IX-B where there is an entry in the official records of the prisoners of wars for "Hartman R." His German identification number was 27608. Roland barely spoke about his military action and refused to discuss his prisoner-of-war experience. It took decades to get to the point where something was said. He never told us why he earned a Silver Star, although he mentioned that he disabled a pillbox before being captured. He believed that his treatment was no worse than that of other captured soldiers. Fortunately, he arrived in February 1945, and the war was over in Europe a few months later.[583]

Not long after his capture, he was reported dead, probably because everyone else in his boat died from artillery fire, and several partial listings of POWs at Stalag IX-B did not have his name on them. He was discovered alive only after the camp was liberated at the beginning of April. Surprised to see him, the people processing the newly liberated soldiers told him that 1,100 troops died on the first night of operations trying to cross the Sauer River into Germany. This number probably relates to the XII US Corps and not the 417th Infantry Regiment. He later claimed there were between 11 to 22 found alive after the crossing, and this is probably a viable estimate for his regiment. Roy Martin thought the number of survivors was 16. For Roland, this meant numerous casualties, and it was personal since he was the one who witnessed these losses. He struggled with these numbers well passed the end of the war. Roland never saw the value in that attempt to cross the river that night, and he continued to hate General George Patton for the February action. He never did see the big picture of the war. It was too personal for him.

Many of the men who survived their individual battle and POW experiences returned home, resumed their lives, and tried to leave the war behind them. For some, the nightmares continued for years. There were little personal stories they could tell, but many of these men did not discuss what they saw and experienced until decades after the end of the war. For many, beginning to talk about their experiences was when the healing began.

It was writing this book chronicling the horrors of the POW experience that gave me a deeper understanding of what my father endured. I am grateful he shared some of his story with me. However, there are still two mysteries I have yet to solve, one being why he received the Silver Star. Recently, I discovered that he should have had an Oak Leaf Cluster attached to his ribbon as he was awarded two Purple Hearts. He also did not have anything related to the Presidential Unit Citation. The other mystery was his initial journey as a POW, which may have taken him to Dietz Castle in addition to another camp instead of the more conventional route of a brief stop for processing at a transit camp. I understand that some of his memories were too difficult to discuss, and perhaps some things are better left in the past. Nevertheless, I still look for general orders for the army during and after World War II, which could provide the answer to why he received his Silver Star.

As the daughter of a soldier in Patton's Third Army, I view my father's service as part of a military unit that successfully forced a crossing over a raging river and then proved that even the extensive defensive system known as the Siegfried Line could be shattered. The cost was high for many men involved, including my father, but their heroic effort paid off.

Strategically, I believe the crossings were necessary as the operation was part of a coordinated, broad-front operation that would take the XII US Corps to Irrel, Trier, Bitburg, and ultimately the west bank of the Rhine River in early March, where they joined other British and American troops along the Allied front. The whole Allied front participated in this action at some point during February and March of that year.

As for George Patton, I find him to be a man of contradictions: a personally flawed individual with the ability to succeed on the battlefield. It is hard for me to totally admire or hate him, and I am not sure how easy it would have been to win the war in Europe without him. Eisenhower's decision not to fire Patton must have been exceedingly difficult to make.

Everyone has their stories. For my father, there was the story of the watch that was taken from him by the German soldiers upon his capture and was retaken by American troops when they captured the German soldier who took it several days later. Somehow, that watch made its way back to Chicago and was returned to my father in New York after the war.

According to family lore, Joe Dunninger - a well-known mentalist and entertainer at that time and a family friend- gave my grandfather an envelope with three dates in it when my father went to war. The first date was my father's nineteenth birthday and was the day my father was captured by the Germans in World War II. The second date was the date Roland was reported dead to my grandfather. But there was a third date listed, which is why my grandfather never told my grandmother that their son was dead. The third date was the date my father came home. Several family members told me this story, and my father verified it. I met Dunninger and saw his performance live, and I never could figure out how he did what he did with an audience he did not know.

Sauer River near Echternach today

In 2015, I visited Luxembourg along the Sauer and Our Rivers and saw a small river meander through a beautiful country scene. I found monuments to the 417th Regiment, the 5th Infantry Division, and the 80th Infantry Division at the approximate crossing sites. If you know where to go over the rivers and over hills and into the forested areas of Germany, you can view the remnants of the pillboxes, trenches, and machine gun nests of the Siegfried Line. Now, most people visit that region for scenic views and hiking instead. You can easily walk from one side of the Sauer River to the other side without even knowing you are moving between different countries. To visit the high plateaus of Biesdorf, Germany, is to see miles of countryside and rolling hills with small towns. It is a beautiful sight. Patton is buried in the American Cemetery in Luxembourg, several miles away. It is hard to imagine that this was once the scene of fierce war.

Appendix A

Military Organization in World War II

The military organization in Europe during World War II consisted of Army, Air Force, and some Navy personnel. In February 1945, The Supreme Headquarters Allied Expeditionary Forces (SHAEF) was commanded by General Dwight D. Eisenhower of the United States; Air Chief Marshal Sir Arthur Tedder of Great Britain served as the Deputy Supreme Allied Commander. Along with the three active army groups in Europe under SHAEF, there were the First Allied Airborne Army and three air force formations under the SHAEF umbrella.

An army group could have 600,000 or more personnel, depending on the number of units within it. The three Army groups in Europe incorporated eight field armies. The Fifteenth US Army, however, was primarily for training and reorganizing units in the Twelfth US Army Group and did not become active in combat until the last few months of the war. Armies were composed of corps, which were composed of divisions. Corps and divisions (with all their units attached) could be detached and reassigned to other units as needed. This would happen for a variety of reasons, including to add strength to a particular action due to changes in the borders between sectors (adjust the border, but leave units in the place assigned to a new parent unit) or to replace a unit that had become inactive for a time or on reserve for future action. By February, there were over twenty corps operating in Europe (one of which was an airborne corps) containing approximately 73 divisions. Within a division, there were regiments that contained battalions that were further divided into companies. All these organizational units had within them administrative and support groups, including medical, engineering, artillery, armored groups, intelligence, planners, and other support personnel.

During World War II, the United States Army defined and standardized the size and organization of these units. The approximate number of personnel in each American unit during the war was:

Military unit	**Approximate number of personnel**
Army Group	600,000 or more, depending on field armies
Field Army	300,000, depending on the number of corps
Corps	75,000, depending on number of divisions
Infantry Division	approximately 15,000
Infantry Regiment	approximately 3300
Battalion	Approximately 900
Company	180-200
Platoon	50
Squad	12

The Twelfth US Army Group, at the beginning of February, had two field armies, the First and Third US Armies, each with approximately 300,000 troops. The Third Army had four corps, and the First US Army had three corps at the beginning of February, but the III US Corps (commanded by Major General John Milliken), which had been part of the Third US Army in January, was reassigned to the First US Army on February 10th.

There was versatility in the makeup of divisions and corps. The composition of each corps might vary, for there were various types of divisions, such as infantry divisions and airborne divisions, as well as armored, cavalry, and mountain divisions. Each type was useful for different types of battles. For example, crossing the Sauer and Our Rivers required infantrymen. Once across, armored divisions were helpful on the battlefield. In addition, there were supporting units within the divisions and regiments. For example, there were engineer battalions composed of approximately 660 men, artillery divisions with 2,200 men, medical battalions with 465 men, and rifle companies with 190 men. In February 1945, the organization of the Allied armies was as follows:

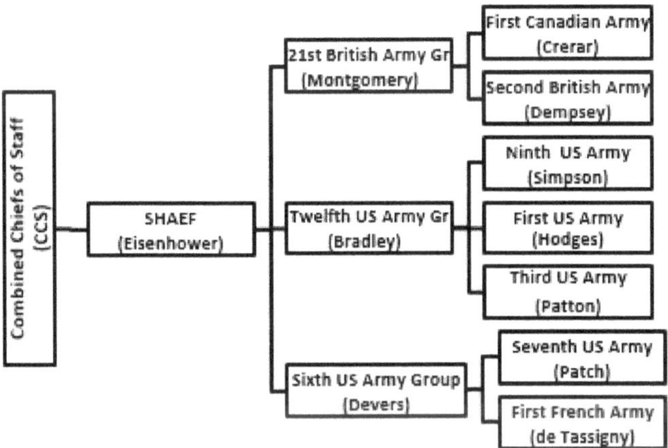

In many ways, divisions were a basic unit. Divisions were independent units that could be reassigned to other corps when additional manpower was needed, and it was the smallest unit that could organize and plan its own operations. Below that level, regiments might be temporarily loaned to another division, but they generally remained with their division through the war. This is what happened to the 417th Regiment when it was attached to the 5th Infantry Division for a few days in February 1945. The parent unit of the 417th Regiment, the 76th Infantry Division, was reassigned several times to different corps during 1945 and ended the war in the VIII US Corps, which was then a part of the First US Army.

At the beginning of February, the Third US Army, part of the Twelfth US Army Group, contained three army corps: the

VIII US Corps under Major General Troy Middleton to the north, the XII US Corps under Major General Manton Eddy in the center and the XX US Corps under Major General Walton Walker on the southern flank. A fourth corps, the III US Corps under Major General John Millikin, was reassigned from the Third US Army to First US Army at the beginning of February.

In the XII US Corps, Major General Eddy's division commanders were Major General Horace McBride for the 80th Infantry Division, Maj General S. Leroy Irwin for the 5th Infantry Division, and Major General William Schmidt for the 76th Infantry Division. The 80th Division included the 305th Engineer Combat Battalion, the 305th Medical Battalion, and the 80th Division Artillery. Part of the 4th Armored Division was also working in support of them. The 5th Infantry Division included the 5th Division Artillery, the 7th Engineer Combat Battalion, and the 5th Medical Battalion. Also attached to the 76th Division were the 76th Division Artillery, 301st Engineer Battalion, and the 301st Medical Battalion. Various cavalry, chemical tank destroyer, armored, and other units could also be assigned to these divisions for specific operations.

The organization of the Third US Army in February, excluding the III US Corps, which was reassigned to another army on February 10th, included the following:

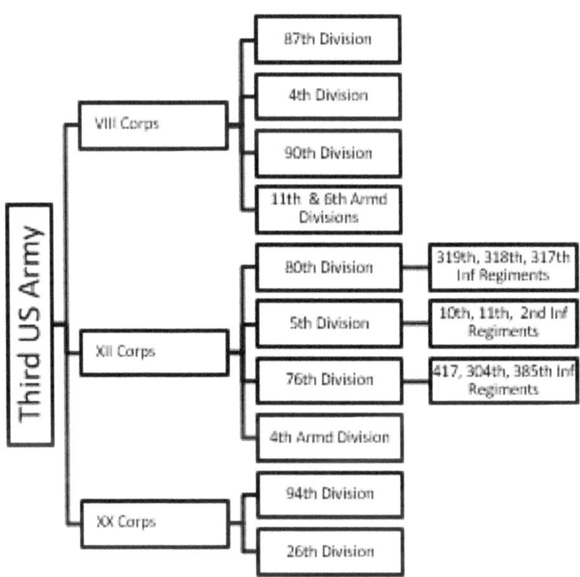

Third US Army
VIII Corps
87th Division
4th Division
90th Division
11th & 6th Armd Divisions
XII Corps
80th Division
319th, 318th, 317th Inf Regiments
5th Division
10th, 11th, 2nd Inf Regiments
76th Division
417, 304th, 385th Inf Regiments
4th Armd Division
XX Corps
94th Division
26th Division

Endnotes

1. On the back of the Silver Star awarded to Roland D. Hartman.

2. Website for the 76th Infantry Division. Online at http://76thdivision.com/417/history_417.html.

3.Roland Hartman, private interview. Unpublished.

4. Roland Hartman, private interview.

5. Deborah Dash Moore. *GI Jews How World War II Changed a Generation*. (Cambridge, Ma: Belknap Press of Harvard University Press, 2004), 83.

6. Handwritten History of the 1st Battalion, 417th Regiment. Department of the Army, United States War College and Carlisle Barracks.

7. Roland Hartman, private interview.

8. Handwritten History of the 1st Battalion, 417th Regiment. Department of the Army, United States War College and Carlisle Barracks.

9. Roland Hartman, private interview.

10. Roland Hartman, private interview.

11. Roland Hartman, private writings. Unpublished.

12. Roland Hartman, private interview.

13. Roland Hartman, private writings.

14. Roland Hartman, private writings.

15. Roland Hartman, private interview.

16. Roland Hartman, private writings.

17. Roland Hartman, private interview.

18. Roland Hartman, private interview.

19. Roland Hartman, private interview.

20. Central Intelligence Agency. *The World Factbook*. Online at https://www.cia.gov/library/publications/the-world-factbook/ [accessed December 31, 2020].

21. Roland Gaul. *The Battle of the Bulge in Luxembourg, The Southern Flank December 1944- January 1945, Volume II: The Americans.* (Atglen, PA: Schiffer Military/Aviation History, 1995), 311.

22. Martin Blumenson and George S. Patton. *The Patton Papers.* (Boston: Houghton Mifflin, 1973), 615.

23. The Far, Far Side" by Harold J "Lindy" Lindberg, Chapter 7 (Through the Siegfried Line)

http://76thdivision.com/indexlindy.html

24. The Far, Far Side" by Harold J "Lindy" Lindberg, Chapter 7 (Through the Siegfried Line)

http://76thdivision.com/indexlindy.html

25. Headquarters, Third US Army, APO 403, Operational Directive, January 26, 1945.

26. Eisenhower, Dwight D. Report by the Supreme Commander to the Combined Chiefs of Staff on the Operations in Europe of the Allied Expeditionary Force, 6 June 1944 to 8 May 1945. Washington: Govt. print. off., 1946. p82-85.

27. Chandler, Alfred D. Jr. Ed. *The Papers of Dwight David Eisenhower: The War Years* Vol. 4. Baltimore: Johns Hopkins University Press, 1970. P2465.

28. United States Army, 417th Inf Regt. Journal, February 45. Source: none listed. RG 407, NARA, College Park, MD. p258.

29. Bradley, Omar N. *A Soldier's Story.* New York: Henry Holt and Company, 1951, p494.

30. George S. (George Smith) Patton, Paul D. Harkins, and Beatrice Ayer Patton, *War as I Knew It.* (Boston: Houghton Mifflin Co.), 1947. 209.

31. Blumenson,*The Patton Papers,* 632.

32. Smith Greenwood. *Normandy to Victory: The War Diary of General Courtney H. Hodges and the First U. S. Army.* (Lexington: University Press of Kentucky, 2008), 277-283 AND Mary H. Williams (Compiled). *United States Army in World War II, Special Studies, Chronology, 1941-1945. (Washington, D.C.: Office of the Chief of Military History, United States Army, 1960),* Jan 29-31.

33. Greenwood, *Normandy to Victory,* 288. And Williams, *Chronology.* And United States Army, First US Army. 1st Army operations. RG 407, NARA, College Park, MD. p44.

34. United States Army, VIII Corps. After Action Report: "Report of the VIII Corps After Action against Enemy Forces in Belgium Luxembourg and Germany, For the Period---- 1-28 February 1945.". Source: Headquarters VIII Corps. RG 407, NARA, College Park, MD. pg 3.

35. United States Army, VIII Corps. After Action Report. RG 407, NARA, College Park, MD. pg 3

36. United States Army, 1st Bn, 319th Inf Regt. After Action Report: "Crossing the Sauer River" 7-28 Feb 1945. Source: Maj Arthur H Clark. 1 RG 407, NARA, College Park, MD. 1.

37. United States Army, 2n Bn, 319th Inf Regt. After Action Report: "Attack across Our River into Siegfried Line" 7-28 Feb 1945. Source: Lt col Paul Bandy, Capt John Leake Jr, and Capt Thomas C. Mason.. RG 407, NARA, College Park, MD. 3.

38. United States Army, After Action Report: "The Crossing of the Sauer River, 7 February, 1945, BY F Co, 318TH Infantry Regt." RG 407, NARA, College Park, MD. 1.

39. Joseph J Hutnik, *We Ripened Fast: The Unofficial History of the Seventy-Sixth Infantry Division.* (Frankfurt: Otto Lembeck, 1946), 61.

40. United States Army, 318th Regiment. After Action Report: "The Crossing of the Sauer River, 7 February, 1945, BY F Co, 318TH Infantry Regt.," RG 407, NARA, College Park, MD 1-2.

41. United States Army., 318th Regiment. After Action Report. "February 1945". RG 407, NARA, College Park, MD. 2.

42. United States Army, 2n Bn, 319th Inf Regt. After Action Report: "Crossing of the Our River by F Company, 2nd Bn, 319th Inf Regt" 7 Feb 1945." Source: not given. RG 407, NARA, College Park, MD. p 1

43. U.S. Army, 2nd Bn, 319th Inf Regt. After Action Report: "Attack across Our River into Siegfried Line" 7-28 Feb 1945. Source: Lt Col Paul Bandy, et al. P2

44. U.S. Army, 2n Bn, 319th Inf Regt. After Action Report: "Crossing of the Our River by F Company, 2nd Bn, 319th Inf Regt" 7 Feb 1945." Source: not given. p2

45. United States Army, 10th Inf Regt. After Action Report: "Sauer River Crossing" 7-15 Feb 1945. Source: Lt Col William Breckinridge. RG 407, NARA, College Park, MD. p2

46. United States Army, 11th Inf Regt. After Action Report: "Crossing of the Sauer River" 6-17 Feb 1945. Source: Major Coghill. RG 407, NARA, College Park, MD. p1

47. United States Army, 11th Inf Regt. History: "Breaching of the Siegfried Line by the 11th Infantry" 1-18 Feb 1945. Source: none listed. RG 407, NARA, College Park, MD.

48. United States Army, 11th Inf Regt. History. RG 407, NARA, College Park, MD. p56

49. United States Army, 1st Bn, 417th Inf Regt. After Action Report: "Crossing of the Sauer River" 5-12 Feb 45. Source: Lt Col Clarence A Mette, Jr. RG 407, NARA, College Park, MD. p2.

50. United States Army, 417th Inf Regt. After Action Report: "Crossing of the Sauer River vicinity Echternach" -17 Feb 45. Source: Lt. Col R. D. Boerem. RG 407, NARA, College Park, MD. p2

51. United States Army, 1st Bn, 417th Inf Regt. After Action Report: "Crossing of the Sauer River" 5-12 Feb 45. Source: Capt Homer O. Schmidt. RG 407, NARA, College Park, MD. p2.

52. U.S. Army, 1st Bn, 417th Inf Regt. After Action Report: "Crossing of the Sauer River, 1st Bn, 417th INF REGT, 7 – 8 February 1945," p1.

53. U.S. Army, 80th Infantry Division. After Action Report- G2. February 1945 RG 407, NARA, College Park, MD p2.

54. States Army, 80th Infantry Division. History of the 80th Infantry Division. February 1945. RG 407, NARA, College Park, MD. p2.

55. United States Army, 166th Engineer Bn. After Action Report: "Crossing of the Sauer River at Dillingen, Luxembourg History." 5-12 February 1945.Source: Capt Dale S. Wallace. RG 407, NARA, College Park, MD. p 1.

56. Third Army AAR, pg 254

57. U.S. Army, 80th Infantry Division. After Action Report: G3. RG 407, NARA, College Park, MD. p2.

58. U.S. Army, 318th Regiment. After Action Report: "The Crossing of the Sauer River, 7 February, 1945, BY F Co, 318TH Infantry Regt." p1-2.

59. U.S. Army, 2nd Bn, 319th Inf Regt. After Action Report: "Attack across Our River into Siegfried Line" 7-28 Feb 1945. Source: Lt Col Paul Bandy, et al. p1.

60. U.S. Army, 318th Regiment. After Action Report: "The Crossing of the Sauer River, 7 February, 1945, BY F Co, 318TH Infantry Regt.," p1

61. Dwight D. Eisenhower, Crusade in Europe. (Garden City, NY: Doubleday and Co., 1948. and New York: Da Capo Paperback, 1983). 325-6.

62. Blumenson, *The Patton Papers,* 586.

63. Blumenson, *The Patton Papers,* 588.

64. Blumenson, *The Patton Papers,* 166.

65. Blumenson, *The Patton Papers,* 615.

66. Eisenhower, *Crusade in Europe,* 321.

67. Blumenson, *The Patton Papers,* 626.

68. Blumenson, *The Patton Papers,* 626.

69. Blumenson, *The Patton Papers,* 630.

70. U.S. Army, 2n Bn, 417th Inf Regt. After Action Report: "Crossing of the Sauer River, 1st Bn, 417th Inf Regt" 7-8 February 1945. Source: none listed. p1.

71. U.S. Army, 2n Bn, 417th Inf Regt. After Action Report: "Crossing of the Sauer River, 1st Bn, 417th Inf Regt" 7-8 February 1945. Source: none listed. p1.

72. U.S. Army, 1st Bn, 417th Inf Regt. After Action Report: "Crossing of the Sauer River" 5-12 Feb 45. Source: Lt Col Clarence A Mette, Jr. p3.

73. Adkins, A.Z. Jr and Andrew Z Adkins, III. You Can't Get Much Closer Than This: Combat with Company H, 317th Infantry Regiment, 80th Division. Havertown, PA: Casemate, 2005. P 50.

74. Neil Short, *Germany's West Wall: The Siegfried Line.* (Oxford: Osprey, 2004), 25.

75. Charles Robert Harmon Collection (AFC/2001/001/64278), Veterans History Project, American Folklife Center, Library of Congress. approx. 30:12. Online at: https://memory.loc.gov/diglib/vhp/bib/loc.natlib.afc2001001.64278

76. Stephen E.Ambrose, *Citizen Soldiers: the U.S. Army from the Normandy Beaches to the Bulge to the Surrender of Germany,* June 7, 1944-May 7, 1945. (New York, NY: Simon & Schuster, 1997), 144. And Adkins, *You Can't Get Much Closer than This,* 116.

77. Engineer soldier's handbook.: Basic field manual ; FM 21-105, 1943. United States. War Department. June 2, 1943. United States. War Department. Engineer soldier's handbook., book, June 2, 1943; Washington D.C.. (https://digital.library.unt.edu/ark:/67531/metadc28313/: accessed June 2, 2021), University of North Texas Libraries, UNT Digital Library,

https://digital.library.unt.edu; crediting UNT Libraries Government Documents Department.

78. Willard J. Chapman Collection (AFC/2001/001/05767), Veterans History Project, American Folklife Center, Library of Congress. 282nd Engineers Combat Bn, Sergeant. Approx 15:00-17:00. Online at: https://memory.loc.gov/diglib/vhp/bib/loc.natlib.afc2001001.5767

79. Thomas G. Manos Collection (AFC/2001/001/94110), Veterans History Project, American Folklife Center, Library of Congress, 104th Engineers Bn, 44th Div; co B, 7th engineer Bn, 5th Div most of war - Lt colonel. Approx 36:30. Online at: https://memory.loc.gov/diglib/vhp/bib/loc.natlib.afc2001001.94110

80. James Powell Carr Collection

(AFC/2001/001/82781), Veterans History Project, American Folklife Center, Library of Congress, 248th Combat Engr Bn, Corporal, approx. 16:00 to 19:00 Online at: https://memory.loc.gov/diglib/vhp/bib/loc.natlib.afc2001001.82781

81. John Snurhowski Collection (AFC/2001/001/43387), Veterans History Project, American Folklife Center, Library of Congress 118 Medical Reg, 17th Airborne -Sergeant. Approx 8:06. Online at: https://memory.loc.gov/diglib/vhp/bib/loc.natlib.afc2001001.43387

82. Stephen E. Ambrose, *Band of Brothers: E Company, 506th Regiment, 101st Airborne from Normandy to Hitler's Eagle's Nest.* (New York, NY: Simon & Schuster, 2001), 181.

83. A.Z. Adkins, Jr. and Andrew Z. Adkins, III. *You Can't Get Much Closer Than This: Combat with Company H. 317th Infantry Regiment, 80th Division.*)Havertown, PA: Casemate, 2005), 139.

84. Marvin C. Kruse Collection (AFC/2001/001/68995), Veterans History Project, American Folklife Center, Library of Congress109th Reg, 28th Div - Technical Sergeant, combat Medic. Approx 2:00-2:10 Online at: https://memory.loc.gov/diglib/vhp/bib/loc.natlib.afc2001001.68995

85. Ben Joseph Antonio Collection (AFC/2001/001/76878), Veterans History Project, American Folklife Center, Library of Congress. approx17:20 to approx16:40 to 18:20Online at: https://memory.loc.gov/diglib/vhp/bib/loc.natlib.afc2001001.76878

86. Ben Joseph Antonio Collection (AFC/2001/001/76878), Veterans History Project, American Folklife

Center, Library of Congress. approx17:20 to 18:30to 18:30. Online at:
https://memory.loc.gov/diglib/vhp/bib/loc.natlib.afc2001001.76878

87. Marvin C. Kruse Collection
(AFC/2001/001/68995), Veterans History Project, American Folklife
Center, Library of Congress109th Reg, 28th Div - Technical Sergeant,
combat Medic. Approx 2:00-2:10 Online at:
https://memory.loc.gov/diglib/vhp/bib/loc.natlib.afc2001001.68995

88. NY times, Feb 10 "Rampaging Rivers Hold up Third Army" p3

89. Jessee G. Dye Collection
(AFC/2001/001/59002), Veterans History Project, American Folklife
Center, Library of Congress. approx. 18:20. Online at:
https://memory.loc.gov/diglib/vhp/bib/loc.natlib.afc2001001.59002

90. Carl Roland Hatfield Collection
(AFC/2001/001/31030), Veterans History Project, American Folklife
Center, Library of Congress. Online at:
https://memory.loc.gov/diglib/vhp/bib/loc.natlib.afc2001001.31030

91. Ben Joseph Antonio Collection
(AFC/2001/001/76878), Veterans History Project, American Folklife
Center, Library of Congress. approx. 20:40. Online at:
https://memory.loc.gov/diglib/vhp/bib/loc.natlib.afc2001001.76878

92. Alexander Ludeke, *Weapons of World War II*, (Bath: Parragon Books,
2007), 36.

93. Ludeke, Weapons of World War II. 37.

94. United States Army, VIII Corps. G-3 Journal File 1-17 Feb 45.
Source: none. RG 407, NARA, College Park, MD. and (Victory, pg 293-4
) and 314th Field Battalion

95. U.S. Army, 1st Bn, 417th Inf Regt. After Action Report: "Crossing of
the Sauer River" 5-12 Feb 45. Source: Lt Col Clarence A Mette, Jr. p2

96. United States Army, 1st Bn, 417th Inf Regt. After Action Report:
"Crossing of the Sauer River, 1st Bn, 417th Inf Regt" 7-8 February 1945.
Source: none listed. RG 407, NARA, College Park, MD. p 1-2

97. U.S. Army, 1st Bn, 417th Inf Regt. After Action Report: "Crossing of
the Sauer River, 1st Bn, 417th Inf Regt" 7-8 February 1945. Source: none
listed. p2.

98. U.S. Army, 1st Bn, 417th Inf Regt. After Action Report: "Crossing of
the Sauer River" 5-12 Feb 45. Source: Lt Col Clarence A Mette, Jr. p3

99. Jackson, 2

100. Hutnik, We Ripened Fast, 77-78.

101. Hutnik, We Ripened Fast, 77-78.

102. Richard Scott, (54:47) WW2 Museum oral history

103. Kinglsey Roberts Jr. (AFC/2001/001/15190), Veterans History Project, American Folklife Center, Library of Congress https://memory.loc.gov/diglib/vhp/bib/loc.natlib.afc2001001.15190

104. Michael J. Debacker Collection (AFC/2001/001/76328), Veterans History Project, American Folklife Center, Library of Congress. Approx. 11:15 Online at: https://www.loc.gov/item/afc2001001.76328 [accessed June 2, 2021]

105. Pollack, Al, Special Contributor. "In his own words: A Levittown WWII vet's remembrance." Burlington County Times, June 6, 2014.

106. Roy Martin. Private interview.

107. U.S. Army, 1st Bn, 417th Inf Regt. After Action Report: "Crossing of the Sauer River" 5-12 Feb 45. Source: Lt Col Clarence A Mette, Jr. p3.

108. U.S. Army, 1st Bn, 417th Inf Regt. After Action Report: "Crossing of the Sauer River, 1st Bn, 417th Inf Regt" 7-8 February 1945. Source: none listed. p2.

109. U.S. Army, 1st Bn, 417th Inf Regt. After Action Report: "Crossing of the Sauer River" 5-12 Feb 45. Source: Lt Col Clarence A Mette, Jr. p3 AND 417th IR Journal, 2/7

110. U.S. Army, 417th Inf Regt. Journal, February 7 45. Source: none listed.

111. U.S. Army, 417th Inf Regt. After Action Report: "Crossing of the Sauer River vicinity Echternach." 17 Feb 45. Source: Lt. Col R. D. Boerem. p 3-4.

112. U.S. Army, 417th Inf Regt. After Action Report: "Crossing of the Sauer River vicinity Echternach." 17 Feb 45. Source: Lt. Col R. D. Boerem. p3.

113. U.S. Army, 1st Bn, 417th Inf Regt. After Action Report: "Crossing of the Sauer River, 1st Bn, 417th Inf Regt" 7-8 February 1945. Source: none listed. p 2.

114. U.S. Army, 1st Bn, 417th Inf Regt. After Action Report: "Crossing of the Sauer River, 1st Bn, 417th Inf Regt" 7-8 February 1945. Source: none listed. p3.

115. U.S. Army, 1ˢᵗ Bn, 417th Inf Regt. After Action Report: "Crossing of the Sauer River, 1st Bn, 417th Inf Regt" 7-8 February 1945. Source: none listed. p3.

116. U.S. Army, 1st Bn, 417th Inf Regt. After Action Report: "Crossing of the Sauer River" 5-12 Feb 45. Source: Lt Col Clarence A Mette, Jr. p4.

117. U.S. Army, 1ˢᵗ Bn, 417th Inf Regt. After Action Report: "Crossing of the Sauer River, 1st Bn, 417th Inf Regt" 7-8 February 1945. Source: none listed. p3.

118. Schmidt, 2

119. U.S. Army, 1ˢᵗ Bn, 417th Inf Regt. After Action Report: "Crossing of the Sauer River, 1st Bn, 417th Inf Regt" 7-8 February 1945. Source: none listed. p3.

120. United States Army, 10ᵗʰ Inf Regt. 10ᵗʰ Infantry Journal. 7 Feb 1945. RG 407, NARA, College Park, MD. AND 121. Breckinridge, 1-2

122. U.S. Army, 10th Inf Regt. After Action Report: "Sauer River Crossing" 7-15 Feb 1945. Source: Lt Col William Breckinridge, p3.

123. U.S. Army, 10th Inf Regt. After Action Report: "Sauer River Crossing" 7-15 Feb 1945. Source: Lt Col William Breckinridge, p3.

124. U.S. Army, 10th Inf Regt. 10th Infantry Journal. 7 Feb 1945.

125. Currivan, Gene. *"American in Assault Boats Beat Torrents and Nazi Fire. February 8, 1945."*

126. U.S. Army, 10th Inf Regt. 10th Infantry Journal. 7 Feb 1945.

127. U.S. Army, 10th Inf Regt. 10th Infantry Journal. 7 Feb 1945.

128. U.S. Army, 10th Inf Regt. 10th Infantry Journal. 7 Feb 1945.

129. U.S. Army, 10th Inf Regt. 10th Infantry Journal. 8 Feb 1945.

130. United States Army, 2nd Bn, 11th Inf Regt. After Action Report: "Sauer River Crossing" 7-18 Feb 1945. Source: Capt W B Wood. RG 407, NARA, College Park, MD. p1.

131. U.S. Army, 2nd Bn, 11th Inf Regt. After Action Report: "Sauer River Crossing" 7-18 Feb 1945. Source: Capt W B Wood. 1ˢᵗ. p1.

132. United States Army, 1st Bn, 11th Inf Regt. After Action Report: "Crossing of the Sauer River" 3-14 Feb 1945. Source: Capt Robert H Williams. RG 407, NARA, College Park, MD. p3. And U.S. Army, 11th Inf Regt. History: "Breaching of the Siegfried Line by the 11th Infantry" 1-18 Feb 1945. Source: none listed. p57.

133. U.S. Army, 11th Inf Regt. History: "Breaching of the Siegfried Line by the 11th Infantry" 1-18 Feb 1945. Source: none listed. 1st. p57.

134. U.S. Army, 1st Bn, 11th Inf Regt. After Action Report: "Crossing of the Sauer River" 3-14 Feb 1945. Source: Capt Robert H Williams. 1st p2.

135. U.S. Army, 11th Inf Regt. History: "Breaching of the Siegfried Line by the 11th Infantry" 1-18 Feb 1945. Source: none listed. p58.

136. U.S. Army, 11th Inf Regt. History: "Breaching of the Siegfried Line by the 11th Infantry" 1-18 Feb 1945. Source: none listed. p58.

137. U.S. Army, 318th Regiment. After Action Report: "The Crossing of the Sauer River, 7 February, 1945, BY F Co, 318TH Infantry Regt. p3.

138. U.S. Army, 318th Regiment. After Action Report: "The Crossing of the Sauer River, 7 February, 1945, BY F Co, 318TH Infantry Regt.," p4.

139. U.S. Army, 318th Regiment. After Action Report: "The Crossing of the Sauer River, 7 February, 1945, BY F Co, 318TH Infantry Regt.," p4.

140. U.S. Army, 318th Regiment. After Action Report: "The Crossing of the Sauer River, 7 February, 1945, BY F Co, 318TH Infantry Regt.," p4.

141. Unnamed interview, 4

142. U.S. Army, 318th Regiment. After Action Report: "The Crossing of the Sauer River, 7 February, 1945, BY F Co, 318TH Infantry Regt.,"

143. U.S. Army, 2nd Bn, 319th Inf Regt. After Action Report: "Attack across Our River into Siegfried Line" 7-28 Feb 1945. Source: Lt Col Paul Bandy, et al. p2.

144. U.S. Army, 2nd Bn, 319th Inf Regt. After Action Report: "Attack across Our River into Siegfried Line" 7-28 Feb 1945. Source: Lt Col Paul Bandy, et al. p3.

145. U.S. Army, 2nd Bn, 319th Inf Regt. After Action Report: "Attack across Our River into Siegfried Line" 7-28 Feb 1945. Source: Lt Col Paul Bandy, et al. p3

146. United States Army, 150th Combat Battalion. History. Feb 7 1945. RG 407, NARA, College Park, MD.

147. U.S. Army, 2nd Bn, 319th Inf Regt. After Action Report: "Attack across Our River into Siegfried Line" 7-28 Feb 1945. Source: Lt Col Paul Bandy, et al. p4.

148. U.S. Army, 1st Bn, 319th Inf Regt. After Action Report: "Crossing of Sauer River" 7-28 Feb 1945. Source: Maj Arthur H Clark. p2.

149. U.S. Army, 1st Bn, 319th Inf Regt. After Action Report: "Crossing of Sauer River" 7-28 Feb 1945. Source: Maj Arthur H Clark. p2.

150. U.S. Army, 1st Bn, 319th Inf Regt. After Action Report: "Crossing of Sauer River" 7-28 Feb 1945. Source: Maj Arthur H Clark. p3.

151. U.S. Army, 2nd Bn, 319th Inf Regt. After Action Report: "Attack across Our River into Siegfried Line" 7-28 Feb 1945. Source: Lt Col Paul Bandy, et al. p4.

152. U.S. Army. Incomplete S-3 interview, 5

153. United States Army, 318th Infantry Regt. History, February 1945," RG 407, NARA, College Park, MD. p5.

154. U.S. Army, 318th Regiment. After Action Report: "The Crossing of the Sauer River, 7 February, 1945, BY F Co, 318TH Infantry Regt.," p4.

155. Patton, *War as I Knew It*, 230.

156. Blumenson, *The Patton Papers*, 638.

157. Blumenson, *The Patton Papers*, 638.

158. Roland Hartman, private interview.

159. Roland Hartman, private writings.

160. Roland Hartman, private writings.

161. Roland Hartman, private writings.

162. Roland Hartman, private writings.

163. Roland Hartman, private writings.

164. Roland Hartman, private writings.

165. Roland Hartman, private interview

166. (RDH private interview)

167. U.S. Army, 1st Bn, 417th Inf Regt. After Action Report: "Crossing of the Sauer River" 5-12 Feb 45. Source: Capt Homer O. Schmidt. p2-3.

168. U.S. Army, 1st Bn, 417th Inf Regt. After Action Report: "Crossing of the Sauer River" 5-12 Feb 45. Source: Capt Homer O. Schmidt. p3.

169. U.S. Army, 1st Bn, 417th Inf Regt. After Action Report: "Crossing of the Sauer River" 5-12 Feb 45. Source: Capt Homer O. Schmidt. p3.

170. U.S. Army, 1st Bn, 417th Inf Regt. After Action Report: "Crossing of the Sauer River, 1st Bn, 417th Inf Regt" 7-8 February 1945. Source: none listed. p4.

171. U.S. Army, 1st Bn, 417th Inf Regt. After Action Report: "Crossing of the Sauer River" 5-12 Feb 45. Source: Lt Col Clarence A Mette, Jr. p4.

172. U.S. Army, 417th Inf Regt. Journal, February 45. Source: none listed. February 8, 1945.

173. U.S. Army, 1st Bn, 417th Inf Regt. After Action Report: "Crossing of the Sauer River" 5-12 Feb 45. Source: Lt Col Clarence A Mette, Jr. p4-5

174. U.S. Army, 417th Inf Regt. Journal, February 45. Source: none listed. February 8, 1945.

175. United States Army, 160th Engr Bn, 1103rd Eng Group. After Action Report: "Assault Crossing of Sauer River at Echternach." 5-8 February 1945. Source: Lt Col George H. Jackson. RG 407, NARA, College Park, MD. p3.

176. U.S. Army, 160th Engr Bn, 1103rd Eng Group. After Action Report: "Assault Crossing of Sauer River at Echternach." 5-8 February 1945. Source: Lt Col George H. Jackson. p5.

177. U.S. Army, 417th Inf Regt. Journal, February 45. Source: none listed. February 8, 1945.

178. U.S. Army, 417th Inf Regt. Journal, February 45. Source: none listed. February 8, 1945.

179. U.S. Army, 1st Bn, 417th Inf Regt. After Action Report: "Crossing of the Sauer River" 5-12 Feb 45. Source: Lt Col Clarence A Mette, Jr. p5.

180. U.S. Army, 1st Bn, 417th Inf Regt. After Action Report: "Crossing of the Sauer River" 5-12 Feb 45. Source: Capt Homer O. Schmidt. p3.

181. U.S. Army, 417th Inf Regt. Journal, February 45. Source: none listed. February 8, 1945.

182. U.S. Army, 1st Bn, 417th Inf Regt. After Action Report: "Crossing of the Sauer River" 5-12 Feb 45. Source: Capt Homer O. Schmidt. p4.

183. Patton, *War as I Knew It*, 211.

184. U.S. Army, 10th Inf Regt. 10th Infantry Journal. February 1945.

185. U.S. Army, 10th Inf Regt. 10th Infantry Journal. 1-12 Feb 1945.

186. United States Army, Headquarters 1335th Engineer Combat Battalion. After Action Report. February 1945. Source: Lt Louis J Merlino. RG 407, NARA, College Park, MD. p2.

187. U.S. Army, 10th Inf Regt. 10th Infantry Journal. 1-12 Feb 1945.

188. U.S. Army, 10th Inf Regt. 10th Infantry Journal. 1-12 Feb 1945.

189. U.S. Army, 11th Inf Regt. History: "Breaching of the Siegfried Line by the 11th Infantry" 1-18 Feb 1945. Source: none listed. p58.

190. U.S. Army, 2nd Bn, 11th Inf Regt. After Action Report: "Sauer River Crossing" 7-18 Feb 1945. Source: Capt W B Wood. p2.

191. U.S. Army, 11th Inf Regt. History: "Breaching of the Siegfried Line by the 11th Infantry" 1-18 Feb 1945. Source: none listed. p59.

192. U.S. Army, 1st Bn, 11th Inf Regt. After Action Report: "Crossing of the Sauer River" 3-14 Feb 1945. Source: Capt Robert H Williams. p4-5.

193. U.S. Army, 11th Inf Regt. History: "Breaching of the Siegfried Line by the 11th Infantry" 1-18 Feb 1945. Source: none listed. p58.

194. United States Army, Headquarters 133D Engineer Combat Battalion. After Action Report. February 1945. Source: none listed. RG 407, NARA, College Park, MD. p3.

195. United States Army. After Action Report: Third US Army, 1 August 1944-9 May 1945. Combined Arms Research Library Digital Library. Online at: https://cgsc.contentdm.oclc.org/digital/collection/p4013coll8/id/2212. pg 260.

196. United States Army, 80th Infantry Division. After Action Report-G2. RG 407, NARA, College Park, MD. Feb 8

197. U.S. Army, 80th Infantry Division. After Action Report: G3. pg 2.

198. United States Army, 319th Infantry Regt. Report: Daily action. February 1-28. Source: none RG 407, NARA, College Park, MD. p5, Feb 8 And U.S. Army. 318th Regiment. After Action Report. "February 1945". p4-5.

199. U.S. Army, 80th Infantry Division. After Action Report: G3. p4.

200. United States Army, 150th Combat Bn. 150th Combat Battalion History,

201. U.S. Army, 319th Infantry Regt. Report: Daily action. February 1-28. Source: none. p5, Feb 8

202. U.S. Army, 318th Regiment. After Action Report. "February 1945". p6.

203. U.S. Army, 318th Regiment. After Action Report. "February 1945". p7.

204. U.S. Army, 318th Regiment. After Action Report. "February 1945". p7.

205. U.S. Army. 318th Regiment. After Action Report. "February 1945". p7.

206. United States Army, 1st Bn 318th Regiment. After Action Report. "Action Northern Luxembourg; Crossing Sauer River". 28 Dec 44 to 25th February 45. Source: Capt Charles D. Cockfield, et al. RG 407, NARA, College Park, MD. p5

207. U.S. Army, 1st Bn, 319th Inf Regt. After Action Report: "Crossing of Sauer River" 7-28 Feb 1945. Source: Maj Arthur H Clark. p3.

208. U.S. Army, 80th Infantry Division. After Action Report: G3. 8 Feb.

209. U.S. Army, 2nd Bn, 319th Inf Regt. After Action Report: "Attack across Our River into Siegfried Line" 7-28 Feb 1945. Source: Lt Col Paul Bandy, et al. p5.

210. U.S. Army, 319th Infantry Regt. Report: Daily action. February 1-28. Source: none. p5, Feb 8. .p7.

211. U.S. Army, 80th Infantry Division. History of the 80th Infantry Division. February 1945. p6.

212. United States Army, 3rd Bn, 417th Inf Regt. After Action Report: "Crossing of the Sauer River and Penetration of Seigfried Line" 7-17 Feb 45. Source: Lt Col Phillip S Greene, etc. RG 407, NARA, College Park, MD. p2

213. U.S. Army, 1st Bn, 417th Inf Regt. After Action Report: "Crossing of the Sauer River" 5-12 Feb 45. Source: Capt Homer O. Schmidt. p4.

214. U.S. Army, 417th Inf Regt. After Action Report: "Crossing of the Sauer River vicinity Echternach." 17 Feb 45. Source: Lt. Col R. D. Boerem. p4.

215. U.S. Army, 1st Bn, 417th Inf Regt. After Action Report: "Crossing of the Sauer River" 5-12 Feb 45. Source: Capt Homer O. Schmidt. p4.

216. U.S. Army, 1st Bn, 417th Inf Regt. After Action Report: "Crossing of the Sauer River" 5-12 Feb 45. Source: Capt Homer O. Schmidt. p4-5.

217. U.S. Army, 1st Bn, 417th Inf Regt. After Action Report: "Crossing of the Sauer River" 5-12 Feb 45. Source: Capt Homer O. Schmidt. p5.

218. U.S. Army, 1st Bn, 417th Inf Regt. After Action Report: "Crossing of the Sauer River" 5-12 Feb 45. Source: Lt Col Clarence A Mette, Jr. p5.

219. U.S. Army, 1st Bn, 417th Inf Regt. After Action Report: "Crossing of the Sauer River" 5-12 Feb 45. Source: Lt Col Clarence A Mette, Jr. p6.

220. U.S. Army, 1st Bn, 417th Inf Regt. After Action Report: "Crossing of the Sauer River" 5-12 Feb 45. Source: Lt Col Clarence A Mette, Jr. p6.

221. U.S. Army, 417th Inf Regt. After Action Report: "Crossing of the Sauer River vicinity Echternach." 17 Feb 45. Source: Lt. Col R. D. Boerem. p4 .

222. United States Army, VIII Corps. G-3 Journal File 1-17 Feb 45. Source: none. RG 407, NARA, College Park, MD.

223. United States Army, 1st Bn, 417th Inf Regt. After Action Report: "Reduction of a Pillbox at Ernzerhof By an Assault Team of the 1st Bn, 417th Inf Regt " Source: not listed. RG 407, NARA, College Park, MD. p3

224, U.S. Army, 1st Bn, 417th Inf Regt. After Action Report: "Crossing of the Sauer River, 1st Bn, 417th Inf Regt" 7-8 February 1945. Source: none listed. p4.

225. U.S. Army, 417th Inf Regt. After Action Report: "Crossing of the Sauer River vicinity Echternach." 17 Feb 45. Source: Lt. Col R. D. Boerem. p5.

226. United States Army, 10th Inf Regt. 10th Infantry Journal. 9 Feb 1945. RG 407, NARA, College Park, MD.

227 U.S. Army, 10th Inf Regt. 10th Infantry Journal. 9 Feb 1945.

228. United States Army, Company L, 3rd Bn, 10th Inf Regt. After Action Report: "Crossing of the Sauer River" 1 Jan - 16 Feb 1945. Source: Lt Louis J Merlino. RG 407, NARA, College Park, MD. p1

229. U.S. Army, 10th Inf Regt. 10th Infantry Journal. 9 Feb 1945.

230. U.S. Army, 11th Inf Regt. History: "Breaching of the Siegfried Line by the 11th Infantry" 1-18 Feb 1945. Source: none listed. p59.

231. U.S. Army, 2nd Bn, 11th Inf Regt. After Action Report: "Sauer River Crossing" 7-18 Feb 1945. Source: Capt W B Wood. p2.

232. U.S. Army, 2nd Bn, 11th Inf Regt. After Action Report: "Sauer River Crossing" 7-18 Feb 1945. Source: Capt W B Wood. p2.

233. U.S. Army, 1st Bn, 11th Inf Regt. After Action Report: "Crossing of the Sauer River" 3-14 Feb 1945. Source: Capt Robert H Williams. p5.

234. United States Army, 11th Inf Regt. 11th IR History. RG 407, NARA, College Park, MD. p60 and U.S. Army, 1st Bn, 11th Inf Regt. After Action Report: "Crossing of the Sauer River" 3-14 Feb 1945. Source: Capt Robert H Williams. p5.

235. United States Army, 7th Engineer Bn. Report: "After Action Report Against the Enemy" 1-28 Feb 1945. Source: Headquarters 7th Engineers Battalion. RG 407, NARA, College Park, MD. p1

236. U.S. Army, 1st Bn, 11th Inf Regt. After Action Report: "Crossing of the Sauer River" 3-14 Feb 1945. Source: Capt Robert H Williams. p5.

237. U.S. Army, 1st Bn, 11th Inf Regt. After Action Report: "Crossing of the Sauer River" 3-14 Feb 1945. Source: Capt Robert H Williams. p5.

238. United States Army, 10th Inf Regt. 10th Infantry Journal. 9 Feb 1945. RG 407, NARA, College Park, MD.

239. U.S. Army, 10th Inf Regt. 10th Infantry Journal. 1-12 Feb 1945.

240. United States Army, 10th Inf Regt. After Action Report: "Sauer River Crossing" 7-15 Feb 1945. Source: Lt Col William Breckinridge. p4.

241. U.S. Army, 10th Inf Regt. After Action Report: "Sauer River Crossing" 7-15 Feb 1945. Source: Lt Col William Breckinridge. p5. And 133rd United States Army, Headquarters 133D Engineer Combat Battalion. After Action Report. February 1945. Source: none listed. RG 407, NARA, College Park, MD. p3

242. U.S. Army, 10th Inf Regt. After Action Report: "Sauer River Crossing" 7-15 Feb 1945. Source: Lt Col William Breckinridge. p5.

243. United States Army, Headquarters 133D Engineer Combat Battalion. After Action Report. February 1945. Source: none listed. RG 407, NARA, College Park, MD. p3

244. U.S. Army, 1st Bn, 11th Inf Regt. After Action Report: "Crossing of the Sauer River" 3-14 Feb 1945. Source: Capt Robert H Williams.

245. U.S. Army, 10th Inf Regt. 10th Infantry Journal. 1-12 Feb 1945.

246. U.S. Army. 318th Regiment. After Action Report. "February 1945". p7.

247. United States Army. After Action Report: Third US Army, 1 August 1944-9 May 1945. Combined Arms Research Library Digital Library. p260 Online at:
https://cgsc.contentdm.oclc.org/digital/collection/p4013coll8/id/2212

248. United States Army, 1st Bn 318th Regiment. After Action Report. "Action Northern Luxembourg; Crossing Sauer River". 28 Dec 44 to 25th February 45. Source: Capt Charles D. Cockfield, et al. p6.

249. U.S. Army. 318th Regiment. After Action Report. "February 1945". p7.

250. U.S. Army, 1st Bn 318th Regiment. After Action Report. "Action Northern Luxembourg; Crossing Sauer River". 28 Dec 44 to 25th February 45. Source: Capt Charles D. Cockfield, et al. p6.

251. U.S. Army, 80th Infantry Division. After Action Report: G3. Feb 9, 1945

252. U.S. Army. 318th Regiment. After Action Report. "February 1945". p7.

253. U.S. Army, 80th Infantry Division. History of the 80th Infantry Division. February 1945. p7.

254. United States Army, 80th Infantry Division. History of the 80th Infantry Division. February 1945. p7.

255. United States Army. 318th Regiment. After Action Report. "February 1945". RG 407, NARA, College Park, MD. p8

256. U.S. Army. 318th Regiment. After Action Report. "February 1945". p8.

257. U.S. Army, 80th Infantry Division. After Action Report: G3. p2.

258. U.S. Army, 80th Infantry Division. After Action Report: G3. Feb 9, 1945.

259. U.S. Army, 3rd Bn, 319th Inf Regt. After Action Report: "Crossing of the Sauer River" 4-28 Feb 1945. Source: Capt Robert J. Bee.   p2-3.

260. U.S. Army, 2nd Bn, 319th Inf Regt. After Action Report: "Attack across Our River into Siegfried Line" 7-28 Feb 1945. Source: Lt Col Paul Bandy, et al. p5.

261. United States Army, 2nd Bn, 319th Inf Regt. After Action Report: "Attack across Our River into Siegfried Line" 7-28 Feb 1945. Source: Lt Col Paul Bandy, et al. p7.

262. U.S. Army, 2nd Bn, 319th Inf Regt. After Action Report: "Attack across Our River into Siegfried Line" 7-28 Feb 1945. Source: Lt Col Paul Bandy, et al. p5-6.

263. U.S. Army, 319th Infantry Regt. Report: Daily Action. February 1-28. Source: none. p5, Feb 8. p8

264. U.S. Army, 2nd Bn, 319th Inf Regt. After Action Report: "Attack across Our River into Siegfried Line" 7-28 Feb 1945. Source: Lt Col Paul Bandy, et al.. p6-7.

265. U.S. Army, 1st Bn, 319th Inf Regt. After Action Report: "Crossing of Sauer River" 7-28 Feb 1945. Source: Maj Arthur H Clark. p3.

266. U.S. Army, 319ᵗʰ Infantry Regt. Report: Daily Action. February 1-28. Source: none p6.

267. U.S. Army, 319ᵗʰ Infantry Regt. Report: Daily Action. February 1-28. Source: none p6.

268. United States Army, 905ᵗʰ Field Artillery Bn. "Unit History for month of February 1945." RG 407, NARA, College Park, MD. p4

269. U.S. Army. 318th Regiment. After Action Report. "February 1945". p8-9.

270. U.S. Army. 318th Regiment. After Action Report. "February 1945". p9.

271. U.S. Army. 318th Regiment. After Action Report. "February 1945". p9

272. U.S. Army. 318th Regiment. After Action Report. "February 1945". p9.

273. U.S. Army 1st Bn, 319th Inf Regt. After Action Report: "Crossing of Sauer River" 7-28 Feb 1945. Source: Maj Arthur H Clark. p3. And U.S. Army, 2nd Bn, 319th Inf Regt. After Action Report: "Attack across Our River into Siegfried Line" 7-28 Feb 1945. Source: Lt Col Paul Bandy, et al. p.7 And U.S. Army, 80th Infantry Division. History of the 80th Infantry Division. February 1945. p9.

274. United States Army. After Action Report: Third US Army, 1 August 1944-9 May 1945. Combined Arms Research Library Digital Library. 10 Feb 1945. Online at: https://cgsc.contentdm.oclc.org/digital/collection/p4013coll8/id/2212

275. U.S. Army, 80th Infantry Division. After Action Report: G3. Feb 10, 1945.

276. U.S. Army, 80th Infantry Division. After Action Report: G3. Feb 11, 1945.

277. United States Army, 3rd Bn, 319ᵗʰ Inf Regt. After Action Report: "Crossing of the Sauer River" 4-28 Feb 1945. Source: Capt Robert J. Bee. RG 407, NARA, College Park, MD. p2

278. U.S. Army, 1ˢᵗ Bn, 319ᵗʰ Inf Regt. After Action Report: "Crossing of Sauer River" 7-28 Feb 1945. Source: Maj Arthur H Clark. p3.

279. United States Army. After Action Report: Third US Army, 1 August 1944-9 May 1945. Combined Arms Research Library Digital Library. Online at:

https://cgsc.contentdm.oclc.org/digital/collection/p4013coll8/id/2212 p262

280. U.S. Army, 150th Combat Bn. 150th Combat Battalion History,

281. U.S. Army, 3rd Bn, 319th Inf Regt. After Action Report: "Crossing of the Sauer River" 4-28 Feb 1945. Source: Capt Robert J. Bee. p2.

282. United States Army, 905th Field Artillery Bn. "Unit History for month of February 1945." RG 407, NARA, College Park, MD. pg 4, Feb 11

283. U.S. Army, 2nd Bn, 319th Inf Regt. After Action Report: "Attack across Our River into Siegfried Line" 7-28 Feb 1945. Source: Lt Col Paul Bandy, et al. p7.

284. Blumenson, *The Patton Papers*, 638-9.

285. U.S. Army 417th Inf Regt. Journal, February 45. Source: none listed.

286. U.S. Army, 1st Bn, 417th Inf Regt. After Action Report: "Crossing of the Sauer River" 5-12 Feb 45. Source: Lt Col Clarence A Mette, Jr. p3.

287. United States Army. Third US Army. Reports: G-1 Daily Periodic Reports. found in XII Corps files,. RG 407, NARA, College Park, MD.

288. U.S. Army, 417th Inf Regt. After Action Report: "Crossing of the Sauer River vicinity Echternach." 17 Feb 45. Source: Lt. Col R. D. Boerem. p6-8.

289. United States Army. XII US Corps. G3 section, Feb 13th. RG 407, NARA, College Park, MD

290. United States Army. XII US Corps. "Report of Operations" 1-28 February 1945." Source: Headquarters XII Corps, Office of the Commanding General APO 312. RG 407, NARA, College Park, MD.. p19

291. U.S. Army, 1st Bn, 417th Inf Regt. After Action Report: "Crossing of the Sauer River" 5-12 Feb 45. Source: Capt Homer O. Schmidt. p7.

292. U.S. Army, 1st Bn, 417th Inf Regt. After Action Report: "Crossing of the Sauer River" 5-12 Feb 45. Source: Capt Homer O. Schmidt. p7-8.

293. U.S. Army, 3rd Bn, 417th Inf Regt. After Action Report: "Crossing of the Sauer River and Penetration of Seigfried Line" 7-17 Feb 45. Source: Lt Col Phillip S Greene, etc. p3.

294. U.S. Army, 3rd Bn, 417th Inf Regt. After Action Report: "Crossing of the Sauer River and Penetration of Seigfried Line" 7-17 Feb 45. Source: Lt Col Phillip S Greene, etc. p3-4.

295. U.S. Army, 3rd Bn, 417th Inf Regt. After Action Report: "Crossing of the Sauer River and Penetration of Seigfried Line" 7-17 Feb 45. Source: Lt Col Phillip S Greene, etc. p4.

296. United States Army. Twelfth Corps. "Report of Operations" 1-28 February 1945." Source: Headquarters XII Corps, Office of the Commanding General APO 312. RG 407, NARA, College Park, MD. p22

297. United States Army, 1st Bn, 10th Inf Regt. After Action Report: "Sauer River Crossing and Penetration of the Seigfreid Line" 10-28 Feb 1945. Source: Major Hays and Lt R L Bezla. RG 407, NARA, College Park, MD. p2

298. U.S. Army, 1st Bn, 11th Inf Regt. After Action Report: "Crossing of the Sauer River" 3-14 Feb 1945. Source: Capt Robert H Williams. p7.

299. United States Army, 11th Inf Regt. 3rd Bn, 11th Infantry Journal. Feb 1945. RG 407, NARA, College Park, MD.

300. U.S. Army, 10th Inf Regt. 10th Infantry Journal. 1-12 Feb 1945.

301. U.S. Army, 11th Inf Regt. History: "Breaching of the Siegfried Line by the 11th Infantry" 1-18 Feb 1945. Source: none listed. p61.

302. U.S. Army, 1st Bn, 11th Inf Regt. After Action Report: "Crossing of the Sauer River" 3-14 Feb 1945. Source: Capt Robert H Williams. p8.

303. United States Army, 11th Inf Regt. 1st Bn, 11th Infantry Journal. Feb 1945. RG 407, NARA, College Park, MD.

304. U.S. Army, 11th Inf Regt. 1st Bn, 11th Infantry Journal. Feb 1945. AND U.S. Army, 2nd Bn, 11th Inf Regt. After Action Report: "Sauer River Crossing" 7-18 Feb 1945. Source: Capt W B Wood. p3. And U.S. Army, 1st Bn, 11th Inf Regt. After Action Report: "Crossing of the Sauer River" 3-14 Feb 1945. Source: Capt Robert H Williams. p9.

305. U.S. Army, 11th Inf Regt. History: "Breaching of the Siegfried Line by the 11th Infantry" 1-18 Feb 1945. Source: none listed. p61.

306. United States Army, 11th Inf Regt. 2nd Bn 11th Infantry Journal. Feb 1945. RG 407, NARA, College Park, MD. AND U.S. Army, 2nd Bn, 11th Inf Regt. After Action Report: "Sauer River Crossing" 7-18 Feb 1945. Source: Capt W B Wood.

307. U.S. Army, 11th Inf Regt. History: "Breaching of the Siegfried Line by the 11th Infantry" 1-18 Feb 1945. Source: none listed. p62.

308. U.S. Army, 11th Inf Regt. 2nd Bn 11th Infantry Journal. Feb 1945.

309. U.S. Army, 11th Inf Regt. 3rd Bn, 11th Infantry Journal. Feb 1945.

310. U.S. Army, 11ᵗʰ Inf Regt. History: "Breaching of the Siegfried Line by the 11ᵗʰ Infantry" 1-18 Feb 1945. Source: none listed. p62.

311. U.S. Army, 11th Inf Regt. 3ʳᵈ Bn, 11th Infantry Journal. Feb 1945.

312. U.S. Army, 11ᵗʰ Inf Regt. History: "Breaching of the Siegfried Line by the 11ᵗʰ Infantry" 1-18 Feb 1945. Source: none listed. p62. AND U.S. Army, 11th Inf Regt. 3rd Bn, 11th Infantry Journal. Feb 1945.

313. United States Army, 3d Bn, 11th Inf Regt. After Action Report: "Sauer River Operation" 6-12 Feb 1945. Source: Capt R M Gill. RG 407, NARA, College Park, MD. p3. AND U.S. Army, 11th Inf Regt. History: "Breaching of the Siegfried Line by the 11th Infantry" 1-18 Feb 1945. Source: none listed. p62. AND U.S. Army, 11th Inf Regt. 3rd Bn, 11th Infantry Journal. Feb 1945.

314. United States Army, 11th Inf Regt. 3rd Bn, 11th Infantry Journal. Feb 1945. RG 407, NARA, College Park, MD.

315. U.S. Army, 11th Inf Regt. 3rd Bn, 11th Infantry Journal. Feb 1945. AND U.S. Army, 3d Bn, 11th Inf Regt. After Action Report: "Sauer River Operation" 6-12 Feb 1945. Source: Capt R M Gill.

316. U.S. Army, 11ᵗʰ Inf Regt. History: "Breaching of the Siegfried Line by the 11ᵗʰ Infantry" 1-18 Feb 1945. Source: none listed. p63.

317. U.S. Army, 11th Inf Regt. 3rd Bn, 11th Infantry Journal. Feb 1945.

318. U.S. Army, 11th Inf Regt. 3rd Bn, 11th Infantry Journal. Feb 1945.

319. Blumenson, *The Patton Papers*, 638

320. Patton, *War as I Knew It*, 215.

321. United States Army. After Action Report: Third US Army, 1 August 1944-9 May 1945. Combined Arms Research Library Digital Library. Online at:
https://cgsc.contentdm.oclc.org/digital/collection/p4013coll8/id/2212 p264

322. United States Army. After Action Report: Third US Army, 1 August 1944-9 May 1945. Combined Arms Research Library Digital Library. Online at:
https://cgsc.contentdm.oclc.org/digital/collection/p4013coll8/id/2212 p26

323. U.S. Army, 80th Infantry Division. After Action Report: G3. p3.

324. United States Army. XII US Army. Report/History "XII Corps: Spearhead of Patton's Third Army." Chapter 12: Siegfried Line to Rhine. 7 Feb 45 – 14 Mar 45. RG 407, NARA, College Park, MD. p17

325. United States Army, 317th Inf Regt. Regimental History 1-28 Feb 1945. Source: Headquarters, 317th Infantry. RG 407, NARA, College Park, MD. p4

326. U.S. Army, 80th Infantry Division. After Action Report: G3. Feb 16.

327. U.S. Army, 317th Inf Regt. Regimental History 1-28 Feb 1945. Source: Headquarters, 317th Infantry. p5.

328. U.S. Army, 80th Infantry Division. After Action Report: G3. AND United States Army, 80th Infantry Division. History of the 80th Infantry Division. February 1945. p17-18.

329. U.S. Army, 317th Inf Regt. Regimental History 1-28 Feb 1945. Source: Headquarters, 317th Infantry. p5. And 80th G-3 history, Feb 17 and 80th Div History, pg 17

330. United States Army, 317th Inf Regt. S-2 Report with daily action. Feb 1945. Source: Headquarters, 317th Infantry. RG 407, NARA, College Park, MD. p5

331. U.S. Army, 80th Infantry Division. After Action Report: G3. 19th Feb. AND United States Army, 317th Inf Regt. Regimental History 1-28 Feb 1945. Source: Headquarters, 317th Infantry. p5.

332. U.S. Army, 80th Infantry Division. After Action Report: G3. Feb 20. AND U.S. Army, 317th Inf Regt. Regimental History 1-28 Feb 1945. Source: Headquarters, 317th Infantry. p5.

333. U.S. Army. 318th Regiment. After Action Report. "February 1945". p10

334. U.S. Army, 1st Bn 318th Regiment. After Action Report. "Action Northern Luxembourg; Crossing Sauer River". 28 Dec 44 to 25th February 45. Source: Capt Charles D. Cockfield, et al.. p6-7. AND U.S. Army, 318th Regiment. After Action Report. "February 1945". "February 1945". p10.

335. U.S. Army, 318th Regiment. After Action Report "February 1945". p12.

336. U.S. Army. 318th Regiment. After Action Report. "February 1945". p12.

337. United States Army, 314th Field Artillery Bn. History of 314th Field Artillery Battalion. RG 407, NARA, College Park, MD.p 4

338. U.S. Army, 80th Infantry Division. After Action Report: G3. Feb 16,

339. U.S. Army, 318th Regiment. After Action Report. "February 1945". p12. AND U.S. Army, 80th Infantry Division. History of the 80th Infantry Division. February 1945. p8.

340. U.S. Army, 318th Regiment. After Action Report. "February 1945". p2. AND U.S. Army, 318th History, pg 8. and U.S. Army, 318th AAR, Feb 18th.

341. U.S. Army, 1st Bn 318th Regiment. After Action Report. "Action Northern Luxembourg; Crossing Sauer River". 28 Dec 44 to 25th February 45. Source: Capt Charles D. Cockfield, et al. p8.

342. U.S. Army, 80th Infantry Division. After Action Report: G3. Feb 20. AND U.S. Army, 318th Regiment. After Action Report. "February 1945". p16.

343. U.S. Army, 3rd Bn, 319th Inf Regt. After Action Report: "Crossing of the Sauer River" 4-28 Feb 1945. Source: Capt Robert J. Bee. p3.

344. U.S. Army, 2nd Bn, 319th Inf Regt. After Action Report: "Attack across Our River into Siegfried Line" 7-28 Feb 1945. Source: Lt Col Paul Bandy, et al. p8.

345. U.S. Army, 319th Infantry Regt. Report: Daily Action. February 1-28. Source: none.

346. United States Army, 905th Field Artillery Bn. "Unit History for month of February 1945." RG 407, NARA, College Park, MD. p5, Feb 14

347. U.S. Army, 3rd Bn, 319th Inf Regt. After Action Report: "Crossing of the Sauer River" 4-28 Feb 1945. Source: Capt Robert J. Bee. p4-5.

348. U.S. Army, 80th Infantry Division. After Action Report: G3. Feb 16.

349. U.S. Army, 80th Infantry Division. After Action Report: G3. Feb 1 - 9. AND U.S. Army, 2nd Bn, 319th Inf Regt. After Action Report: "Attack across Our River into Siegfried Line" 7-28 Feb 1945. Source: Lt Col Paul Bandy, et al. p8.

350. U.S. Army, 80th Infantry Division. After Action Report: G3. 19th Feb.

351. U.S. Army, 80th Infantry Division. After Action Report: G3. 20th Feb.

352. U.S. Army, 150th Combat Bn. 150th Combat Battalion History, p2.

353. U.S. Army, After Action Report: G3. RG 407, NARA, College Park, MD. Feb 13

354. Eisenhower, Dwight D. Report by the Supreme Commander to the Combined Chiefs of Staff on the Operations in Europe of the Allied Expeditionary Force, 6 June 1944 to 8 May 1945. Washington: Govt. print. off., 1946. P88.

355. Greenwood, *Normandy to Victory*, 296.

356. United States Army, Ninth US Army After Action Report. RG 407, NARA, College Park, MD. p3.

357. Greenwood, *Normandy to Victory*, 298.

358. U.S. Army, Ninth US Army After Action Report. p3.

359. United States Army, First US Army Operations Report. RG 407, NARA, College Park, MD. p50.

360. United States Army, VIII US Corps Operations After Action Report. RG 407, NARA, College Park, MD. p4.

361. U.S. Army, VIII US Corps Operations After Action Report.

362. U.S. Army, VIII US Corps Operations After Action Report. p7.

363. United States Army, VIII US Corps G3 Report, February 9, 1945. RG 407, NARA, College Park, MD.

364. Greenwood, *Normandy to Victory*, 309.

365. Greenwood, *Normandy to Victory*, 306.

366. United States Army, VIII US Corps History. RG 407, NARA, College Park, MD. p11.

367. U.S. Army, VIII US Corps After Action Report. p13.

368. POW Info Bureau Subject File, Stalag 9B, RG 389, Box 2150. NARA, College Park, MD.

369. Troy H. Kimmel, written account as a POW. Online at: http://www.indianamilitary.org/German%20PW%20Camps/Prisoner%20of%20War/PW%20Camps/Stalag%20IX-B%20Bad%20Orb/TroyKimmel/TroyKimmel.htm p2

370. Myron "Mike" Klingman, written account as a POW. "German Prisoner No. 25708" Online at: http://www.indianamilitary.org/German%20PW%20Camps/Prisoner%20of%20War/PW%20Camps/Stalag%20IX-B%20Bad%20Orb/Myron%20Klinkman/Klingman-Myron.pdf p18

371. Sam Higgins, *Survival: Diary of an American POW in World War II*, (Central Point OR: Hellgate Press, 1999), 3.

372. "Gertrude Sanford Legendre: The Socialite Spy," online at fishersisland.net/2016/10/gertrude-sanford-legendre-socialite-spy/ and "Gertrude Sanford Legendre, 97, Socialite Turned Hunter and Prisoner," New York Times, March 13, 2000, and Foy, David A. *For You the War is Over, American Prisoners of War in Nazi Germany*. New York: Stein and Day, 1984 p46-7.

373. Foy, David A. *For You the War Is Over: American Prisoners of War in Nazi Germany*. New York: Stein and Day, 1984. p45

374. Roland Hartman, private interview

375. Roland Hartman, private interview.

376. Stalag XII-A files, RG 389, NARA, College Park, MD.

377. ICRC #632 - Stalag XII – Limburg. A. Date of Visit: November 15th 1944 .Signed Werner Uchmueller. RG 389, NARA, College Park, MD.

378. Letter in XII file Dec 29 1944

379. Hoffmann, Bob. "From Stalag XIIA to Camp Lucky Strike: A POW Story." In Voyageur, summer/fall, 2003.

380. Hoffmann, Bob. "From Stalag XIIA to Camp Lucky Strike: A POW Story." In Voyageur, summer/fall, 2003.

381. International Committee of the Red Cross. Geneva. Stalag XII A. Visited by Mr Kleiner on February 11, 1045. RG 389, NARA, College Park, MD. p2

382. International Committee of the Red Cross. Geneva. Stalag XII A. Visited by Mr Kleiner on February 11, 1045. p6.

383. Higgins, *Survival: Diary of an American POW in World War II*, 58.

384. Roland Hartman, private interview.

385. Roger Cohen, Soldiers and Slaves : American POWs Trapped by the Nazis' Final Gamble (New York: Knopf, 2005), 70.

386. "The Treatment of Soviet POWs: Starvation, Disease, and Shootings, June 1941–January 1942," United States Holocaust Memorial Museum, Washington, DC. Online at: https://www.ushmm.org/wlc/en/article.php?ModuleId=10007183 [accessed 6/30/22]

387. Max Hastings, *Armageddon : the Battle for Germany, 1944-45*. (New York: Vintage Books, 2005). 235.

388. Higgins, Survival: Diary of an American POW, 7.

389. Higgins, Survival: Diary of an American POW, 40-41.

390. Higgins, Survival: Diary of an American POW, 72.

391. Higgins, Survival: Diary of an American POW, 30.

392. U.S. Army Military Intelligence Service War Department, Report, "Stalag IX-B American Prisoners of War in Germany, Stalag 9 B- Bad Orb, Germany." RG 389, Entry A1 460A; Records of the Provost Marshal General. American Prisoner of War Information Bureau. 1942 – 1946, National Archives, College Park, MD. Online at: http://www.indianamilitary.org/German%20PW%20Camps/Prisoner%20of%20War/PW%20Camps/Stalag%20IX-B%20Bad%20Orb/History.htm [accessed 5/23/2023]

393.   Hal LaCroix, Journey Out of Darkness: the Real Story of American Heroes in Hitler's POW Camps, An Oral History. (Westport: Praeger Security, 2007), 20.

394. U.S. Army Military Intelligence Service, Report, "Stalag IX-B German Prisoner of War Camp Bad Orb, 3.

395. International Committee of the Red Cross, "Translation by the London Delegation. Reservelazarett, Stalag IX-B. Visited by Dr. Landholt and Mr Wyze. 25th August 1944. Report on hospital." RG 389, Entry A1 460A; Records of the Provost Marshal General. American Prisoner of War Information Bureau. 1942 – 1946, National Archives, College Park, MD.

396. International Committee of the Red Cross, "Report No. 690: IX B. Visited by Werner. Buchmueller, January 24, 1945." RG 389, Entry A1 460A; Records of the Provost Marshal General. American Prisoner of War Information Bureau. 1942 – 1946, National Archives, College Park, MD.

397. AS-473. Incoming Telegram 1945 to Secretary of State. "American Interests Germany POWs regarding inferior conditions at Stalag IX B. Signed by Harrison, dated February 15." RG 389, Entry A1 460A; Records of the Provost Marshal General. American Prisoner of War Information Bureau. 1942 – 1946, National Archives, College Park, MD.

398. U.S. Army, Military Intelligence Service. Report, "Stalag IX-B German Prisoner of War Camp Bad Orb.

399. U.S. Army, Military Intelligence Service. Report, "Stalag IX-B German Prisoner of War Camp Bad Orb.

400. Higgins, Survival: Diary of an American POW, 70.

401. LaCroix, *Journey Out of Darkness*, 20.

402. Higgins, *Survival: Diary of an American POW*, 46.

403. Higgins, *Survival: Diary of an American POW*, 95.

404. Higgins, Survival: *Diary of an American POW*, 71.

405. Higgins, Survival: *Diary of an American POW*, 128.

406. Kakacek, Frank. "Grandpa, What Did You do in the War? My Child, I took a Tour of the Rhine River Valley of Germany," Library of Congress. Online at: http://memory.loc.gov/diglib/vhp/story/loc.natlib.afc2001001.01580/ 189. [accessed June 20, 2022]

407. Klingman, "German Prisoner No. 25708," 30.

408. Higgins, *Survival: Diary of an American POW*, 40.

409. Klingman, "German Prisoner No. 25708," 22.

410. Kakacek, "Grandpa, What Did You do in the War?" *18-19*.

411. Kakacek, "Grandpa, What Did You do in the War?" 18.

412. Higgins, *Survival: Diary of an American POW*, 136.

413. Kakacek, "Grandpa, What Did You do in the War?" 18.

414. Klingman, "German Prisoner No. 25708," 22, 32.

415. Kakacek, "Grandpa, What Did You do in the War?" 18.

416. Higgins, *Survival: Diary of an American POW*, 70.

417. Kakacek, "Grandpa, What Did You do in the War?" 18.

418. Higgins, *Survival: Diary of an American POW*.

419. Higgins, *Survival: Diary of an American POW*, 23.

420. Higgins, *Survival: Diary of an American POW*, 54.

421. Battle of the Bulge Company C's (424th Regiment, 106th Infantry Division) Story in honor of Donald E. Doubek, Collected stories by Bonnie L (Doubek) McNunn. Online at: http://www.indianamilitary.org/German%20PW%20Camps/Prisoner%2 0of%20War/PW%20Camps/Stalag%20IX-B%20Bad%20Orb/Donald%20E.%20Doubek/Donald%20Doubek.htm 6. [accessed June 20, 2022]

422. Higgins, *Survival: Diary of an American* POW, 39.

423. Excerpts of Articles by POWs, Morale Good Online at:
http://www.indianamilitary.org/106ID/Publications/CubInReview/06-
PrisonerOfWar.htm

424. Klingman, "German Prisoner No. 25708," 28.

425. Higgins, *Survival: Diary of an American POW*, 69.

426. Excerpts of Articles by POWs, unpublished manuscript by Father
Cavanaugh in Yank magazine Jul-Aug Sept 1978. Morale Good Online at:
http://www.indianamilitary.org/106ID/Publications/CubInReview/06-
PrisonerOfWar.htm [accessed June 2, 2921]

427. Higgins, *Survival: Diary of an American POW*, 49.

428. Higgins, *Survival: Diary of an American POW*, 139.

429. David Ririe, *One-Man Mission: An American POW's Struggle to Survive
Hitler's Nazi Prison Camp*. (Idaho Falls: Teton Crest: 2012), 117.

430. Higgins, *Survival: Diary of an American POW*, 1.

431. Higgins, *Survival: Diary of an American POW*, 93.

432. Russell Hoff, oral history. Digital Collection, National World War II
Museum. Online at: https://www.ww2online.org/view/russell-d-
hoff#becoming-a-pow [accessed June 2, 2022]

433. Klingman, "German Prisoner No. 25708," 23.

434. U.S. Army, Military Intelligence Service Report, "Stalag IX-B
German Prisoner of War Camp Bad Orb, 23.

435. Klingman, "German Prisoner No. 25708," 23.

436. Roger Cohen, "The Lost Soldiers of Stalag IX-B." New York Times,
Magazine Section, February 27, 2005. Online at:
https://www.nytimes.com/2005/02/27/magazine/the-lost-soldiers-of-
stalag-ixb.html [accessed June 2, 2022].

437. Cohen, "The Lost Soldiers of Stalag IX-B."

438. Cohen, "The Lost Soldiers of Stalag IX-B."

439. Cohen, "The Lost Soldiers of Stalag IX-B."

440. Cohen, "The Lost Soldiers of Stalag IX-B."

441. Johann Carl Friedrich Kasten, IV Collection
(AFC/2001/001/12002), Veterans History Project, American Folklife
Center, Library of Congress Online at:
https://memory.loc.gov/diglib/vhp/bib/loc.natlib.afc2001001.12002 5.
[accessed June 2, 2022]

442. Johann Carl Friedrich Kasten, IV Collection (AFC/2001/001/12002), 5.

443. U.S. Army, Military Intelligence Service Report: "Stalag IX-B German Prisoner of War Camp Bad Orb.

444. Roddie Edmonds, The Righteous Among the Nations Database. Online at: https://righteous.yadvashem.org/?searchType=righteous_only&language=en&itemId=11025207&ind=0 [accessed June 2, 2022]

445. Higgins, *Survival: Diary of an American POW*, 65-67.

446. Higgins, *Survival: Diary of an American POW*, 110.

447. Klingman, "German Prisoner No. 25708," 29.

448. Klingman, "German Prisoner No. 25708," 32.

449. Higgins, *Survival: Diary of an American POW*, several times in book.

450. Higgins, *Survival: Diary of an American POW*, 51.

451. Kakacek, "Grandpa, What Did You do in the War?" 20.

452. Higgins, *Survival: Diary of an American POW*, 149.

453. Higgins, *Survival: Diary of an American POW*, 147.

454. Roland Hartman, private interview.

455. Higgins, *Survival: Diary of an American POW*, 152.

456. Higgins, Survival: Diary of an American POW, 163.

457. Higgins, Survival: Diary of an American POW, 138.

458. Higgins, Survival: Diary of an American POW, 157.

459. Higgins, Survival: Diary of an American POW, 39 and 152.

460. Higgins, Survival: Diary of an American POW, 150.

461. Higgins, Survival: Diary of an American POW, 166.

462. Higgins, Survival: Diary of an American POW, 163.

463. Higgins, Survival: Diary of an American POW, 150.

464. Klingman, "German Prisoner No. 25708," 31.

465. U.S. Army, Military Intelligence Service Report: "Stalag IX-B German Prisoner of War Camp Bad Orb.

466. U.S. Army, Military Intelligence Service Report: "Stalag IX-B German Prisoner of War Camp Bad Orb.

467. Klingman, "German Prisoner No. 25708," 32.

468. Klingman, "German Prisoner No. 25708," 32.

469. Kakacek, "Grandpa, What Did You do in the War?"

470. Klingman, "German Prisoner No. 25708," 35.

471. Klingman, "German Prisoner No. 25708," 1.

472. Klingman, "German Prisoner No. 25708," 36.

473. U.S. Army, Military Intelligence Service Report: "Stalag IX-B German Prisoner of War Camp Bad Orb.

474. M. Williams, *Chronology*, 1-2 April 1945.

475. "POW camp (Stalag IXB) near Bad Orb with American and Allied Prisoners," Original film can be found at the National Archives in College Park Maryland. A film with excerpts is available online at U. S. Memorial Holocaust Museum, online at https://collections.ushmm.org/search/catalog/irn1004536.[Accessed October 3, 2022].

476. Photographs of Stalag IX-B in Bad Orb, Germany, Lone Sentry Website. Online at http://www.lonesentry.com/badorb/. [Accessed October 3, 2022].

477. SHAEF, "SCAF 212, Ref S-79573, Allied Prisoners of War is Subject regarding the movement of prisoners out of camps, Feb 18, 1945." RG 389, Entry A1 460A; Records of the Provost Marshal General. American Prisoner of War Information Bureau. 1942 – 1946, National Archives, College Park, MD.

478. U. S. Army, J.S.M. Washington. JSM 560, "Reference JSM 559 and SCAF 212" 20 Feb 1945." RG 389, Entry A1 460A; Records of the Provost Marshal General. American Prisoner of War Information Bureau. 1942 – 1946, National Archives, College Park, MD.

479. Letter to Dr. Carl Burkhardt, President of ICRC from Major General R.N. Barker. 20 Feb 1945. RG 389, Entry A1 460A; Records of the Provost Marshal General. American Prisoner of War Information Bureau. 1942 – 1946, National Archives, College Park, MD.

480. International Committee of the Red Cross. Ref Index 1628. "Report: signed by Harrison to US regarding over 100,000 prisoners being forced to march along northern Germany, dated February 28, 1945." RG 389, Entry A1 460A; Records of the Provost Marshal General. American Prisoner of War Information Bureau. 1942 – 1946, National Archives, College Park, MD. AND SHAEF Cable. "S79573 to Combined Chiefs of

Staff regarding the movement of prisoners on marches around Germany and a proposal to solve the problem. Dated February 28, 1945." RG 389, Entry A1 460A; Records of the Provost Marshal General. American Prisoner of War Information Bureau. 1942 – 1946, National Archives, College Park, MD.

481. U.S. Army, SHAEF, European Theater of Operations, Message from SHAEF to Army Groups, "SCAF 248" Regarding agreed outline plan for POWs 3 April 1945." RG 389, Entry A1 460A; Records of the Provost Marshal General. American Prisoner of War Information Bureau. 1942 – 1946, National Archives, College Park, MD.

482. WW2 US Medical Research Center. "R A M P Administrative Repatriation Procedures & Evacuation and Disposition of Recovered Allied Military Personnel." Online at: https://www.med-dept.com/articles/r-a-m-p/ [accessed 5/23/23]

483. WW2 US Medical Research Center, "R A M P Administrative Repatriation Procedures."

484. WW2 US Medical Research Center, "R A M P Administrative Repatriation Procedures."

485. Higgins, Survival: Diary of an American POW,189.

486. Higgins, Survival: Diary of an American POW, 197-8.

487. Greenwood, *Normandy to Victory*, 315-320.

488. Omar Nelson Bradley and Clay Blair, *A General's Life : an Autobiography* (New York: Simon and Schuster, 1983), 405-407.

489. Greenwood, *Normandy to Victory*, 330.

490. Bradley and Blair. *A General's Life*, 401.

491. VIII U.S. Corp, 3rd Information and Historical Services, Captain Wm. J. Dunkerley interview of Lt Col Hester, Report on 76th Infantry Division. "Miscellaneous Information. March 29 1945." RG 407, Entry A1 460A; Records of the Adjutant General. World War II Operations Reports, 1940-48, National Archives, College Park, MD.

492. Ririe, One-Man Mission, 176-7.

493. Ririe, One-Man Mission, 177.

494. Roland Hartman, private interview.

495. WW2 US Medical Research Center, "R A M P Administrative Repatriation Procedures."

496. Ririe, One-Man Mission, 176-7.

497. U. S. Army, "Interviews by Bahn with ARC Staff and Hospital Personnel, May 1945." RG 389, Entry A1 460A; Records of the Provost Marshal General. American Prisoner of War Information Bureau. 1942 – 1946, National Archives, College Park, MD.

498. US Army, Interviews with ARC Staff and Hospital Personnel.

499. US Army, Interviews with ARC Staff and Hospital Personnel.

500. George F. Horne, "1,975 Arrive here from Nazi Prisons," New York Times, April 29, 1945, 16.

501. Signed Security Certificate signed by Anthony Acevedo, April 5, 1945, Online at: https://californiarevealed.org/islandora/object/cavpp%3A121992, accessed 9/13/22.

502. Hearing before the Judiciary Committee of the U.S. Senate on Determining Who Profited from the Forced Labor of American World War II Prisoners on June 28, 2000, Senate Hearing 106-585, (From the U.S. Government Printing Office) Online at: https://www.govinfo.gov/content/pkg/CHRG-106shrg65766/html/CHRG-106shrg65766.htm. [accessed 9/13/22].

503. Cohen, "Soldiers and Slaves."

504. Eisenhower, Report by the Supreme Commander to the Combined Chiefs of Staff, 87.

505. George Patton, Diary, February 7, 1945, in the file the Patton Papers, Library of Congress, Washington, DC.

506. Omar N. Bradley. A Soldier's Story. (New York: Henry Holt and Company,1951). 502.

507. United States Army, Twelfth Army Group Letter of Instructions #14, 24 January 1945. RG 407, Entry A1 460A; Records of the Adjutant General. World War II Operations Reports, 1940-48, National Archives, College Park, MD.

508. Chandler, The Papers of Dwight David Eisenhower: The War Years. Letter #2270, 2465.

509. US Army, Third US Army, Operations Report: "The Eifel to the Rhine and the Capture of Trier" 29 January to 12 March 1945. RG 407, Entry A1 460A; Records of the Adjutant General. World War II Operations Reports, 1940-48, National Archives, College Park, MD, 1.

510. Omar Nelson Bradley, A Soldier's Story. (New York: Holt, 1951), 501.

511. Bradley, A Soldier's Story, 501.

512. Ralph Ingersoll, Top Secret. (New York: Harcourt, Brace and Company, 1946), 290.

513. Charles B. MacDonald, US Army in World War II. European Theater of Operations: The Last Offensive. (New York: Barnes & Noble Books, 1995), p67-8. AND Bradley, A Soldier's Story, 50.

514. New York Times, February 8, 1945, 1.

515. 80th Inf Div, Lt Col Miller and Maj Croker, Asst, Engr, Observer's Report No 78, "XII Corps, Crossing Our and Sauer Rivers, 7 February to 11 February." RG 407, Entry A1 460A; Records of the Adjutant General. World War II Operations Reports, 1940-48, National Archives, College Park, MD.

516. US Army, 417th Inf Regt, Infantry Journals.

517. Michael J. Debacker Collection (AFC/2001/001/76328), approx. 11:1.

518, 417th Inf Regt, AAR by Boerem, "Crossing of the Sauer River vicinity Echternach, 7-17 Feb 45," 6.

519. Hutnik, We Ripened Fast.

520. US Army, Third US Army, Reports, "G-1 Daily Periodic Reports," (found in XII Corps files).

521. US Army, 11th Inf Regt, "After Action Against the Enemy Report for Period 1 February to 28 February 1945" Inclusive. RG 407, Entry A1 460A; Records of the Adjutant General. World War II Operations Reports, 1940-48, National Archives, College Park, MD.

522. US Army, Inf Regt, 3rd Bn, AAR by Gill, S-3. "Sauer River Operation for 6-12 Feb 1945," 3.

523. 7th Engineer Bn, Report, "After Action Report Against the Enemy," 1-28 Feb 1945, 1.

524. US Army, 10th Inf Regt. After Action Report: "Sauer River Crossing" 7-15 Feb 1945. Source: Lt Col William Breckinridge, 4-5.

525. Blumenson, The Patton Papers, Letter dated February 6, 1945, 636.

526. Blumenson, The Patton Papers, Letter dated February 13, 1945, 636.

527. Patton, War as I Knew It, 212.

528. War Department, General Orders, No19: Battle Orders, 10 February 1947. RG 407, Entry A1 460A; Records of the Adjutant General. World

War II Operations Reports, 1940-48, National Archives, College Park, MD.

529. U.S. Army, XII Corps. Corps commendation, February 1945. Records of the Adjutant General. World War II Operations Reports, 1940-48, National Archives, College Park, MD.

530. Bradley and Blair, *A General's Life,* 394.

531. Norman J. Feitelson Collection (AFC/2001/001/76487), Veterans History Project, American Folklife Center, Library of Congress. Corporal-11th Regiment, Co A- 34;40. Online at: https://memory.loc.gov/diglib/vhp/bib/loc.natlib.afc2001001.76487 [accessed June 6, 2022].

532. Hank I. Sherr Collection (AFC/2001/001/55521), Veterans History Pr oject, American Folklife Center, Library of Congress. Online at: https://memory.loc.gov/diglib/vhp/bib/loc.natlib.afc2001001.55521 [accessed June 6, 2022].

533. George Monroe Ketner, Jr. Collection (AFC/2001/001/39243), Veterans History Project, American Folklife Center, Library of Congress Approx 27:00 Online at: https://memory.loc.gov/diglib/vhp/bib/loc.natlib.afc2001001.39243 [accessed June 6, 2022].

534. Arthur Staymates. Digital Collection at the World War II Museum. Online at: https://www.ww2online.org/view/arthur-staymates-0#encounter-with-general-patton [accessed June 6, 2022].

535. Arthur Staymates. Digital Collection at the World War II Museum.

536. Arthur W. Kramer Collection (AFC/2001/001/72699), Veterans History Project, American Folklife Center, Library of Congress. Battery B, 609th field Artillery Bn, 71st Div. Approx 20:20. Online at: https://memory.loc.gov/diglib/vhp/bib/loc.natlib.afc2001001.72699 [accessed June 6, 2022].

537. Thomas G. Manos Collection (AFC/2001/001/94110), Veterans History Project, Approx 26:40.

538. Alan Moskin, Digital Collection at the World War II Museum. Online at: https://www.ww2online.org/view/alan-moskin#general-patton [accessed June 6, 2022].

539. Abraham Baum, Digital Collection at the World War II Museum. Online at: https://www.ww2online.org/view/abraham-abe-baum#segment-4 [accessed June 6, 2022].

540. Hubert Essame, Patton: a Study in Command (New York: Scribner, 1974), 256.

541. Essame, Patton: a Study in Command, 259.

542. Robert S. Allen, Lucky Forward, the History of Patton's Third U.S. Army (New York: MacFadden-Bartell, 1971), 27.

543. Col. Charles R., Drive (Boston: Little, Brown, 1957), 144.

544. Carlo D'Este, Patton: A Genius for War (New York: HarperCollins Publishers, 1995), 811.

545. Chandler, The Papers of Dwight David Eisenhower: The War Years. #1205, Aug 24 1943, 1353.

546. Chandler, The Papers of Dwight David Eisenhower: The War Years, #1205, Aug 24, 1943, 1353.

547. Allen, Lucky Forward, 28.

548. Bradley, A Soldier's Story, 405.

549. Blumenson, The Patton Papers, 538. AND   Patton, War as I Knew It, 119.

550. Harry Yeide, Fighting Patton: George S Patton Jr. Through the Eyes of His Enemies (Minneapolis: Zenith Press, 2014), 420.

551. Yeide, Fighting Patton, 415-6.

552. Yeide, Fighting Patton, 419.

553. Codman, Drive, 159-160.

554. Essame, Patton: a Study in Command, 255.

555. Essame, Patton: a Study in Command, 255.

556. Allen, Lucky Forward, 33.

557. Blumenson, The Patton Papers, 851.

558. Essame, Patton; a Study in Command, 209.

559. Essame, Patton; a Study in Command, 258.

560. Ladislas Farago, Patton : Ordeal and Triumph (New York: Dell Publishing, 1963), 880.

561. Allen, Lucky Forward, 29.

562. Allen, Lucky Forward, 31.

563. Codman, Drive, 187.

564. Codman, Drive, 160.

565. Blumenson, The Patton Papers, 849.

566. Essame, Patton: a Study in Command, 142.

567. Essame, Patton: a Study in Command, 236-7.

568. Codman, Drive, 271.

569. D'Este, Patton: A Genius for War, 811.

570. Blumenson, The Patton Papers, 849.

571. Essame, Patton, a Study in Command, 259.

572. Farago, Patton, Ordeal and Triumph, 795.

573. Farago, Patton, Ordeal and Triumph, 795.

574. "Instructions to the Third United States Army, Letter of Instructions #2, 2 April, 1944." Found in George S Patton, Jr. and Charles M. Province (ed), Military Essays and Articles, (San Diego, CA: The George S. Patton, Jr. Historical Society, 2002), Online at: https://www.pattonhq.com/pdffiles/vintagetext.pdf [Accessed September 22, 2022]. 66-75.

575. "Instructions to the Third United States Army, Letter of Instructions #2, 2 April, 1944," 66-75.

576. "Instructions to the Third United States Army, Letter of Instructions #2, 2 April, 1944," 66-75.

577. U.S. Army, Military Intelligence Service War Department Report, "Stalag IX-B German Prisoner of War Camp Bad Orb, Germany History," compiled in November 1945. RG 407, Entry A1 460A; Records of the Adjutant General. World War II Operations Reports, 1940-48, National Archives, College Park, MD. 88. Online at: http://www.indianamilitary.org/German%20PW%20Camps/Prisoner%20of%20War/PW%20Camps/Stalag%20IX-B%20Bad%20Orb/History.htm [accessed September 22, 2022].

578. U.S. Army, Military Intelligence Service. Report: "Stalag IX-B German Prisoner of War Camp, 89.

579. Garcia, J. Malcolm, "German POWs in the American Homefront, " Smithsonian Magazine, September 15, 2009. Online at German POWs on the American Homefront | History | Smithsonian Magazine. [Accessed September 22, 2022.]

580. *George G. Lewis and John Mehwa*, "History of Prisoner of War Utilization by the United States Army 1776-1945" *(PDF), (Washington, DC:*

Center of Military History, United States Army, 2004), 103. Online at: https://history.army.mil/html/books/104/104-11-1/cmhPub_104-11-1.pdf [Accessed September 2022]. AND Michael Farquhar, "Enemies Among Us: German POWs in America." The Washington Post, September 10, 1997. Online at https://www.washingtonpost.com/archive/1997/09/10/enemies-among-us-german-pows-in-america/e606d338-4d69-4298-9c4a-3ab4ad0d6336/   [Acessed on September 22, 2022]

581. *Lewis and Mehwa.* "History of Prisoner of War Utilization," *103.*

582. Barbara Schmitter Heisler, "Returning to America: German Prisoners of War and the American Experience," The Johns Hopkins University Press German Studies Review, Vol. 31, No. 3 (Oct. 2008), 537-556. Online at: https://www.jstor.org/stable/27668591. [Accessed October 6, 2022]

583. Roland Hartman, private interviews.